The Belchambers
From the parishes of Kirdford and L...

John Belchamber

I dedicate this book to my lovely wife Tricia for her patience.

(c) John Belchamber 2012

Published 2013 by www.belchamber.co.uk

Printed by Lulu.Com

ISBN 978-1-291-12751-5

Front Cover: The Belchamber coat of arms in stained glass by Tricia Belchamber.

Rear Cover:John Belchamber and June Evans

THE NAME

The sources I have used for my information have been many and varied. The recording of Baptisms, Marriages and Burials in Parish Registers only began in 1538 and many parishes did not make a start in recording this vital information until much later. Over the centuries some parish registers have been lost altogether, or in part from the ravishes of time and neglect.

While working on this research I have come across some very early references to the name. It is not possible to piece together these references into family units because the documents recording them seldom give any indication of relationship. They are useful however in giving some indication of the age of the name, its early distribution and giving some pointers to its origin. These will be discussed more fully later.

First we must enter into some discussion of the meaning and origin of the name Belchamber. Many books have been written over the years on this subject but I shall cite just three, which I have used to support my argument.

(1)   C. W. Bardsley   Dictionary of British Surnames

(2)   P. H. Reaney   Dictionary of English Surnames

(3)   R. A. McKinley   Surnames of Sussex

C. W. Bardsley believed that the surname was local i.e. a place name, its origin being in the village of Bellencumbre, in the arrondissement of Dieppe in Normandy, France. However Bardsley does not give any firm evidence for his opinion and as you will read later I can find only circumstantial evidence but it seems to give a firmer conclusion than the alternatives.

P. H. Reaney in his book of Dictionary of English Surnames, although highly rated as an authority on surnames, does not seem to be able to give any clear conclusion. He offers suggestions but does not seem to be able to come out on one side of the argument or the other.

R .A. McKinley who confines his study in this particular volume to the Surnames of Sussex, states that the first reference in Sussex is a Richard Belechambr or Belechombre before 1285 who was a tenant of a virgate of land in Slindon. Although he mentions an earlier instant of the name, which he connects to France, he does not make the leap from the French connection to the later references to the name in England.

Having researched the name now for many years and making my own assessment of the various sources available I have come to the conclusion that the origin of the name is in fact French and that Bel(l)chamber(s) is what finally became the anglicised version of the French place name Bellencumbre. I have to admit that I have no proof positive that this is so, but when one looks at the very few early references and the variation in the spelling it does not seem to be a gargantuan leap from Bellencumbre to Bellchambers.

Before I go into a more detailed explanation of the evidence supporting my conclusion I must give some reasons why I reject the idea of the 'Bell Tower' theory and its association with bell ringing. I cannot imagine anybody living in the 'Bell Tower' it would be an absolute nightmare, having to live with the sporadic ringing of bells, which would have been a much more regular occurrence in those early years than it is today. It could be that the Bellchamber name was connected, not to living in the Bell Tower, but being responsible for the upkeep of the tower and maybe even for the ringing of the bells. However, I do not think that this is feasible either, my argument being that every parish the length and breath of the country had its own church, so it would be expected that the name would be fairly evenly distributed throughout the country, and this is not so, apart from one or two mentioned in Suffolk, Norfolk, Hertford, and Oxford, several in Essex and the inevitable one or two in London, the name does not appear at all North of the River Thames until the early part of the nineteenth century.

The evidence for concluding that the name is a place name in origin is as stated previously, nothing if not flimsy, but it is all I have at the present time and it may be that more will be revealed in due course.

I shall begin with the very early history of the tiny village called Bellencombre, because I believe this is relevant to my argument. It is situated on the west bank of the river Varrene about 35 kilometres from Dieppe and about the same distance from Rouen. The village consists of one single broad street at the southern end of which was a large and imposing castle, now sadly only a mound of rubble. However some idea of its size and beauty can be obtained from the few sketches and tapestries that survive.

Early in the eleventh century a French nobleman named William de Warenne built this castle and made his home there. When William the Conqueror came to England in 1066, William de Warenne was among those who came and gave him support. Once the conquest had taken place William de Warenne was awarded large tracts of land, over a large part of southern England. William de Warenne remained in England and made his headquarters at Lewes in the County of Sussex where he built a castle, which still stands to this day. William de Warenne later married the daughter of William the Conqueror named Grundrada, by whom he had at least one son also named William, who succeeded his father as the 2nd Earl Warenne.

William de Warenne 1st Earl with all these lands to administer would have needed a team of faithful and trustworthy men to assist him in running all the estates he had been granted. It would not have been very surprising then that among the team would perhaps have been a member of the entourage who had come over from de Warenne's seat in France, logically it would also not be surprising if in order to distinguish one team member from another that coming from Bellencombre he was given the name de Bellencombre, bearing in mind that at that time hereditary surnames had not yet come into being.

From 1066 to 1500 I have found only a small number of references to the name, but few of those refer to any family groups. The reason the number of references are so small are several, the population of the country was scanty in comparison to modern times, very few of these could read or write and materials such as paper, pens and ink were very difficult to procure and very expensive. There was no law that required the registration of, births, marriages or deaths, so apart from the odd references to disputes in a Court or references to transfers of land, very little documentation was produced. I will therefore list references that I have found between these dates to give some idea of the continuity of the name.

(1)   Rudolph de Bellencombre held the manor of Cuckfield, County of Sussex around 1066.

       (History of the Parish of Cuckfield)

(2)   Bernard de Bellencombre held land in Suffolk 1086

('The Norman People' published by the Genealogical Co. Inc. Baltimore 1875 and reprinted 1985 page 156)

(3)   William de Bellencombre, 1165 witness to two charters granted by Isabella, Countess of Surrey to Lewes Priory. Isabella was the widow of William de Warenne, 2nd Earl Warenne.

       (original charters at East Sussex Record Office, Lewes)

(4)   William Belencumbre 1235 unpublished Assize Rolls (P.H. Reaney)

(5)   Presentation of Robert de Belencumbre to the church of Merewe (now Merrow in the County of Surrey) in the

       Diocese of Winchester 1st July 1249 (Calendar of Patent Rolls)

(6)   William de Belencumbre County of Essex 1272   (Feet of Fines)

(7)   Robert de Belencumbre County of Essex 1272 (Feet of Fines)

(8)   John de Belencumbre County of Essex 1273 (Hundred Rolls)

(9)   Robert de Belencumbre County of Essex 1273 (Hundred Rolls)

(10)   Robert de Belencumbre property worth 6 marks in rent in Felstead County of Essex also property at Finchingfield County of Essex (Feet of Fines 1285 – 1286 Vol. ii)

       The property in Finchingfield is now known as Belcumber Hall.

(11) John de BelencumbreFinchingfield County of Essex 1285 – 1286 (Feet of Fines)

(12) Richard Belchambre tenant of a virgate of land in Slindon County of Sussex 1285 (Feet of Fines)

(13) Robert de Belencombre, Alice his wife and John his son. 1 messuage - 20 acres of land worth 2 shillings and 5½ pennies Finchingfield County of Essex 1313 – 1314 (Feet of Fines)

(14) Robert de Belencumbre and Alice his wife 1 messuage – 16 acres of land, 1 acre of pasture at Bumstede

Helyum, FinchingfieldEssex 1315 – 1316 (Feet of Fines)

(15) Robert de Belencumbre of Finchingfield County of Essex was granted a pardon 11th June 1318 after being committed to the Kings prison at Colchester County of Essex for disseisin   (Calendar of Patent Rolls)

(16) John son of Robert de Belencombre 1 messuage – 8 acres of land, 5 acres of meadow and 1 acre of pasture plus 3 acres of wood and 85 shillings rent in Finchingfield County of Essex 1321 – 1322 (Feet of Fines)

(17) Walter de Bellencombre held land in Kirdford County of Sussex 1st December 1333 (Calendar of Patent Rolls)

(18) Thomas Belchambre 10th May 1369 names of armed men and archers sent for the defence of the Country at the King's request by the Mayor and Alderman of the City of London   (London Letter Book G. page 244)

(19) Thomas Belchambre 18th January 1385 – one of three people named as giving evidence regarding the use of unlawful fishing nets on the River Thames (London Letter Book H.)

(20) Richard Belechambre of Chichester County of Sussex 16th May 1395 owed 20 marks by Hugh Richardson of Southampton   (Calendar of Patent Rolls)

(21) John Belechambre mentioned as one of a large number of protesters who prevented, by force, the parson and a number of his parishioners from passing over a meadow and the bridge over the River Tow to the Chapel of St Lawrence County of Devon on 10th August 1397 (Calendar of Patent Rolls)

(22) John Belechambre of Bushey County of Hertfordshire, a warrener, in dispute over a debt 28th November 1418

(Calendar of Patent Rolls)

(23) PCC will of John Belencombre of St George the Martyr Hardingham County of Norfolk 1451

(24) John Belchambers mentioned as a scholar of New College Oxford 24th April 1507

(25) Will of John Belchamber the elder of Basingstoke County of Hampshire 1512

(26) Will of Richard Belchamber of the manor of Stoke and Pypering in the County of Surrey 1527

This list contains all the disconnected references to the name over the first 500 years since the conquest, but we haven't yet reached the date of the commencement of the first Parish Registers. In order to bridge the gap I have had to use Court records and any available wills etc. Using these sources has enabled me to produce a family tree generation to generation from this time to the present day.

 (c) June Evans 2009

Introduction

Let me introduce myself, my name is John Belchamber the author of this book. I know the book is not going to win any literary prizes or top any best seller charts, but it is my interpretation of my family. It is not the definitive family tree, and by no means is it finished. You never stop researching family history like life it goes' on, people are being born, getting married and dying all the time and so adding their own identities to an ever increasing family. All my research has been proved and verified I have not listed all sources. The pre-1837 research has been from Parish Records of Northchapel, Kirdford, Wisborough Green and Horsham to name but a few, all post 1837 civil registrations has been researched by Birth, Marriage and Death certificates. I have some census records 1841-1911; these have yet to be thoroughly researched A note about census records especially the ages listed, a persons age in a census can vary by sometimes five years or more. If a person did not know his or her birth date the enumerator would guess at an age, so if someone was a youthful looking 25 he may have been listed as 20 and so on.

Some records have been duplicated, I have done this to maintain continuity and help you read and understand the contents easily.

I have not included in the book two sections of the tree because I have not had time to do any research on them, one being the line of William and Ann Belchamber nee Lucas. I think William Belchamber who married Ann Lucas was from my tree born 1768 the son of William and Elizabeth Belchamber nee Foyce baptized in Kirdford, Sussex 27th March 1768.
Further to that a daughter of William and Elizabeth Belchamber nee Foyce married in Godalming.Sarah Belchamber married James Gill 25th July 1784 Sarah being baptized 22nd December 1765.
Another son of William and Elizabeth, Edward Belchamber married Elizabeth Stenning in Shalford,Surrey on the 6th November,1824,one of their witness's was a Robert Bellchamber who if its the Robert son of William and Ann he would have been Edward's cousin.

The other being the family of John and Ann Belchamber nee Boulton. When John and Ann married in Kirdford, John listed himself as "of this parish" research has proven there was no baptism record for him in the parish. John put his age as being born in 1798.The only John recorded was a twin born to William and Sarah Bellchamber in Chichester,Sussex,the other twin being a Thomas Belchamber, so where the Kirdford connection is, as yet to be established.

Way back in the late 1950's when my grandparents and their siblings got together they told stories of my late great-grandfather George Belchamber, about his shed which nobody dare go into unless he said so, his funny ways, his strictness etc. Sunday afternoons was high tea for Dorothy and James when Aunt Kit and Uncle Ron, Uncle Gordon and Aunt Lydia and Aunt Etty and her husband Harold would visit us and laugh and joke about the old days. I cannot remember any of these stories now which makes me sad, but I can even now hear the raucous laugher. I was only 3.5 when he died, but I remember him and that he called me "his little Mate" he took me for walks and I remember helping him collect willow from Coombe Court for his basket making of which the only surviving example to my knowledge is in Canada with his grandson Jim Belchamber.

George always took me to two white marker stones along Coombe Lane, Chiddingfold near to what we called Spain Cottages, and there he would tell me wondrous stories. The only one I can remember was about a fox hunt and the fox being killed, which made me cry, my grandfather Jim also told the story. I can remember the day Granddad died, I don't know how I remember I just do, panic in the house, my Mum rushing up stairs, I wasn't allowed to go up, I knew my Granddad had died.

It was remembering these times that got me interested in my family and the Belchamber name. After attending an evening class on family history run by Eric Restall, I started taking genealogy seriously in the mid-1990, s and set out to find my ancestors.1997 I set about writing to everyone with the Surname Belchamber I could find. I got some replies mostly from Belchambers who were not from my line, some very kert; I remember someone sent an advert for a book on the Belchambers published by Burkes.

One reply was very interesting though, I remember it was from a Margaret Jarvis living in Hambledon,Surrey,it was my family tree from my 2nd Great Grand Parents back to the late 1600's the thing I found most exciting was they all lived and died in the parish of Kirdford. I had always thought the family were from Dunsfold where my Grandfather James had been born, even though I had researched the Dunsfold Parish Records and had not found any apart from a marriage in 1815 between a John Belchamber and Martha Wood from my Belchamber line.

The first trip to the West Sussex Record Office in Chichester was an eye opener so much to see and do, I eventually settled down in front of a microfiche reader and began to look through the Kirdford Parish Records starting with births I remember they just kept on jumping out at me, Margaret Jarvis's tree had checked out and I was able to add more ancestors. At the same time as starting my research I had joined a few Genealogical Forums on the internet, and had a reply from a Margaret Zietzke who was related through an ancestor from Northchapel, Sussex. Margaret sent me the catalyst of a family tree from the village of Northchapel, Sussex.

It was also about this time I made contact with June Evans, and June was doing a one name study of the Belchamber name and all its variants and a member of GOONS, The Guild of One Name Studies. I had just to ask and June could have given me my complete family tree on day one, I said to her "do not tell me anything" "I want to find out for myself, I only want clues". I must say there have been times when I have been really stuck she has helped me, thanks June.

From their beginnings in the parishes of Northchapel and Kirdford we now have a totally international family of Belchambers from England, Canada and the USA, to date there is no evidence of any family in Australia or New Zealand, but that's not to say there isn't. A cousin did emigrate in the 1960's but returned to live in the UK, some years ago.

I have only recorded the male line of the family, other researchers tell me I should include the female line, to be honest it's been fifteen years to get this far just researching the male lines, maybe I will do the female side later.

To save any copyright issues I have transcribed all Birth, Marriage and Death certificates, you may notice that some spellings differ, John Belchamber could be born spelt with one L,married spelt with two LL's and died with two LL's and sometimes an S on the end. That is because who ever recorded the certificate spelt it that way.

To help you follow the Family Tree,the principal people are in bold type with a list of christain names followed by a number,this is a list of ancestors:

Example:
John Belchamber(Ivy14,James13,George 12 back to John1)
This will tell you that I am John Belchamber my mother is Ivy14,my grandfather is James13 and great-grandfather is George12 and so on back to John and Agnes in Generation 1. Everyone in our family goes back to John and Agnes Belchamber

Kirdford

Kirdford parish comprised of Plaistow, Ebernoe, Balls Cross and Strood Green until the beginning of the 20th Century. The area was mainly agricultural, which was a source of income for most of my ancestors. Earlier there were Glass and Iron industries going on in the area, there is no evidence of any Belchambers involved. The parish is the largest in the county, with a width of 6 miles and a breadth of 4 miles.
My ancestors gave their residence as Kirdford, but from what I can see according to the census records they lived in Plaistow, especially from the mid to latter part of 19th Century and well into the middle of the 20th Century.
Although my grand uncle Jehu and his wife Rosina lived in Kirdford at Foresters Cottage till the middle of the 20th Century.

Northchapel

Like Kirdford Northchapel was mainly agricultural with earlier industries of Glass working and iron smelting. Northchapel was part of the parish of Petworth until 17th March, 1717 so early research was from the parish records for Petworth. Although the earliest Belchambers were recorded living in the village from the 1500's they could have been living there earlier. If I ever get a chance to use a time machine, I would go back to that time and ask my 12th Great-Grandfather John Belchamber who his father and grandfather were.

Wisborough Green

Wisborough Green is south of Kirdford about 5 miles away. Some of the Belchamber family lived there mainly in the late 19th and early 20th century. William James Belchamber was postman there in the early 20th Century. John and Harriet Belchamber nee Sheppard also lived there and their grandson Frederick Streeter also a Postman he worked alongside William James. I wonder whether they knew that they were related.

Garlands

My ancestors lived in Northchapel on a farm named Garlands, Garlands is a timber framed house probably built in the 15thcentury, and it is situated on the outskirts of the village along Pipers Lane. Once a farm with outbuildings and barns the property has now been reduced in size and the outbuildings were removed and sent to The Frontier CultureMuseum, Staunton, Virginia, USA.Shonks is another farm and once part of Garlands, it can also be seen in the village, across the green near the playground. Rita Bedford the owner of Garlands invited me to look around the house a few years ago, what a feeling to walk in the footsteps of your ancestors; the house has many of its original features including an original Tudor panel, oh yes! And a ghost who apparently walks around in the upstairs area.

WSRO and the SHC

Over the last 15 years I have spent many happy and sometimes thwart hours at The West Sussex Record Office in Chichester researching, and would like to thank the staff for their help and guidance over the years.
The same can be said of The Surrey History Centre in Woking, again I would like to thank the staff.

New friends and family

While researching family history I have met some wonderful people including family members. Family and Non-family members include June Evans, Margaret Zietzke, Bill Bellchambers, Judy Black, Jill Bowden, Dorothy Belchamber, Jean Madgwick, Audrey Winson, Robin Belchamber, Beryl Knowles, Ivy Boughton and many more not listed, thank you one and all for your help.

Now let's get started with my 12th great grand parents John and Agnes Belchamber nee Payne:

Generation1

John Belchamber was born in Northchapel,Sussex circa 1485/90 and died 1550 he married Agnes Payne probably about 1510c,they had four children James,Sybil,Roger and Robert.Robert was the youngest and heir to his grandfather Robert Payne.
John Belchamber made a will in 1550 leaving his wife Agnes as Executrix.
In 1524 John was listed in the Lay Subsidy for Petworth,which included Northchapel at that time.
The Subsidy was imposed upon persons according to the reputed value(moderate estimate)of their estates. The rate at one time was fixed as 4s for land and 2s 8d for goods. The word subsidy is used to define a specific set of records as well as an umbrella name for a group of records. Lay Subsidies Rolls included the taxes assessed against the laity("common people").Clerical Subsidies were similary collected at the rate of 4s assessed on ecclesiastical preferments,and made by the clergy in Convocation and afterwards confirmed by Parliament.

John's will was proved on 23rd July,1550,his wife Agnes was sole executrix.In the will John mentions 4 children Robert,James,Sybble and Roy(Roger),he also left money to his godson John Belchamber and every other godchild of his and a cow to John Belchamber?,at the moment these people cannot be identified.

John Belchambers Will 1550

In the name of god Almighty the 21 of Apprill In the year of our Lord god one thousand five hundreth and fifty and in the fourthe year of our sovraigne Edward to sixth by grace of god king of England France and Ireland Defender of the faithe and of the Churche of England and also Ireland in earth the Supreme Lord.
I John Belchamber of the parishe of Northchaple in the countie of Sussex being sicke in body hole and perfect in rememberance thanks be to god after this manner and forme folowing I do make this my testament and last will first I bequeathe my soull to all mighty god trusting to the meritte of his Glorius passion that my soull shall (obtain ?) everlasting life and my body to be buryed - the grave yard of North Chaple a for said item I give to the pore viii s (8s) Chy est(perhaps Chichester) ii s (2s)
Item I give to John Belchamber my god sone xii d (12d) and to any other god child of mine iid (2d) Item I give to Thomas Morley my best cowe to John Morley his sone the first calfe of the same cowe Item I give to John Belchamber a cowe Item I give to Robt my sone one stere iii yere old Item to James Belchamber my sone a heffer of ii yeres old Item I give to Syblle Belchamber my daughter a stere of ii yere old Item I give to Roger Belchamber my sone a bullocke of a yere old / all other residue of my goods moveable and unremoveable unbequeathed I give to Agnes Belchamber my wife whom I do make my soull Executrix / my (trustees?) here of that this is my last and trew will - at -- -- William Hosbourne and Thomas Alwyn !

Agnes Payne was the daughter of Robert and Margery Payne she was born about 1485c.Agnes Belchamber died in the August and was buried at Petworth,Our lady of pity on the 25th of August,1561.

John Belchamber and Agnes Payne had the following Children:
i   James Belchamber was born about 1511 in Northchapel,Sussex
          Notes for James Belchamber
          In 1550 James was left a 2 year old heffer in his father's will

ii   Sybil Belchamber was born about 1513 in Northchapel,Sussex
          Notes for Sybil Belchamber
          In 1550 Sybble was left a 2 year old steer in her father's will,and in 1551 she was a beneficiary in the will of her maternal grandfather Robert Payne,he left her his best cow.

iii   Roger Belchamber was born about 1517 in Northchapel,Sussex.He Married unknown.

iv   Robert Belchamber was born about 1520 in Northchapel,Sussex.He died in 1571.He married Margery,she died in 1582 in Northchapel,Sussex.

Generation 2

Roger Belchamber(John1) was born about 1517 in Northchapel,Sussex,he
Married unknown
Notes for Roger Belchamber
In 1550 Roy(Roger) was left a 1 year old bullock in his father's will.

Roger Belchamber and Unknown had the following children:

i   Elizabeth Belchamber was born about 6th April,1623.
       Notes for Elizabeth Belchamber
       Elizabeth could have been the Elizabeth Belchamber who married Henry
       Young on the 30th November,1661 in Petworth,Sussex

ii   Margaret Belchamber was born on 22nd March,1629

iii   Roger Belchamber was born on the 12th May,1639

iv   Joan Belchamber was born about 12th May,1639
       Notes for Joan Belchamber
       Joan married Cornelus Johnson on the 24th June,1679

Robert Belchamber 11th Great Grandparents
(John1) was born about 1520 in Northchapel,Sussex.He died in 1571.He married
Margery,she died in 1582 in Northchapel,Sussex

       Notes for Robert Belchamber
       Robert Belchamber my 11th GGP was born about 1520,he was a yeoman
       farmer,he married Margerie.Robert obtained copyhold of 80 acres of land
       called Garlands and 15 arces of land called Shonks in 1547 as the heir of
       Robert Payne,providing he gives a room and 10 shillings a year to his parents
       John and Agnes. In 1550 Robert was left a 2 year old steer in his father's
       will,and in 1551 when Robert Payne died he left Robert one bull and the
       residue of is goods and named him as executor.
       From the Petworth Manor Court Rolls in 1550 Robert was ordered to make a
       ditch and fence against the property of Stephen Holwey,and in 1565 he was
       ordered to repair his house and barn,Robert was fined 12 shillings for failing
       to do this.
       In 1571 Robert surrenders out of court land called Shonks part of Garlands,to
       be regranted to his son John Belchamber.Robert died in 1571 and Margerie
       was admitted to her bench.Next heir is his son Robert,the custom of Petworth
       Manor was that the youngest son became heir,a custom known as"Borough
       English". Robert's will is in all probability lost,it is not listed in the archives
       of the West Sussex Record Office.
       Margerie would have taken her place in the manor court until her son was of
       age. In the 1575 survey she is noted as a widow occupying lands called
       Garlands,a tenement and orchard.Margerie died in 1582 leaving a will,her son
       Robert as executor.Margerie left her 3 daughters and her son John
       livestock,her son Robert was left the rest of the goods,which would have
       included 80 acres of land called Garlands.

Robert could have been the Robert Belchamber who on the 29th October,1567 was juror for the inquest of Ralph Morley late of Northchapel who hanged himself from a beam in a room of his dwelling.

Margaret or Margerie Belchamber Will 1582

In the name of god amen the 30th day of may in the year of our Lord god 1582 and in the 23rd year of the reign of our sovereing Lady Elizabeth by grace of god queene of England France and Ireland defender of the faith I Margorie Belchamber widow of the parish of Petworth in the countie of Sussex sick in body but of hole and perfect mynd and memory thanks be given to god and therefore do ordainen and make this my last will and testament in manner and from as herewith / First I bequeath my soule unto Almightie god who graces me and my bodie to be buried in the churchyard at Northchapell / To the high church of Chichester.

I give - and to the poore in Northchapell - / I give to John Belchamber my son my eldest maoe one eawe and one lamb I give to Jane my eldest daughter that is now marryed one cowe or bullock of one year age which of the two she will one eawe and one lamb/ I give to Margaret Belchamber my daughter one cowe and eawe and one lamb/ I give to Joanne Belchamber my youngest daughter one cowe one eawe and one lamb/ I give to (Anne ?) (Morly) one eawe and one lamb/ I give to James Stente one lamb/ I give to John Coles one lamb/ The rest of all my goods my debts having been paid I give to Robert Belchamber my son whence I do make him executor to dispose these my goods as is in this my last will proscribed - also this and the debts that I do owe:

To my son John Belchamber 40sh
To John Fry of Petworth 3s 8d
To Richard Haman 4s 8d
To Mrs Margaret Blackwell 2 bushells of rye
Also I do make Henry Apsley and Henry Gardiner supervisors to see that this my last will perfomrd and kept / and I do give each of them for there paynes 3s 4d
Henry Apsley Henry Gardener

Robert Belchamber and Margery had the following children:

i   John Belchamber(Robert2,John1) was born about 1550 in Northchapel,Sussex. He married Joan,she died 1612

ii   Jane Belchamber(Robert2,John1) was born in 1554 in Northchapel,Sussex. She married Henry Voice the son of William and Agnes Voice in 1575.Henry Voice was born about 25th March,1551 in Horsham,Sussex

iii   Robert Belchamber(Robert2,John1) was born about 1556 in Northchapel,Sussex. He died in 1612.He married Constance Goodair in November 1609 in Northchapel,Sussex.Constance died in 1621.

iv   Margaret Belchamber(Robert2,John1) was born about 1562 in Northchapel,Sussex. She married Rafe Gray on 7th September,1589 in St.Nicholas,Guildford,Surrey

v   Joane Belchamber(Robert2,John1) was born about 1562 in Northchapel,Sussex. She married Nicholas Socher on 3rd November,1663 in Kirdford,Sussex
Notes for Joane Belchamber
In 1571 her brother John inherited 15 acres of land in Northchapel called Shonks and in 1582 her brother Robert inherited 80 acres of land called Garlands.
In 1582 Joane the youngest daughter of Margery was left one cow,one ewe and one lamb in her mother's will.

Generation 3

John Belchamber(Robert2,John1) was born about 1550 in Northchapel,Sussex.
He died in 1606 in Northchapel. He married Joan.She died 1612.

Notes for John Belchamber
Born 1550c the son of Robert and Margery.In 1571 John's father surrended15 acres of land to him called Shonks,part of Garlands and in 1582 when his mother died she left him her eldest mare,one ewe,one lamp and 40s that she owed him.

On the 19th September,1606 administration of John's goods etc. amounting to the sum of £82.18s was granted to his widow Joan Belchamber. When Joan died in 1612 she left her son Richard 50s,her daughter Joan(Miles) 10s,the 4 children of her son Richard 35s between them and the residue of money,good and chattels to her son John and her daughter Susan, John and Susan were also her executors.
I presume that her son Henry wasn't a beneficiary of her will because he had already inherited Shonks after his father died in 1606.

John Belchamber and Joan had the following children:

i   Henry Belchamber(John3,Robert2,John1) was born about 1575 in Petworth,Sussex. He died about 29th March,1638 in Northchapel,Sussex. He married Mary.

ii   Richard Belchamber(John3,Robert2,John1) was born about 1577 in Petworth,Sussex. He married Mary.

iii   Joane Belchamber(John3,Robert2,John1) was born about 1579 in Petworth,Sussex. She married Miles.
Notes For Joane Belchamber
Born 1579c the daughter of John and Joan.In 1612 when Joane(Miles) mother died she left her 10s in her will.

iv   James Belchamber(John3,Robert2,John1) was born about 4th April,1581 in Petworth,Sussex. He died about 7th March,1581. Notes for James Belchamber
James was buried on 17th March,1581 and Although the baptism and burial dates suggest the James died before he was born,he was actually 11 months old because before 1752 the year began on 25th March and ended on 24th March.

v   John Belchamber(John3,Robert2,John1) was born about 30th November,1583 in Petworth,Sussex. He married Elizabeth Wood.

vi   Susan Belchamber(John3,Robert2,John1) was born about 23rd December,1587 in Petworth,Sussex. She married John Wells.

Jane Belchamber(Robert2,John1) was born in 1554 in Northchapel,Sussex. She married Henry Voice in 1575.

Notes For Jane Belchamber
In 1582 Jane the eldest daughter of Margery,who is now married was left a 1 year old cow or bullock,one ewe and one lamb in her mother's will.

Henry Voice and Jane Belchamber had the following children:

i   Joane Voice. She married Thomas Dongatt on 29th June,1586 in Horsham,Sussex.

Robert Belchamber 10th Great Grandparents
 (Robert2,John1) was born about 1556 in Northchapel,Sussex. He died in 1612.He married Constance Goodair in November,1583c. She died in 1612.

Notes for Robert Belchamber
Robert was born mid 1500s at Garlands,Northchapel he was a yeoman farmer and my 10th GGF he married Constance Goodair about 1583c. The 1610 survey shows Robert occupying Garlands,80 acres. Constance his wife was executor to his will when he died in 1612.

At this time Northchapel was a hamlet in the parish of Petworth and events should have been entered in the Petworth registers but were not. The chapel must have kept it's own registers but these are lost. We have only to rely on the Bishops Transcripts,a yearly return by the parish priest to the bishop,and only some of these have come to light.Northchapel became a parish in 1716.

Robert Belchamber and Constance Goodair had the following children:

i   Rose Belchamber(Robert3,Robert2,John1) was born in February 1584 in Northchapel,Sussex. She married Ralphe Constable about 1600 in Northchapel,Sussex.

ii   Robert Belchamber(Robert3,Robert2,John1) was born about 1586 in Northchapel,Sussex. He died about 2nd May,1666.He married Elizabeth.
Notes for Robert Belchamber
Robert married Elizabeth,no baptisms appear in the few surviving parish records for children of Robert and Elizabeth
From his mother's will 1621 he received the sum of 40s and a cow,and to Elizabeth she bequeaths"A payne of flaxon sheets of clothe which is at the weavers.

iii   Henry Belchamber(Robert3,Robert2,John1) was born on 12th May,1589 in Northchapel,Sussex. He died on 29th March,1638. He married Mary.

iv   Richard Belchamber(Robert3,Robert2,John1) was born about 1592 in Northchapel,Sussex. He died about 6th September,1637. He married Katherine Tickner on 10th February,1624 in Northchapel.

v   Edward Belchamber(Robert3,Robert2,John1) was born about 1594 in Northchapel,Sussex. He died about 5th May,1645 in Kirdford,Sussex. He married Mary about 1624.
Notes for Edward Belchamber
Born 1594c the son of Robert and Constance ,a yeoman farmer.In 1612 when Edward's father died,he left all his goods to be equally divided between Edward and his 5 brothers Robert,Henry,Richard,Thomas and William providing that they each pay their sister Rose(Constable) 20s which would amount to £6. Note:His father did not bequeath anything to his brother John,because he knew that he would inherit the house and land called Garlands when his mother died. In 1621 when Edward's mother died she left him and his 3 brothers,Richard,Thomas and William equal shares of the residue of her goods etc.Richard was also her executor.
Edward was noted in the 1641 protestation returns for Kirdford.

vi   Thomas Belchamber(Robert3,Robert2,John1) was born about 1596 in Northchapel,Sussex. He married Joan Mellersh in 1626 in Lurgashall,Sussex.

vii   William Belchamber(Robert3,Robert2,John1) was born about 1598 in Northchapel,Sussex. He died about 1660 in Kirdford,Sussex. He married Elizabeth Forman on 6th February,1630 in Northchapel.

viii   John Belchamber(Robert3,Robert2,John1) was born about 1602 in Northchapel,Sussex. He died in 1661. He married Alyce Strudwicke.

Margaret Belchamber(Robert2,John1) was born about 1560 in Northchapel,Sussex. She married Rafe Gray on 7th September,1589 in St.Nicholas,Guildford,Surrey

Notes for Margaret Belchamber

Born 1560c the daughter of Robert and Margery.In 1582 Margaret was left one cow,one ewe and one lamb in her mother's will.
In the Guildford parish registers there were two children buried 30th August,1590 to Rafe Gray.The records for the years 1593 to 1597 are missing,so no other children were recorded.

Rafe Gray and Margaret Belchamber had the following children:

i   John Gray was born on the 23rd October,1590

Generation 4

Henry Belchamber (John3, Robert2, John1) was born about 1575 in Petworth, Sussex. He died about 29th March,1638 in Northchapel, Sussex.
He married Mary.

Notes for Henry Belchamber:
Born 1575c the son of John and Joan.According to Petworth Copyholds,Henry inherited 15 acres of land called Shonks(part of Garlands) from his father,and when Henry died his daughter Mary (Feilder) inherited Shonks,so it was no longer in the Belchamber Family. Petworth Copyholds also confirm it was Henry son of John and Joan who died 1638 no age given.

Notes for Mary.

No death details have been found for Mary.

Henry Belchamber and Mary had the following child:

i   Mary Belchamber was born about 1602

Richard Belchamber(John3,Robert2,John1) was born about 1577 in Petworth,Sussex. He married Mary.No death found.

Notes for Richard Belchamber:
Born 1577c the son of John and Joan. In 1612 when Richard's mother died she left him 50s in her will,she also bequeathed 35s between his 4 children John,Elizabeth,Margaret and William. His sister Joan(Miles) got 10s,his brother John and sister Susan were left the residue of the money,goods and chattels.John and Susan were also executors.

Richard Belchamber and Mary had the following children:

i   John Belchamber was born about 7th August,1603 in Petworth,Sussex. He died in 1662.

ii   Margaret Belchamber was born about 1605 in Petworth,Sussex.She married Christopher Maybanck in 1630 in Petworth,Sussex.

Notes for Margaret Belchamber:
Born 1605c the daughter of Richard and Unknown. In 1612 Margaret was a beneficiary of her grandmother's will(Joan Belchamber) she received 5s,her father Richard received 50s,her sister Elizabeth and 2 brothers John and William all received 10s.
In 1662 John Belchamber of Petworth had a will proved,in the will he leaves £15 To William Belchamber and 10s to Christpher Maybanck. I think this is Margaret's brother born 1603,because they also had a brother William.

iii   Elizabeth Belchamber was born about 10th April,1608 in Petworth,Sussex.

iv   William Belchamber was born about 30th February,1611 in Petworth,Sussex.

John Belchamber(John3,Robert2,John1) was born about 30th November,1583 in Petworth,Sussex. He married Elizabeth Wood.

Notes for John Belchamber:
Born 1583c the son of John and Joan. In 1612 when John's mother died,she left him and his sister Susan the residue of money,goods and chattels after giving his brother Richard 50s,Richard's 4 children 35s between them and his sister Joan(Miles) 10s. John and Susan were also the executors.No death found for John or Elizabeth at the moment.

John Belchamber and Elizabeth Wood had the following children:

i   John Belchamber was born about 6th May,1614 in Horsham,Sussex.

ii   Elizabeth Belchamber was born about 21st July,1616 in Horsham,Sussex. She died in 1617 in Horsham,Sussex.

Rose Belchamber(Robert3,Robert2John1) was born in February,1584 in Northchapel,Sussex. She married Ralphe Constable about 1600 in Northchapel

Notes for Rose Belchamber:
Born 1585 the daughter of Robert and Constance Belchamber,Robert was a yeoman farmer.In1612 when Rose's father died,he left all his goods and chattels to be equally divided between her 6 brothers Robert,Henry,Richard,Edward,Thomas and William provided that they each pay Rose 20s each,which would amount to £6. Note:her father did not bequeath anything to her brother John,because he knew that he would inherit the house and lands called Garlands when her mother died. In 1612 when her mother did die,she left her daughter Rose £3,her clothes,a feather bed,bedding and 40s each for her 6 children.

Ralphe Constable and Rose Belchamber had the following children:

i   Richard Constable was born about 26th June,1601 in Kirdford,Sussex

ii   Robert Constable was born in 1608 in Kirdford,Sussex

iii   Jane Constable was born about 28th February,1615 in Kirdford,Sussex

iv   William Constable was born about 10th April,1618 in Kirdford,Sussex

v   Francis Constable was born about 5th December,1619 in Kirdford,Sussex

vi   Elizabeth Constable was born about 20th February,1624 in Kirdford,Sussex. She was buried in Northchapel 2nd March 1633. Elizabeth was not born when Rose's mother died in 1621,so who was the sixth child mentioned in her will? And from the wording in her mother's will,I think Rose was having another baby.
In 1666 when Rose's brother Robert died without issue,he left £10 for each of the children of Francis Constable when they reach the age of 18 years.Edward Belchamber and Robert Constable were the executors of his will and beneficiaries of the residue of his goods and chattels which included livestock.

Henry Belchamber(Robert3,Robert2,John1) was born on 12th May,1589 in Northchapel,Sussex. He married Mary.

Notes for Henry Belchamber:
Born 1589 the son of Robert Belchamber and Constance Goodiar.

Henry Belchamber and Mary had the following children:

i   Mary Belchamber was born 1602 in Petworth,Sussex. She married William Feilder in 1623 in Petworth,Sussex.
Notes for Mary Belchamber:
Born 1602c the daughter of Henry and Mary. According to Petworth Copyholds Mary inherited land called Shonks(part of Garlands) after her father died,so it was no longer in Belchamber family.

Richard Belchamber(Robert3,Robert2,John1) was born about 1592 in Northchapel,Sussex. He died on 6th September,1637. He married Katherine Tickner on 10th February,1624 in Northchapel,Sussex.

Notes for Richard Belchamber:
Richard Occupation farmer,married Katherine Tickner. His mother in her will bequeathed to him"one pewter platter and one fourth of the residue of her estate unbestowed after her debts have been paid". If Richard and Katherine had one child the few parish records that survive reveal no more.
Richard died leaving a will but only his inventory and administration survive. His was probably a small farm judging form his stock and crops.He dies in early February,1637 during an epidemic,the bishops transcripts for that year show many more burials than normal. It was winter with frosts and possibly snow,with little or no crops in the ground. Most of his wheat,hay and

straw were stored in the house and barn. His house appears to have four rooms and was sparsely and poorly furnished. No death found for Katherine.

Richard Belchamber and Katherine Tickner had the following child:

i   Catherine Belchamber was born about 1627 in Northchapel,Sussex.

Thomas Belchamber 9th Great Grandparents
(Robert3,Robert2,John1) was born about 1596 in
Northchapel,Sussex. He married Joan Mellersh in 1626 in Lurgashall,Sussex.

Notes for Thomas Belchamber:
Thomas was born in 1596 the son of Robert Belchamber and Constance Goodiar.Thomas was noted in the 1641 protestation returns for Northchapel.

Notes for Joan Mellersh
Joan was noted as a spinster of the parish of Lurgashall,Sussex. No death details found.

Thomas Belchamber and Joan Mellersh had the following children:

i   Edward Belchamber was born about 30th November,1634 in
         Northchapel,Sussex. He died about 20th June,1688. He married
         Elizabeth. She died about 23rd September,1693 in Northchapel,Sussex.

ii   John Belchamber was born about 29th Decemeber,1639 in
         Northchapel,Sussex. He married Anne. She died on 12th April,1687.

iii   Alice Belchamber was born about 1645 in Northchapel,Sussex.
         Notes for Alice Belchamber:
         In 1666 Alice daughter of Thomas was left £10 in her Uncle Robert
         Belchamber's will.

iv   Mary Belchamber was born about 1650 in Northchapel,Sussex.She
         married Thomas Hobye about 1671 in Northchapel,Sussex.
         Notes for Mary Belchamber:
         In 1666 Mary daughter of Thomas was left £10 in her uncle Robert
         Belchamber's will,to be paid to her when she reaches the age of 18
         years.
         Married by licence to Thomas Hobye,the marriage took place in
         Horsham,Sussex.

William Belchamber(Robert3,Robert2,John1) was born about 1598 in Northchapel,Sussex. He died about 1660 in Kirdford,Sussex. He married Elizabeth Forman on 6th February,1630 in Northchapel,Sussex.

Notes for William Belchamber:
Born 1598c the son of Robert Belchamber and Constance Goodair.William was noted in the 1641 protestation returns for Kirdford. On 8th November,1660 administration of the goods etc.of William Belchamber of

Kirdford was given to his natural and lawful son Robert.

Notes for Elizabeth Forman:
No death details found for Elizabeth but probably before 1660.

William Belchamber and Elizabeth Forman had the following children:

i   William Belchamber was born in 1633

ii   John Belchamber was born about 31st March.1635 in Kirdford,Sussex. He married Mary Agates about 1662 in Horsham,Sussex.

iii   Ann Belchamber was born about 14th February,1640 in Kirdford,Sussex. She married John Morock on 13th January,1667 in Horsham,Sussex.
Notes for Ann Belchamber:
Ann the daughter of William and Elizabeth Forman. She was noted as a spinster of this parish when she married John Morock a Yeoman of this parish by licence.

iv   Robert Belchamber was born about 1637 in Kirdford,Sussex. He died in 1664 in Kirdford. He married Katherine Hudson.
Notes for Robert Belchamber:
Born 1637c the son of William Belchamber and Elizabeth Forman.On 8th November 1660 Robert was granted administration of his father William's goods etc.Robert died 1664 age about 27. On 1st August,1664 administration of the goods etc.of Robert Belchamber of Kirdford amounting to the sum of £295.10s was given to his natural and lawful brother John after Robert's widow Katherine renounced the burden of administration.

John Belchamber(Robert3,Robert2,John1) was born about 1602 in Northchapel,Sussex. He died in 1661. He married Alyce Strudwicke.

Notes for John Belchamber:
The youngest son of Robert and Constance Belchamber,he was born in Garlands,Northchapel. He married Alyce Strudwicke. John was a yeoman farmer and the last Belchamber to have copyhold of Garlands. After his death his daughter Elizabeth Baker inherited and the house stayed in the Baker family until the Earl of Egremont purchased Garlands in 1820. His mother's will 1621"to John my youngest sone the heir of my house and land,one bedstead standing in the parlour and all that belong unto it,a cupboard,a table and bench and stowing in the hall,a long table,a frame and a chest standing in the parlour to tablecloths to the table,two bedsteads and a chest standing in the supper chamber,a iron cauldron,a trivet and a dropping panne,a great brass pott which I will to youngest son"

John was noted in the 1641 protestation returns for Northchapel.

On 3rd December,1661 administration of John's goods etc.amounting to the sum of £20.10s was granted to Jane King alias Belchamber his natural and lawful daughter.

Deed Poll of Grant.ADD Mss 44815 17th February,1637/8

> (a) John Strudwicke of Lurgashall and Elizabeth his wife.John Belchamber of Northchapel,yeoman and Alice his wife.
> (b) Alice Strudwicke daughter of Thomas Strudwicke of WisboroughGreen,butcher and Alice his wife.
> All right and interest in cottage at Betelisham in Lurgashall,in occupation of Joseph Smythe,gent and also the garden adjoining(1/2r)adjoining Ebernoe Common to(b)after death of John Strudwicke and Elizabeth his wife and the longest liver.
> With remainder,for lack of heirsto(b) to Thomas Strudwicke her brother and his heirs,then to William Strudwicke her brother and his heirs.
> Witness's Robert Hollinwood,Ralphe Browne.
>
> NB:Deed Poll of Grant were used to transfer a Corporeal Hereditament to another person.The transfer of Corporeal Hereditaments were transferred by an act or deed such as handing over the key to the property or other parts of the property such as a piece of turf from the land to the new owner.
>
> Note for Alyce Strudwicke:
> No death details found for Alyce.

John Belchamber and Alyce Strudwicke had the following children:

i   John Belchamber was born about 1628 in Northchapel,Sussex. He died about 5th October,1630 in Northchapel.

ii   Mary Belchamber was born about 1630 in Northchapel,Sussex. She died about 6th October,1630 in Northchapel.

iii   Jane Belchamber was born about 1632 in Northchapel,Sussex. She married Unknown King.
Notes for Jane Belchamber
On 3rd December,1661 administration of her father John's goods etc.amounting to the sum of £20.10s was granted to Jane King alias Belchamber his natural and lawful daughter, Jane's father John had inherited 80 acres of land called Garlands in Northchapel from his parents Robert and Constance.

iv   Elizabeth Belchamber was born about 19th March,1634 in Northchapel,Sussex. She married Richard Baker.
Notes for Elizabeth Belchamber
Born 1632 the daughter of John and Alyce.

v   Anne Belchamber was born about 20th September,1637 in Northchapel,Sussex. She died on 19th September,1638 in Northchapel.

vi   Katherine Belchamber was born about 9th December,1638 in
        Kirdford,Sussex.

Generation 5

Edward Belchamber(Thomas4,Robert3,Robert2,John1) was born about 30th
November,1634 in Northchapel,Sussex. He died about 20th June,1688. He
married Elizabeth. She died about 23rd September,1693 in Northchapel.

Notes for Edward Belchamber
Edward was born 1634 in Northchapel the son of Thomas and Joane Mellersh
he married Elizabeth,there are only three baptisms for children born to Edward
and Elizabeth in the Northchapel Bishops Transcripts. The registers to 1716
are lost.In1716 Northchapel became a parish in it's own right,before it was a
hamlet in the parish of Petworth. The transcripts do not cover all years.

In 1666 Edward Belchamber and Robert Constable were the executors and
beneficiaries of the residue of their uncle Robert Belchamber's goods and
chattels which included livestock. Edward's daughter Elizabeth was also
bequeathed £5 when she reaches the age of 18 years.Edward died 1688c.

Notes for Elizabeth:
Elizabeth died 1688 the parish register for Elizabeth's burial in Northchapel
does actually read "widow of Edward" but Edward was buried 5 years earlier
in Kirdford. This needs further investigation.

Edward Belchamber and Elizabeth had the following children:

i   William Belchamber was born about 2nd March,1662 in
        Northchapel,Sussex.

ii   Ann Belchamber was born about 28th September,1666 in
        Northchapel,Sussex. She died about 4th May,1687 in
        Northchapel,Sussex.

iii   Elizabeth Belchamber was born about 1656 in Petworth,Sussex. She
        married Thomas Smith about 1675 in Northchapel.
        Notes for Elizabeth Belchamber
        Born 1656c in Petworth,Sussex, the daughter of Edward and
        Elizabeth.In 1666 Elizabeth daughter of Edward was left £5 in her
        great uncle Robert Belchamber's will,to be paid to her when she
        reaches the age of 18 years. Her father Edward was one of the
        executors and one of the beneficiaries to get the residue of his goods
        and chattles which included livestock.

John Belchamber 8th Great Grandparents
 (Thomas4,Robert3,Robert2,John1) was born about 29th
December,1639 in Northchapel,Sussex. He married Anne. She died 12th

April,1687.

Notes for John Belchamber:
Born 1639 the son of Thomas and Joane Mellersh. In 1666 John was left £10 in his uncle Robert Belchamber's will. No death details for John

Notes for Ann or Annis:
She died 1687 no age given.I Think John and his wife Ann were both buried in Northchapel in 1687 but because no age is recorded,it could be any John or Ann.

John Belchamber and Ann had the following children:

i   Joanne Belchamber was born about 13th March,1665 in Northchapel,Sussex.

ii   Edward Belchamber was born about 2nd December,1668 in Northchapel,Sussex. He died 20th May,1748. He married Mary Stodman on 30th April,1703 in Kirdford,Sussex. She died on 8th February,1736. He married Mary Chandler on 15th May,1740 in Kirdford,Sussex. She died about 4th May,1750 in Kirdford.

iii   John Belchamber was born about 20th October,1672 in Northchapel,Sussex. He died about 7th May,1687 in Northchapel.

iv   Mary Belchamber was born about 1675 in Northchapel,Sussex.

v   William Belchamber was born about 1st December,1678 in Northchapel,Sussex.

William Belchamber(William4,Robert3,Robert2,John1) was born 1633

Notes for William Belchamber:
William was born 1633,I do not know his wifes name but they had one child,Elizabeth born in Kirdford,Sussex.

William Belchamber and unknown wife had the following child:

i   Elizabeth Belchamber was born about 11th May,1673 in Kirdford,Sussex.

John Belchamber(William4,Robert3,Robert2,John1) was born about 31st March,1635 in Kirdford,Sussex. He married Mary Agates 1662 in Horsham,Sussex.

Notes for John Belchamber:
John Belchamber born 1635 in Kirdford the son of William and Elizabeth Forman. He married Mary Agates,John and Mary had 5 child,there may have been more but the registers for Kirdford are not always readable.

On 1st August,1664 administration of the goods etc.of John's brother Robert Belchamber of Kirdford was granted to him after Robert's widow Katherine(Hudson) renounced the burden of administration.

Notes for Mary Agates:
Mary Agates of Nuthurst,Sussex.No death details found to date.

John Belchamber and Mary Agates had the following Children:

i   Elizabeth Belchamber was born about 30th September,1663 in Horsham,Sussex.

ii   William Belchamber was born about 30th March,1669 in Kirdford,Sussex.

iii   Joahn Belchamber was born about 14th February,1671 in Kirdford,Sussex. She died in 1696 in Northchapel.

iv   Elizabeth Belchamber was born about 31st March,1674 in Kirdford,Sussex.

v   John Belchamber was born about 23 January,1675 in Kirdford,Sussex.

Generation 6

Edward Belchamber 7th Great Grandparents
(John5,Thomas4,Robert3,Robert2,John1) was born
about 2nd December,1668 in Northchapel,Sussex. He died 20th May,1748. He married(1) Mary Stodman on 30th April,1703 in Kirdford,Sussex. She was born in Kirdford. She died 8th February,1736 no age given. Edward then married(2) Mary Chandler on 15th May,1740 in Kirdford,Sussex. She died about 4th May,1750 in Kirdford,no age given. When Mary died in 1750 she was recorded as the widow of Edward Belchamber.

Edward Belchamber and Mary Stodman had the following children:

i   Edward Belchamber was born about 25th February,1702 in Kirdford,Sussex. He died on 3rd March,1703 in Kirdford.

ii   Mary Belchamber was born about 29th April,1705 in Kirdford,Sussex.

iii   Jane Belchamber was born about 17th November,1706 in Kirdford,Sussex. She married John Ayling on 1st May,1732 in Kirdford.

iv   Edward Belchamber was born about 19th September,1708 in Kirdford,Sussex. He died 12th March,1785 in Kirdford. He married Mary Boxall on 2nd November,1738 in Kirdford. Mary was the daughter of William Boxall and Elizabeth Newland,she was born in Kirdford in 1702 and died there on 15th October,1789,no age given.

v   Sarah Belchamber was born about 29th April,1712 in Kirdford,Sussex. She married John Wood on 16th November,1735 in Kirdford.

Notes for Mary Chandler:
Mary Chandler a widow died about the 4th May 1750 no age was given,she was recorded as the widow of Edward Belchamber

Generation 7

Jane Belchamber(Edward6,John5,Thomas4,Robert3,Robert2,John1) was born about 17th November,1706 in Kirdford,Sussex .She married John Ayling on 1st May,1732 in Kirdford,Sussex.

John Ayling and Jane Belchamber had the following child:

i   Mary Ayling was born 19th October,1735

Edward Belchamber 6th Great Grandparents
(Edward6,John5,Thomas4,Robert3,Robert2,John1) was
born about 19th September,1708 in Kirdford,Sussex. He died 0n 12th March,1785 in Kirdford. He married Mary Boxall on 2nd November,1738 in Kirdford.

Notes for Edward Belchamber
The son of Edward and Mary Studman he died about 12th March,1785,no age given,he was buried in St.John the Baptist,Kirdford.

Edward Belchamber and Mary Boxall had the following children:

i   Edward Belchamber was born about 7th October,1739 in Kirdford,Sussex. He married Ann Booker in Slinfold,Sussex on the 27th April,1769.

ii   William Belchamber was born about 30th March,1741 in Kirdford,Sussex. He died 26th April 1817 in Kirdford. He married Elizabeth Foyce on 19th May,1763 in Kirdford. Elizabeth Foyce was born about 1741,she died in Kirdford on 24th October,1823.

iii   John Belchamber was born about 1st July,1744 in Kirdford,Sussex. He died there on the 14th April,1805.

iv   James Belchamber was born about 10th August,1746 in Kirdford,Sussex. He died in Kirdford on 23 December,1801 .He married Mary Voice on 13th June,1773 in Pulborough,Sussex.

v   Jenney Belchamber was born about 14th July,1751 in Kirdford,Sussex. She married Henry Standage on 27th April,1780 in Kirdford.

Notes for Jenney Belchamber:
Listed as a spinster of this parish(Kirdford) when she married Henry Standage of Petworth,Sussex by banns in Kirdford their witness's were Robert Moodey and Ann Goodring.
Jenney was a witness to the marriage of her brother James when he married Mary Voice.

vi   A unnamed male child was born about 28th March,1749 in Kirdford,Sussex.

Sarah Belchamber(Edward6,John5,Thomas4,Robert3,Robert2,John1) was born about 29th April,1712 in Kirdford,Sussex. She married John Wood on 16th November,1735 in Kirdford.

Notes for Sarah Belchamber:
Born 1712 the daughter of Edward and Mary Stodman.

John Wood and Sarah Belchamber had the following children:

i   Sarah Wood was born about 3rd October,1736.

ii   Mary Wood was born about 18th March,1738

iii   Ruth Wood was born about 24th August,1739
NB:All born in Kirdford,Sussex.

Generation 8

Edward Belchamber(Edward7,Edward6,John5,Thomas4,Robert3,Robert2, John1) was born about 7th October,1739 in Kirdford,Sussex. He married Ann Booker in Slinfold,Sussex on 27th April,1769. No death details found for Edward to date.

Edward Belchamber and Ann Booker had the following Child:

i   Edward Belchamber was born 1771. He died about 23rd November,1823 in Horsham,Sussex. He married Fanny Briggs on 18th May,1794 in Horsham.Fanny was the daughter of Charles Briggs and Ann Dench. Fanny died in the city of London on 21st July,1837

William Belchamber 5th Great Grandparents
(Edward7,Edward6,John5,Thomas4,Robert3,Robert2,John1)was born about 30th March,1741 in Kirdford,Sussex. He died 26th April,1817 age 76 in Kirdford. He married Elizabeth Foyce on 19th May,1763 in Kirdford,Sussex by banns which were read 1st,8th and 15th May. Witness was John Nightingale.

Notes for Elizabeth Foyce:
Born about 17th July,1743 in Billingshurst,Sussex,the daughter of Robert and Elizabeth Foyce. She died 1823 aged 82.

William Belchamber and Elizabeth Foyce had the following children:

i   Mary Belchamber was born about March,1764 in Kirdford,Sussex. She married George Linnegar on 14th May,1784 in Witley,Surrey. Whoever recorded the event wrote Mary's surname as Belchymores. Assuming the recorder was hard of hearing and maybe Mary had a strong Sussex accent the word Belchymores can sound like Belchamber if said quickly, also Mary could not write as she left her mark on the register, so probably could not read either, George Linnegar also left his mark so I presume he was illiterate also, so they both signed the register not realizing the mistake There are no Belchymores in Witley or in fact on the IGI and a Google search also comes up with zero So I think that it is safe to say that Mary Belchymore is in fact Mary Belchamber.

ii   Sarah Belchamber was born about 22nd December,1765 in Kirdford,Sussex. She married James Gill on 25th July,1784 in Godalming,Surrey.

iii   William Belchamber was born about 27th March,1768 in Kirdford,Sussex. He died on the 3rd August,1844 in Godalming. He married Ann Lucas 16th August,1795 in Godalming. Ann Lucas was born 1773. She died in Godalming on 16th July,1846 in Godalming.

iv   Patience Belchamber was born about 26th February,1774 in Kirdford,Sussex. She died about 24th February,1869 in Kirdford. She married Thomas Wood on 24th May,1792 in Kirdford.

v   Jenny Belchamber was born about 1st December,1776 in Kirdford,Sussex.

vi   James Belchamber was born about 5th September,1779 in Kirdford,Sussex. He died 13th December,1856 in Wisborough Green,Sussex. He married Jane Downer in Kirdford on 24th May,1804.Jane was born in 1782,she died in Wisborough Green 25th June,1866.

vii   Ann Belchamber was born about 2nd June,1782 in Kirdford,Sussex. She married James Faulkner on 21st June,1808 in Dunsfold,Surrey.James was born 1774 and died 1851.
Notes for Ann Belchamber:
Born 1782 the daughter of William and Elizabeth Foyce. In 1859 Ann(Faulkner) was the only beneficiary of her Brother John's will.

vii   Edward Belchamber was born about 15th May,1785 in Kirdford,Sussex. He died on 19th October,1865 in Kirdford,Sussex. He married Elizabeth Stenning on 6th November,1824 in Shalford,Surrey. She was born about 1800 and died 25th January,1867 in Kirdford.

ix   John Belchamber was born about 16th March,1788 in Kirdford,Sussex. He died 5th March,1859 in Rooks Hill,Bramley,Surrey. He married Martha Wood in Dunsfold,Surrey on 2nd February,1815. Martha died 22nd September,1846 in Shalford.

JamesBelchamber
(Edward7,Edward6,John5,Thomas4,Robert3,Robert2,John1)
Was born about 10th August,1746 in Kirdford,Sussex .He died 23rd December,1801 in Kirdford. He married Mary Voice on the 13th June,1773 in Pulborough,Sussex.

Notes for James Belchamber:
When their sons William and Richard were born,James and Mary were listed as paupers. James was buried in Kirdford 0n 23rd December,1801 aged 51. When James married Mary Voice the banns were read on 23rd and 30th May and 6th June.James's sister Jenny Belchamber and Daniel Searle were witness's.

Notes for Mary Voice:
Born in Billingshurst,Sussex and baptisted on 20th March,1755.

James Belchamber and Mary Voice had the following children:

i   Sarah Belchamber was born about 8th March,1778 in Kirdford,Sussex. She married John Reeves on 7th June,1796 in Wisborough Green,Sussex.

ii   Mary Belchamber was born about 9th September,1781 in Kirdford,Sussex. She married Thomas Wood on 29th October,1811 in Kirdford.

iii   Ann Belchamber was born about 29th June,1783 in Kirdford,Sussex. She married Thomas Duke on 26th September,1812 in Lyminster,Sussex.
        Notes for Ann Belchamber:
        In 1857 Ann(Duke) of Wick,Sussex was left 20 in her brother James' will.

iv   James Belchamber was born about 25th September,1785 in Kirdford,Sussex. He died on 10th June,1857 in Littlehampton,Sussex. He married Charlotte Cobby on 9th December,1806 in St.Mary Littlehampton,Sussex. She died 28th April,1850 in Littlehampton.
        Notes for Charlotte Cobby:
        She was the daughter of James and Susanna Cobby,born about 24th June,1781 in Walberton,Sussex.

v   Jane Belchamber was born about 15th September,1788 in Kirdford,Sussex.

vi   John Belchamber was born about 15th September,1788 in Kirdford,Sussex. Twin to Jane Belchamber.

vii   William Belchamber was born about 27th March,1791 in Kirdford,Sussex. He died 3rd May,1838 in Luth House,Wisborough Green,Sussex. He married Sarah Barnes on 13th September,1814 in St.Mary Littlehampton,Sussex. She died on 5th October,1849 in Wisborough Green.

viii Richard Belchamber was born about 30th December,1792 in Kirdford,Sussex.

Richard Belchamber Convict:
Richard Belchamber could have been the son of James and Mary Belchamber nee Voice baptized 30th December 1792 in Kirdford, Sussex.
He enlisted in the 39th Dorsetshire Regiment and at some point was posted to Upper Canada prior to 1815. He deserted the regiment and on the 3rd of May 1815 was sentenced to be transported as a felony. He came back to England on HMS Dido arriving 9th of October 1815 and was goaled in a Prison Hulk in Portsmouth Harbour (Langstone Harbour) until he was put aboard HME Atlas 111 to be transported to Port Jackson, NSW, Australia 1816. There are three possible Prison Hulks he was on the Coromandel,Perseus or Laurel.
HMS Atlas departed Portsmouth on the 23 January 1816 and arrived 22 July 1816, she was carrying 194 male Prisoners; there were 187 prisoners when she arrived, 7 prisoners had died on route, and 60 prisoners were under 21 years of age. Her Master was Walter Meriton and Patrick Hill was the Surgeon Superintendent.
Richards was sentenced alongside two other man, Job Hamilton and James Fitzpatrick all labourers, both these men were given Conditional Pardons, although there is no record of Richard receiving one. He did obtain two Tickets of Leave in 1828 and 1830 for the districts of Bathurst and Prospect. (This meant he was free to travel from these districts, probably for work. Richard cannot be found in the 1828 NSW Census.
At this moment I cannot find him marrying or dying.
The indent does state his native place was Sussex, that he was 23 when he arrived and that he had Brown Hair, Hazel eyes and a fair sallow complexion. The three prisoners could have deserted after or during the Battle of Lundy's Lane, where the British army suffered Huge loses of men and lack of supplies.
NB:
There is a Richard Belchamber who is another possible candidate,he was born in Lyminster,Sussex in 1794

ix   George Belchamber was born about 3rd April,1796 in Kirdford,Sussex. He married Elizabeth Henley in St.Mary Littlehampton on 27th January,1818.

Generation 9

Edward Belchamber

(Edward8,Edward7,Edward6,John5,Thomas4,Robert3,Robert2,John1)
Was born in 1771. He died about Nov,1823 age 52 in Horsham,Sussex. He
married Fanny Briggs on 18th May,1794 in Horsham by banns.
Notes for Edward Belchamber;
Edward was buried in St.Marys Church,Horsham,Sussex. The service was
conducted by W Pearse.
Notes for Fanny Briggs:
Possibly born about 22nd November,1772 in Horsham,Sussex the daughter of
Charles Briggs and Ann Dench. She died on 21st July,1837 in the City of
London.

Edward Belchamber and Fanny Briggs had the following childen:

i   Edward Belchamber was born on 27th May,1795 in Horsham,Sussex.
He died on 16th January,1878 in Camberwell Infirmary. He married
Ann Sayer on 24th April,1814 in Horsham. She died on 13th
October,1857 in Camberwell.

In the 1841 census Ed and Ann Belchamber were in Horsham living at Northchapel
House,Chapel Street. Ed was 46 and an Ag.Lab Ann was 45 their children were
Samuel 12,Jane 8 and Lucy 6.

Edward and Ann were living in Camberwell at Baily Grove in the 1851 census with
their children. Edward was a Gardener aged 55 as was Ann.The children were Jane
18,William 16,Lucy 16 and nephew William 5.

Ned (Edward Belchamber) aged 66 and his nephew William aged 15 were living with
his neice Jane Shobbock and her family in Camberwell in 1861

Edward 75 a widower and Gardener was head of household in the 1871 census,he
was living at 12 Rupell Terrace in Camberwell. Living with him was his daughter
Jane Shobbock a Laundress aged 37 and a widow and her Children and William
Belchamber listed as Edward's nephew,William was 24 and a Solicitors Clerk.

Death Certificates:
Edward Belchamber died of decay on the 16th of January,1878 at the Camberwell
Infirmary. Listed as a Gardener aged 83,the death was registered by C.W Gregory on
the 18th of January.J Thompson,Matron at the Infirmary was the informant.

62 year old Ann Belchamber died of an Ovarian Tumour(5 Years) Certified on the
13th of October,1857.Ann was listed as the wife of Edward Belchamber a Jobbing
Gardener,E Belchamber probably her son was informant and present at death. The
death was recorded on the 13th of October by the registrar Charles Nicolles.

ii   Fanny Belchamber was born on 2nd April,1797 in Horsham,Sussex.

iii   Sarah Belchamber was born on 9th June,1799 in Horsham,Sussex. She died on
the 21st September,1873 in Hounslow. She married Samuel Ferdinand Morris
on 29th August,1825 in Lothbury,London.

iv   Ann Belchamber was born on 7th May,1802 in Horsham,Sussex. She died in 1831 in Horsham. She married William Cottington on 28th August,1822 in Horsham.

Sarah Belchamber

(Edward8,Edward7,Edward6,John5,Thomas4,Robert3,Robert2,John1) was born about 22nd December,1765 in Kirdford,Sussex. She married James Gill on 25th July,1784 in Godalming,Surrey
Notes for Sarah Belchamber:
Sarah was born 1765 the daughter of William and Elizabeth Foyce.
The banns for their wedding were called on the 4th,11th and 18th of July.Witness' were Joseph Hord and Henry Coston.

James Gill and Sarah Belchamber had the following child:

i   Henry Gill,he married Lydia.

William Belchamber

(Edward8,Edward7,Edward6,John5,Thomas4,Robert3,Robert2,John1) was born about 27th March,1768 in Kirdford,Sussex.
It is probable that this William was the William Belchamber who married Ann Lucas in Godalming,Surrey on the 16th August,1795.This needs further investigation and no data is included in this book.

Patience Belchamber

(Edward8,Edward7,Edward6,John5,Thomas4,Robert3,Robert2,John1) was born about 26th February,1774 in Kirdford,Sussex. She died about 24th February,1869 in Kirdford. She married Thomas Wood on 24th May,1792 in Kirdford by banns.
Notes for Thomas Wood:
A Bricklayer by trade he married Patience Belchamber by banns in Kirdford.Witness' were William Belchamber and James Bryder. Thomas died in 1855.

Thomas Wood and Patience Belchamber had the following children:

i   Elizabeth Wood born about 21st April,1799.

ii   Richard Wood born about 12th February,1804.

iii   Arthur Wood born about 15th May,1808.

iv   James Wood born about 14th October,1810.

v   Edward Wood born about 15th January,1815

vi   Charles Wood born about 23rd August,1818.
      All born in Kirdford,Sussex.

James Belchamber 4th Great Grandparents

(Edward8,Edward7,Edward6,John5,Thomas4,Robert3,Robert2,John1) was born about 5th September,1779 in Kirdford,Sussex. He died on 13th December,1856 in

Wisborough Green,Sussex. He married Jane Downer on 24th May,1804 in Kirdford.She was born in 1782 She died on 25th June,1866 in Wisborough Green.
Notes for James Belchamber:
Born 1779 the son of William and Elizabeth Foyce.James married Jane Downer by banns which were called 29th April,6th May and 13th May. Witness'were Mary Sopp,John Durrant and Elizabeth Downer. Mary signed her name but John and Elizabeth made their mark.

In the 1841 Census James and Jane were in Lakers Lodge Cottage,Wisborough Green. James aged 61 ,Jane aged 59 and their son Edward 25 was unmarried and a Agricultural Labourer

In the 1851 census James and Jane were in Malthurst Farm Cottage Wisborough Green with them was their unmarried son Edward aged 34 a Agricultral Labourer.James aged 71 and Jane aged 69 were also Agricultural,Labourers. Also James' brother John Belchamber aged 62 a widower and Agricultural Labourer.

In 1861 widow Jane Bellchamber aged 79 was living in Wisborough Green,Sussex at Foxes,she was listed as a pauper. Edward her son aged 44 and a Agricultural Labourer was also living with her.

James Belchamber was buried at Wisborough Green on the 21st of Dec 1856 aged 77,Jane Belchamber aged 84 was also buried at Wisborough Green on the 28th of June 1866.
James Belchamber Died of diarohea(Certified) on the 13th of December,1856 at Wisborough Green,Sussex. James was a 77 year old Agricultral Labourer. Present at death and informant was Susan Remnant also of Wisborough Green. Henry Boxall the registrar for Petworth registered the death on the 15th of December.

Jane Belchamber aged 84 died in the workhouse in Kirdford on the 25th of June,1866,cause of death was Apoplexy which was certified. Jane was listed as the widow of James Belchamber Farm Labourer,the informant and present at death was Eliza Pullen of the Workhouse,Kirdford. The death was recorded at Petworth on the 5th of July by George Wells Registrar.

James Belchamber and Jane Downer had the following children:

i   James Belchamber was born about 2nd June,1805 in Kirdford,Sussex. He died 11th May,1875 in Plaistow,Sussex. He married Mary Denyer on 26th May,1831 in Kirdford. She was born in 1812 in Kirdford. She died 13th December,1891 in Plaistow.
James Belchamber and Mary Denyer were married in St John the baptist,Kirdford on the 29th of May 1831,by banns the ceremony was performed by Robert Ridsdale vicar. James and Mary put their marks on the register and Henry Young and Elizabeth Belchamber were witness`s they both signed their names.

ii   Elizabeth Belchamber was born about 24th July,1808 in Kirdford,Sussex. She married John Lee on the 5th October,1834 in St.Marys,Guildford,Surrey. He was born in 1804 in Woking,Surrey.

iii   John Belchamber was born about 27th October,1811 in Kirdford,Sussex. He died 7th December,1893 in The Union Workhouse,Leytonstone. He married Sarah Sopp on 11th October,1840 in Holy Trinity,Westminister. She died 15th January,1877 in 50 Marsham Street,Westminister.

iv   William Belchamber was born 18th May,1814 in Wisborough Green,Sussex. He died 28th August,1872 in Ovingdean,Sussex. He married Barbara Hannah Westgate on 21st August,1846 in The Parish Church,Sheffield,Yorkshire. She was born in 1822 in Patcham,Sussex. She died 19th April,1895 in Brighton, Sussex.

v   Edward Belchamber was born about 11th June,1816 in Wisborough,Green. He died on 24th June 1871 in The Kirdford Workhouse. Edward never married.

Death Certificate:
Edward Belchamber aged 55 died of Chronic Hepatitis on the 24th June,1871 in the Kirdford Workhouse. The informant and present at the death was Ann Luff. Henry Boxall the registrar for Petworth recorded the death on the 27th June.

vi   Mary Belchamber was born about 16th May,1819 in Alfold,Surrrey. She married John Mason on the 7th November,1849 in St.Clement Dane, Westminister.

Marriage Certificate:
Mary Belchamber and John Mason married at the parish church St.Clement Danes,Middlesex on the 7th of November,1849 by license.Bachelor John and spinster Mary were of full age,John was a Builder by trade,their abode was 23 Stoughton Street. Their fathers were John Mason a Builder and James Belchamber a Bailiff. The witness's were Hannah Linnegar and James Linnegar.J Harkwell performed the ceremony.

vii   Ann Belchamber was born about 9th November,1819 in Wisborough Green Sussex. She died there in 1824

Edward Belchamber
(William8,Edward7,Edward6,John5,Thomas4,Robert3,Robert2,John1) was born about 15th May,1785 in Kirdford,Sussex. He died on 19th October,1865 aged 82 in Kirdford,Sussex. He married Elizabeth Stenning on 6th November,1824 in Shalford,Surrey. She was born about 1800. She died 31st January,1867 in Kirdford.
Notes for Edward Belchamber:
Born 1785 he was listed as a Agricultural Labourer when he married Elizabeth Stenning. In 1825 he was a witness at the marriage of his brother John who married Martha Woods.
Notes for Elizabeth Stenning:
She was born about 1800 in Dunsfold,Surrey. When she married Edward she was listed as a spinster of the parish of Dunsfold. Witness' to the marriage were Lynsey Sturt and Robert Bellchamber. I think Robert was Edward's nephew,the son of his brother William and his wife Ann nee Lucas.

Census:
In 1841 Elizabeth was in Kirdford at Pound Common with two sons William 10 and John 5.Elizabeth was aged 35. Her husband Edward must have been away working as there is no mention of him.

In the 1851 census Edward and Eliza were in Kirdford living at Pound Common. Edward was aged 64 and a Agricultural Labourer,Eliza was 48. Their son William 28 was a Agricultural Labourer,also living with them was a lodger Henry Hillyer aged 32 a former Shoemaker.

In the 1861 census Edward and Elizabeth were in Kirdford,living in Pound Common Cottage.Edward was 76 and Agricultural Labourer,Elizabeth was 63 from Dunsfold,Surrey. Sons William 28 and John 25 were both Agricultural Labourers.

Death certificates;
Edward Belchamber died in Kirdford,Sussex on the 19th of October,1865 aged 82,cause of death was Diarrhoea and old age. Informant was Henry Boxall.Registrar George Wells recorded the death for Petworth on the 16th of November.

Elizabeth Belchamber died in Kirdford aged 67 on the 25th of January,1867. Cause of death was Bronchitis.Henry Boxall was informant and present at Death.Elizabeth was listed as the wife of Edward Belchamber a Farm Labourer. The death was registered on the 14th of February by George Wells the registrar for Petworth.

Edward Belchamber and Elizabeth Stenning had the following children:

i   Mary Ann Belchamber was born about 9th July,1826 in Kirdford,Sussex. She married Pacey Tribe on 16th April,1854 in All Saints,Wandsworth,Surrey.

Marriage Certificate:
Mary Anne Belchamber aged 27 and Pacey Tribe aged 33 were married at All Saints,Wandsworth,Surrey on the 16th of April,1854. Pacey Tribe was a Carpenter from Wandsworth as Mary also listed her abode at the time of marriage. Witness's were George and Mary Day. The fathers were James Tribe a Carpenter and Edward Belchamber a Labourer.Stephen J Gower performed the service.

ii   William Belchamber was born about 3rd April,1831 in Kirdford,Sussex. He died 10th February,1886 in The Workhouse,Petworth,Sussex. William did not marry.

Death Certificate:
Farm Labourer William Belchamber died in the Petworth Workhouse on the 10th of February,1886. Cause of death was Stranglated Hernia operation and exhaustion certified by J Wilson Hogg MRC.William Holt the Master of the Workhouse was Informant. C G Hill the registrar for Petworth registered the death on the 18th of February.

iii   John Belchamber was born 22nd November,1835 in Kirdford,Sussex. He died 10th December,1883 in Kirdford. He married Sophia Older on 3rd October,1865 in Kirdford. She was the daughter of William Whittick Older and Sophia Southerton. She was born about 1ˢᵗ March,1840 in Wisborough Green,Sussex. She died on 13ᵗʰ April,1920 in The Village,Kirdford.

John Belchamber

(William8,Edward7,Edward6,John5,Thomas4,Robert3,Robert2,John1) was born about16ᵗʰ March,1788 in Kirdford,Sussex. He died 5ᵗʰ March,1859 in Rooks Hill,Bramley,Surrey. He married Martha Wood on 2ⁿᵈ February,1815 in Dunsfold,Surrey. She died 22ⁿᵈ September,1846 in Shalford.

Marriage Licence:
John Belchamber and Martha Woods were married in the parish church Dunsfold,Surrey by banns on the 12th day of February,1815. John was a bachelor and of this parish and Martha a spinster of this parish. They both signed the license with their mark. Witmess' were John Voller and Edward Belchamber who signed with his mark. The Rev.Bartholmew performed the service.

Census:
John and Martha were living at Quarry Hill in Shalford,Surrey in the 1841 census.Both aged 50 John was a Carrier. Living with them was their son William aged 20 a Carpenter by trade.

In 1851 John was living with his Brother James and wife Jane in Loxwood,John was 62 and a Agricultural Labourer.

Death Certificates:
The death of John Belchamber a Carrier took place at Rooks Hill,Bramley on the 5th March 1859. John died of Bronchitis,Mary Worsfold was informant and present at the death,which was registered on the 9th March.

Martha Belchamber died on the 22nd of September 1849 in Shalford,Surrey aged 59.Her occupation was listed as Wife of John Belchamber carrier. Martha died of Fever Typhoides(3 weeks)Mary Belchamber her daughter in law was informant and present at death. The death was registered on the 25th September.
Martha was buried in Shalford,Surrey on the 27ᵗʰ September,1846 aged 59.

John made a will leaving everything to his sister Ann Faulkner,he died aged 71

John Belchamber's will:
On the 16ᵗʰ day of July 1859
Letters of administration,with the will and codicals thereto annexed
Of all and singular the personal estate and effects of John Belchamber late of Rooks Hill,Bramley near Guildford in the county of Surrey
Deceased who died on the 5ᵗʰ day of March,1859 at Rooks Hill aforesaid.
Were granted at the principal registry of her majesty's court of probate
To Ann Faulkner of Rooks Hill widow
Aforesaid the sister of the deceased
The Legatee named in the said will,she having been first sworn duly to administer.No executor being named in the said will

John Belchamber and Martha Wood had the following children:

i   Ann Belchamber was born about 4th October,1815 in Guildford,Surrey. She died on 8th May,1825 in Shalford.

ii   John Belchamber was born about 20th August,1817 in Shalford,Surrey and died there on 13th October,1819.

iii   William Belchamber was born about 20th August,1820 in Shalford,Surrey. He married Mary Welch on 23rd March,1846 in the parish of Putney. She died 1st November,1880 in 49 Lower Park Street,Greenwich,Kent.

iv   Mary Belchamber was born about 2nd February,1823 in Shalford,Surrey. She died there 6th December,1838 in Shalford.
Notes for Mary Belchamber:
15 year old Mary Belchamber died of consumption on the 6th December,1838 in Shalford. She was recorded as the daughter of John Belchamber a Waggoner. Her mother was informant,the death was registered on the 7th of December by Deputy Registrar Robert Sutcliffe for Hambledon Union. Mary was buried on the 12th December at St.Marys,Shalford.

v   Henry Belchamber was born about May,1825 in Shalford,Surrey. He died about 5th June,1825 in St.Marys,Shalford.

Sarah Belchamber
(James8,Edward7,Edward6,John5,Thomas4,Robert3,Robert2,John1) was born about 8th March,1778 in Kirdford,Sussex. She married John Reeves on 7th June,1796 in Wisborough Green,Sussex.

Notes for Sarah Belchamber:
Listed as the daughter of James and Mary Voice. In 1857 Sarah Reeves of Wisborough Green was left £20 in her brother James' will,he also left to her and her daughter Sarah Reeves a house each,located in Littlehampton,Sussex. Other members of Sarah's family were also beneficiaries.

John Reeves and Sarah Belchamber had the following children:
i   Mary Reeves born 1799
ii   James Reeves born 1800
iii   William Reeves born 1801
iv   Thomas Reeves born 1803
vi   Arthur Reeves born 1804
vii   Elizabeth Reeves born 1808
viii   Harriet Reeves born 1812
All born in Kirdford,Sussex.Sometimes known as Rives.

James Belchamber
(James8,Edward7,Edward6,John5,Thomas4,Robert3,Robert2,John1) was born about 25th September,1785 in Kirdford,Sussex. He died in Littlehampton,Sussex on the 10th June,1857. He married Charlotte Cobby on 9th December,1809 in St.Marys,Littlehampton,Sussex. She was the daughter of James Cobby and Susanna. She was born on 24th June,1781 in Walberton,Sussex. She died 28th

April,1850 in Littlehampton. James and Charlotte were married by banns,the witness'
were Elizabeth Cobby and Thomas Heward.

In the 1841 census James 60 and Charlotte 61 were living in Littlehampton on the
Beach with Susan and Henrietta Grey both 20

Death Certificate:
Master Carpenter James Belchamber aged 73 died at Littlehampton on the 10th of
June 1857,cause of death was Water on the chest.Charlotte Skinner was informant and
present at death. The death was registered on the 12th of June by George Grant
registrar for Worthing.

James Belchamber of Littlehampton died of the 10th June,1857 leaving a will which
is transcribed below:

This is the last will and testament of me James Belchamber of Littlehampton in the
county of Sussex.
I appoint Mr Henry Lock of Littlehampton,Schoolmaster and Mrs Charlotte Skinner
as my Exacutor and Exacutrix od this my will.I give to Mr Henry Locke as my
acting Exacutor all power to take my money from the savings bank in Arundel
and other monies of mine in my procession at the time of my death.I allow
him twenty pounds of the same out of which he shall pay all my funeral and
other necessary expenses attendant thereon.I give him power to receive from
Mr Edward Landers the sum due to meet with interest thereon as the named
mortgage deed on the brig Elizabeth of the port of Arundel or the right to sell
the above named brig to recover the principal and interest due thereon.
(and if my estate will allow to give to the undernamed persons the following sum of
the proportional parts of the same,within six months after I decease.
To Mrs Reeves of Littlehampton fifty pounds,to Fanny Landers of Wick ten pounds,to
Mary Matthews ten pounds,to Ann Dannaway ten pounds,to Sarah Cockerel
five pounds,to Charles Duke five pounds all the above named persons of
Wick.To John Reeves of Brighton ten pounds and a watch,to Eliza Carpenter
of Wick ten pounds.To Elizabeth Belchamber the daughter of my brother five
pounds and to her mother five pounds.To Emily Gravett(widow of
Littlehampton) five pounds and her daughter five pounds,to Mrs
Kennard(widow five pounds.
The remainder of my money I leave and give to the exacutor Mr Henry Lock to give
to my two sisters Ann Duke of Wick and Sarah Reeves of Wisborough
Green(both in Sussex the sum of twenty pounds each) if the estate will allow
or a proportionit part.I also empower my exacutor Mr Henry Lock to give to
John Belchamber of Wisborough Green ten pounds and to my niece now
living at Wisborough Green(whose maiden name was Ellen Reeves ten pounds
or proportional part of the same.Of my leasehold property I give to Mrs
Skinner of Littlehampton the house in which she is now living and the garden
belonging thereto(except a piece ten foot wide from north to south at the well
end thereof the house Mrs Lupper lives in.I give to Sarah Reeves the younger
the house that Thomas Leggett lives in.I give to Sarah Reeves the elder (both
of Littlehampton) to be disposed of,at her as she pleases(subject to the spirit of
the lease)

The house that I James Belchamber live in joining Mrs Skinner I give to Mary Clark my niece of London during her lifetime and at her death to go to John Reeves of Littlehampton and if he is not of age at the tome of her death the money to be taken as rent by Mr Henry Lock or by Mrs Skinner and put into a bank until he is of age(and if he die before he comes of age to go the William Reeves his brother.

I leave my household furniture,a large glafs over the parlour fireplace to Sarah Reeves the younger,to Mrs Skinner I leave my clock,to Luke Reeves the best bed,bed furniture and bedstead belonging thereto and of the rest of my furniture Sofa,Writing Desk,Dining Table and seats and a chest of draws.I give to Mrs Reeves. The remainder of my furniture I empower my exacutor to sell to defray the expenses of proving my will and other incidental expenses.

I now declare this is my last will and testament and I revoke all former will or wills,in witness's hereof(in the presence of two undernamed witness's and in the presence of each each other(after my name is written) I affix my mark and seal on the ninth day of May one thousand eight hundred and fifty seven.

James Belchamber mark,James Albon,William S Lock

Effects swain	The will was proved on the
Under £600	25th day of June 1857 before
	The Rev'd William Miller Clerk Surrogate
Leaseholds	vc of the oaths of Henry Lock
	And Charlotte Skinner the exacutors
Testator dies	therein named to whom a day was given
10th June 1857	for exhibiting an inventory

Death Certificate:
Charlotte Belchamber died in Littlehampton aged 69 on the 23rd of April 1850,cause of death was Atrophy(3 weeks certified),she was listed as the wife of James Belchamber a Carpenter. Informant and present at death was Christiana Lewray of Littlehampton. Registrar George Grant recorded the death on the 26th of April for Worthing.

Charlotte Cobby had the following child:

i   Sarah Cobby.

William Belchamber
(James8,Edward7,Edward6,John5,Thomas4,Robert3,Robert2,John1) was born about 27th March,1791 in Kirdford,Sussex. He died on 3rd May,1838 in Luth House,Wisborough Green,Sussex. He married Sarah Barnes on 13th September,1814 in St.Marys,Littlehampton,Sussex. She died on 5th October,1849 in Wisborough Green.Witness's to the marriage of William and Sarah were James Belchamber and John Page.

Census:
Sarah and her two daughters were living in Wisborough Green,Sussex at the Luth in the 1841 census.Sarah was 50 Louisa 25 and Fanny 14. Also living with them were William Barnes aged 73 and Sarah Barnes 71 her parents

Death Certificates:
47 year old Labourer William Belchamber died on the 3rd 0f March 1838 of Dropsey. William died at Luth House,Wisborough Green,Sussex,his wife Sarah Belchamber was informant and present at death. Henry Turner the registrar for Petworth Union recorded the death on the 4th of March.

58 year old Sarah Belchamber died on the 5th of October,1849 in Wisborough Green,Sussex. She was the widow of William Belchamber a Labourer.Informant and present at death was her daughter Louisa Belchamber. Cause of death was Paraplexy,the death was registered by Henry Boxall the registrar for Petworth Union.

William Belchamber and Sarah Barnes had the following children:

i   Louisa Belchamber was born on 9th July,1815 in Kirdford,Sussex. She married James Puttick on the 9th October,1857 in Kirdford.

Marriage Certificate:
Louisa Belchamber and James Puttick were married at Kirdford on the 9th of October,1857,both were of full age and from Kirdford. James Puttick was a widower and Louisa a spinster. Witness's were Benjamin and Eliza Pacy,both Louisa and James signed the licence with their mark. The fathers were James Puttick a Labourer and William Belchamber a Farmer.

ii   John Belchamber was born 27th August,1818 in Kirdford,Sussex. He died 2nd December,1900 in Cray Hill,Pulborough,Sussex. He married Harriet Sheppard on 5th May,1840 in Wisborough Green. She died 4th February,1901 in Cray Hill Cottages,Pulborough.

iii   Sally Belchamber was born 14th January,1821 in Kirdford,Sussex. She died 4th February,1849 in Wisborough Green.

iv   Mary Belchamber was born 16th November,1823 in Wisborough Green,Sussex. She died in 1855 in Petworth,Sussex. She married Luke Towes 6th August,1840 in Wisborough Green.

Marriage Certificate:
Luke Towse a Miller and spinster Mary Belchamber married at the parish church Wisborough Green on the 6th of August 1840. Luke was of full age and Mary a minor. Witness's were Robert Woods and Sally Belchamber,Mary's sister.John Thornton the vicar performed the marriage. The fathers were Thomas Towse a Farmer and William Belchamber a Labourer. Luke gave his abode as Billinghurst and Mary's Wisborough Green.

v   Fanny Belchamber was born 23rd July,1826 in Wisborough Green,Sussex. She married Edward Edwin Bookham

Marriage Certificate:
Edward Edwin Bookham a Bricklayer and Fanny Belchamber married on the 11th June,1851 by banns in The Parish Church,Shalford,Surrey. Witness's were Henry

Wilkinson and Mary Ann Brookes. John Gifford performed the service. Edward's father was Charles Bookham a Servant. Fanny gave her father as James Belchamber a Labourer,now her father was William Belchamber. Fanny's grandfather was a James Belchamber so whether the vicar misheard or Fanny wanted James to be listed as her father we will never know.

Generation 10

Edward Belchanber

(Edward9,Edward8,Edward7,Edward6,John5,Thomas4,Robert3,Robert2,John1) was born 27th May,1795 in Horsham,Sussex. He died on 16th January,1878 in Camberwell Infirmary. He married Ann Sayer on 24th April,1814 in Horsham. She died 13th October,1857 in 4 Hardens Road,Camberwell,Surrey.

Edward Belchamber and Ann Sayer had the following children:

i   Edward Belchamber born 4th September,1814 in Horsham,Sussex. He died 18th October,1892 in Ambra Gate House,Clifton,Bristol. He married Sarah Brockless on 11th July,1850 in Holywell,Oxford. She died in 1865.

Census:
Edward aged 25 was living in Chelsea as a manservant for Elizabeth Hughes at Greenes Row

Marriage Certificate:
Edward Belchamber,bachelor of full age married Sarah Brockless,spinster of full age on the 11th of July 1850 by banns, at the parish church,Holywell,Oxford. Both were residing in Holywell. Witness's were John Lovell and Jane Wrixson. Vicar Arthur H Hadden.Fathers Edward Belchamber was a gardener and Samuel Brockless was also a gardener.

After Sarah died Edward remarried to Comfort Evans on 30th June,1877 in Holy Trinity,Bridgewater,Somerset. She was born in Bode.

Census:
In 1851 Edward 36 is still working for Elizabeth Hughes as a manservant still in Chelsea in Greenes Row.
Also now working as a Servant is Sarah Brockless but like Edward she is listed as unmarried,Edward and Sarah probably didn't tell Elizabeth Hughes they were married for fear of losing their jobs(Edward and Sarah married in 1850 in Oxford)

Marriage Certificate:
Widower Edward Belchamber a Grocer of full age married Spinster Comfort Evans again of full age at the Holy Trinity,Bridgewater,Somerset on the 30th of June 1877 by banns. The witness's were John Davey and Mary Dyer. Edward gave his residence as Bridgewater and Comfort as St.Marys,Clyst. The vicar George Green performed the marriage service. Edwards father gave his name as Ned Belchamber a gardener and Comfort's father William Harris Evans was a Bailiff .

Census:
They are in the 1881 census living in Ambra Hill,Gloucester. Edward is a Grocer aged 66 and Comfort is a Grocers wife aged 39.Living with them are Ann and James Macegins,James is a Brother-in-law and Ann is a Masons wife from Low Gerra,Cornwall, James is from Cardiff and a Confectioners Porter. Also living at that address 1881 were Sarah Gray, widow aged 49 from Tiverton, Devon a Dressmaker, Sarah Florence Gray her daughter aged 14 from Belfast an Assistant Dressmaker and Eve Emily Gray aged 13 and a Scholar also from Belfast.

In the 1891 census Edward and Comfort were living in Clifton, Bristol at Ambra Gate House. Edward was 76 and Comfort was 47.Edward was a Grocer and Beer Licencee.

In the 1901 census Comfort Belchamber aged 57 was living in Bristol at 3 Berkely Road,living with her was Martha Bradfield a lodger aged 81. Comfort was listed as "living on her own means"

Death Certificate:
Edward Belchamber aged 77 died at Ambra Gate House,Clifton on the 18th of October,1892. Listed as a Master Grocer,His wife Comfort Belchamber was informant and present at death. Cause of death was Cardiac disease and bronchitis certifed by Arthur F Blagg MRCS. The death was recorded by Edward Tedder registrar for Barton Regis on the 19th of October.

Belchamber Edward of Ambra Gate House,Ambra Vale,Clifton,Bristol retired Grocer and Beerseller died 18th October 1892.Probate Bristol 16 November to Comfort Belchamber widow Effects £155.10s

Edward Belchamber's Will 1882
Comfort Belchamber-Executive.AlbertGrubble-Commissioner
THIS IS THE LAST WILL AND TESTMENT
Of me EDWARD BELCHAMBER of Ambra Gate House,Ambra Vale in the city and county of Bristol. Grocer and Beerseller
I give devise and bequeath my messuage or dwellinghouse and hereditament in which I reside and all and every my household & furniture,stock in trade,ready money sercurities for money goods and chattels and all and every other my estate and effects whatsoever and wherever both real and personal whether in possession or reversion remainder or expectancy unto my dear wife Comfort Belchamber for her sole and separate use and benefit absolutely and independently of any future husband subject never the less to any mortgage or other debts affecting the same as the time of my decease. I devise and bequeath all estates vested in me as a trustee or mortgage unto the said Comfort Belchamber her heirs executors and administrators subject to the trusts and equity affecting the same respectively and I appoint the said Comfort Belchamber sole executrix of this my will and hereby revealing and making void all former wills I do declare this to be my last will and testament IN WITNESS whereof I said Edward Belchamber have hereto set my hand this twenty first day of February one thousand eight hundred and eight two.

Signed and declared by the
Above named Edward Belchamber
The testator as and for this last will

And testament in the presence of us
Present at the same mine who in his
Presence at his request and in
The presence of each other have
herewith subscribed our names as
Witness's the interlineations between the 16th,
17th, and 18th lines in the first page opposite
To which our initials are placed in the margin
Nowing been first made.
WILLIAM JEFFERIESSolictor Bristol
RICHARD BUSHIN 41 ColstonStreet,Bristol.

Proved at Bristol the sixteenth day of November,1892 by the
Oath of Comfort Belchamber widow the relict of the deceased the
Sole executrix to whom administration was granted.
The testator Edward Belchamber was late of Ambra Gate House,AmbraVale,Clifton
in the city and county of Bristol retired Grocer and Beerseller and died on the
eighteenth day of October,1892 at Ambra Gate House,Ambra Vale
Aforesaid
Gross Value £155.10.0   W Jefferies
Under £200   Solictor   Bristol

G L Belchamber   Percy J Peacock
Executor   A Commisioner of oaths

After Edward's death in 1892 Comfort Belchamber married Thomas Ridley Bryant.

Marriage Certificate:
Widower Thomas Ridley Bryant aged 57 of 31 Somerset Street,Bishopston and
widow Comfort Belchamber aged 59 of 3 Berkely Avenue married in The Parish
Church,Bishopston,Bristol on the 2nd of June,1902. Thomas was a Commission
Agent and Comfort had no occupation listed. Witness were George and Mary
Evans,the fathers were John Bryant a Schoolmaster and William Harris Evans a
Bailiff. Charles Henry Dickinson curate performed the service.

ii   Sarah Belchamber was born about 3rd September,1815 in Horsham,Sussex.
          She died on 24th January,1851 in East Dulwich Grove,Camberwell.

iii   William Belchamber was born about 23rd November,1817 in Horsham,Sussex,
          he died 15th August,1863 in Horsham. He married Frances Sarah Wale 15th
          February,1858 in The Parish Church,Paddington,Middlesex.

Marriage Certificate:
William Belchamber and Frances Sarah Wales married by banns on the 15th of
February,1858 in the parish church,Paddington. William a bachelor was a Servant and

Frances Sarah a spinster both were of full age(over 21). At the time of the marriage William was living in Brook Street and Frances Sarah in Bayswater Tavern. Their witness's were George Henry Field and Lucy Belchamber William's sister. Fathers Edward Belchamber was a Gardener and William Wale a Licensed Victualler. Curate Beauchamp Tyneshill preformed the ceremony.

Census:
In the 1861 census William and Frances were in St.Pancras living at The Bulls Head as Licenced Victuallers. William aged 42 and Frances 41 employed Henry Turner 21 a Barman,Alfred Piggot 28 a Potman and Ann Winson 41 a House Servant,all living at The Bulls Head.

Death Certificate:
William Belchamber aged 46 died on the 15th of August,1863 at The Station Inn,Horsham,Sussex. Cause of death was Gout,Bronchitis,Disease of the liver and Rupture of blood vessels.(certified). William was listed as a Licensed Victualler at The Duke of Cambridge Inn,Cumberland St.Hackney Road,London. Ellen Pollard of North Street,Horsham was informant and present at the death which was registered on the 17th of August in Horsham.

Belchamber William 30 September Effects under £ 3000 The will of William Belchamber formerly of the "Bucks Head"public house High Street,Camden Town but late of the "Duke of Clarence"public house Cumberland Street,Hackney Road both in the county of Middlesex Licensed Victualler deceased who died 15 August 1863 at Horsham in the county of Sussex was proved at the Principal Registry by oath of Frances Sarah Belchamber of the "Duke of Clarence"public house aforesaid widow the relict the sole executrix.

After William Died Frances Sarah Belchamber remarried to William John Wilson.

Marriage Certificate:
Frances Sarah Belchamber aged 46 remarried on the 22nd of May 1865 listed as a widow and Licenced Victualler she married 30 year old bachelor William John Wilson also a Licenced Victualler at the Parish Church,Shoreditch. Witness were William Walter Wale and Amy Emma Field. The fathers were William Wale a Licenced Victualler and William Wilson a Mariner. Both gave their abode as 13 Murray Street,Shoreditch. George Docoty? curate performed the service.

iv   Fanny Belchamber was born about 13th December,1819 in Horsham. To date no marriage or death information as been found for Fanny.

v   David Belchamber was born about 9th December,1821 in Horsham,Sussex. He died 25th Febuary,1902 in 46 Archbishop Place,Brixton Hill. He married Jane Elliott 25th October,1845 in Amberley,Sussex. She was born in Pulborough,Sussex. She died 17th October,1897 at 46 Archbishop Place,Brixton Hill.

vi   Mary Belchamber was born about 23rd May,1824 in Horsham,Sussex. She died on 29th July,1844 in Northchapel House,North Street,Horsham,Sussex.

Death Certificate:
Mary Belchamber died aged 20 years on the 29th of July 1844 of Consumption, at Northchapel House,North Street,Horsham. Edward Belchamber her father was informant and present at death,Registrar J Lawman registered the death on the 2nd of August.

vii John Belchamber was born about 2nd September,1827 in Horsham,Sussex. He died 6th October,1913 in 126 St.James Road,Bermondsey. He was possibly married 3 times first although no marriage certificate as been found to date he may have married Amelia Farge at some time. She died 27th August,1855 in 12 Charles Street,Newington.

viii Samuel Belchamber was born about 13th September,1830 in Horsham,Sussex. He died 11th June,1896 in 19 Barland Road,Fulham. He married Ann Worman on 15th March,1853 in St.Nicholas,Deptford,Kent. She died 13th January,1886 in 59 Beauchamp Place,Kensington.

ix Jane Belchamber was born about 14th September,1833 in Horsham,Sussex. She married Henry Shobbrook on 13th July 1852 in St.Pauls,Deptford,Kent.

Marriage Certificate:
Bachelor and Labourer Henry Shobbrook married Jane Belchambers a spinster and minor at St.Pauls,Deptford,Kent on July 23,1852,both were of this parish. Fathers Philip Shobbrook was a Farrier and Edward was a Gardener. Thomas Fields and Naomi Jupp were the witness'.

x Lucy Belchamber was born about 14th September,1834 in Horham,Sussex. To date no marriage or death information as been found for Lucy.

Ann Belchamber
(Edward9,Edward8,Edward7,Edward6,John5,Thomas4,Robert3,Robert2,John1) was born 7th May,1802 in Horsham,Sussex. She died 1831 in Horsham. She married William Cottington on 28th August,1822 in Horsham.

William Cottington and Ann Belchamber had the following children:

i Ann Cottington born about 20th April,1823

ii William Cottington born about 27th March,1825

iii John Cottington was born about 10th June,1827

iv Samuel Cottington was born about 18th October,1829
All born in Horsham,Sussex.

James Belchamber 3rd Great Grandparents
(James9,William8,Edward7,Edward6,John5,Thomas4,Robert3,Robert2,John1) was born about 2nd June,1805 in Kirdford,Sussex. He died on the 11th May,1875 in

Plaistow,Sussex. He married Mary Denyer on the 26th May,1831 in Kirdford. She was born 1812 in Kirdford. She died in Plaistow on the 13th December,1891.

Notes for James Belchamber:

When James married Mary the service was conducted by Robert Ridsdale the vicar of Kirdford. They had two witness' Henry Young and James' sister Elizabeth Belchamber. James and Mary signed the marriage certificate with a cross,neither could write.

Census:

In the 1841 Census James and Mary were in Kirdford living in Oakhurst with three chidren,Mary 6,Ann 4,James aged 1.

In the 1851 Census James and Mary are in Plaistow,James in 49 and a Agricultural Labourer,Mary is 48 and a Labourer's Wife their children are James 11 a Plough Boy,Jane 8,William 6 and daughter Fanny aged 2

In the 1861 census James and Mary were living in the hamlet of Plaistow,with children James,William and Fanny.

In the 1871 census they were still there but without any children.

James and Mary were living in the hamlet of Plaistow, Kirdford,Sussex. James a Labourer was 67 and Mary 59.

Death Certificates:

70 year old James Belchamber died on the 11th of May,1875 in Plaistow,Sussex. James an Agricultural Labourer died of Dropsy which was certified by Henry Boxall FBCS. The death was recorded on the 11th of May by Henry Boxall Registrar. Son James Belchamber was informant and in attendance of Dunsfold,Surrey.

Mary Belchamber Aged 79 died in Plaistow on the 13th of December,1891 cause of death was Senile Decay which was certified by R Humphfrey MRCS. Mary was listed as the widow of James Belchamber a Labourer. Mary's daughter-in-law Abigail Belchamber was informant,Abigail signed her mark,stating she was of Plaistow also. The death was recorded by George Brookfield the registrar for Petworth on the 16th of December.

Census:

In 1881 Mary was living in Plaistow Street,Plaistow as a widow aged 69 and listed as a Annuitant(Pensioner/Living off own means)

In 1891 Mary aged 79 was in Plaistow living at Fox Street.

James Belchamber and Mary Denyer had the following children:

i   Male child was born on the 10th August,1837 and died the same day.

ii   Mary Belchamber was born on the 14th December,1834 in Kirdford,Sussex.
         She married George Strudwick on the 23rd October,1852 in Kirdford.

Census:
In the 1841 census Mary Belchamber aged 15 was in the household of James Mills a Farmer in Crouch Lane. There is no occupation for Mary,but it's likely she was some sort of Servant.

Marriage Certificate:
George Strudwick and Mary Belchamber both of Kirdford married on the 23rd of October,1852 at Kirdford by banns. George was a bachelor and Labourer of full age,Mary was a minor and spinster. Witness's were Charles Strudwick and Ann Belchamber,Mary's sister both made their mark on the register,as did the groom George. The fathers were John Strudwick and James Belchamber both Labourers. Mary signed her name on the the register. J.F Cole was the vicar.

iii   Ann Belchamber was born on the 15th January,1837 in Kirdford,Sussex. She married Frederick Phillips on the 10th November,1855 in Kirdford. Frederick was the son of James and Ann Phillips born 13th March,1836.
Baptised 15th January, 1837.

iv   James Belchamber was born on the 14th November,1839 in Foxbridge, Kirdford,Sussex. He died on the 8th November,1905 in Plaistow,Sussex.
He married Abigail Pennicard on the 1st June,1864 in Kirdford.Abigail was the daughter of Robert and Ruth Pennicard she was born on the 15th June,1845. She died in Plaistow on the 18th December,1903.

v   Jane Belchamber was born on the 22nd May,1842 in Lyons Farm,Kirdford, Sussex. She married Israel Cooper on the 17th November,1860 in Kirdford. He was born on the 15th March,1840 in Kirdford.
Jane was baptised on the 26th June, 1842

vi   William Belchamber was born on the 20th October,1844 in Plaistow,Sussex. He died 14th May,1923 in Rose Cottage,Plaistow. He married Eliza Greenfield on the 30th June,1866 in Kirdford,she was the daughter of William Greenfield and Susannah Remnant born about 18th April,1847 in Kirdford. She died on the 29th April,1930 in Rose Cottage,Plaistow.
Baptised 20th October, 1844

vii   Fanny Belchamber was born on the 28th May,1848 in Kirdford,Sussex. She died on the 30th June,1905. She married Alfred Cooper on the 23rd November,1867 in Kirdford.the son of Clement Cooper and Emma Rapley born about the 20th June,1847.
Fanny's baptism took place on the 25th June, 1848.

viii   Another male child was born on the 9th August,1851 and died two hours later the same day.

James and Mary had a son born on the 9th of August 1851 in Plaistow,Sussex.George Wells recorded the birth for Petworth on the 13th of September.
Sadly James and Mary's male child died on the 9th of August,cause of death was Convulsions(medical attendant),the child was only 2 hours old. Mary was informant

and present at the death. George Wells registered the death on the 13th of September for Petworth District.

Elizabeth Belchamber
(James9,William8,Edward7,Edward6,John5,Thomas4,Robert3,Robert2,John1) was born about the 24th July,1808 in Kirdford,Sussex. She married John Lee on the 5th October,1834 in St.Marys,Guildford,Surrey. He was born 1804 in Woking,Surrey.

Census:
In the 1881 census John and Elizabeth were living in The High Street,Windlesham,Surrey with one son Edward aged 23 and a Carpenter by trade. John aged 77 was a Farm Bailiff and Elizabeth was aged 72.

John Lee and Elizabeth Belchamber had the following children:

i   Mary Lee born 1839 in Horsell,Surrey

ii   James Lee born 1840 in Knaphill,Surrey

iii   Martha Lee

iv   Sarah Lee born 1849 in Knaphill,Surrey

v   George Lee

vi   Edward Lee born 1858 in Windlesham,Surrey

John Belchamber
(James9,William8,Edward7,Edward6,John5,Thomas4,Robert3,Robert2,John1) was born about the 27th October,1811 in Kirdford,Sussex. He died on the 7th December,1893 in The Union Workhouse,Leytonstow. He married Sarah Sopp on the 11th October,1840 in Holy Trinity,Westminster. She died on the 15th January,1877 in 50 Marsham Street,Westminster.

Marriage Certificate:
John Belchamber and Sarah Sopp were married by banns at Holy Trinity, Westminster on the 11th of October 1840. Both were of full age, neither had an occupation listed, the witness's were Thomas Sopp and Mary Coy. Their fathers were James Belchamber and John Sopp again with no occupations listed.

Death Certificates:
Sarah Belchamber age 60 died on the 15th of January 1877 of Bronchitis and Emphysema at 50 Marsham Street, Westminster her daughter Charlotte Darby was informant, and present at death, Charlotte was living at 65 Tufton Street.

John Belchamber Snr. Age 82 died of Bronchitis certified by E Wallace MRCS on the 7th of December,1893 at the Union Workhouse Leytonstone, John`s daughter Louisa Brazell of 71 Fisher Street, Canning Town was informant and in attendance. The death was recorded by J Miller the registrar for West Ham

Census:
In the 1841 Census there is a John Belchamber aged 25 in the District Westminster Hospital in St.Margarets Westminster listed as a Agricultural Labourer.

In the 1851 census John and Sarah were living in Westminister at 29 Marks Street. John a was a Labourer aged 19,Sarah was 24. With them were their children Mary 9,Louise 5 and Sarah aged 12

To date I have not been able to find any census information for John and Sarah in the 1861 census,it is possible that the family just wasn't counted for some reason.

John and Sarah were living at 4 Devon Place,Westminister in 1871.Contractor Foreman John was 59,Sarah was 54. Their children living with them were Mary 30 and unmarried,John 19 a Carman and Rosa aged 11.

In 1881 John a widower aged 69 was an inmate in the West Ham Union Workhouse,John was listed as a Farm Labourer from Cayford,Sussex it of coarse should read Kirdford,Sussex.

In the 1891 census John was still an inmate in the West Ham Union Workhouse,Leyton,now aged 79 and listed as a Carman from Brighton Sussex.

John Belchamber and Sarah Sopp had the following children:

i   Mary Ann Belchamber was born on the 11th November,1841 in 55 Vine Street Westminster. She died on the 13th July,1895 in The Union Workhouse, Leytonstow.

Birth Certificate:
Mary Ann Bellchamber was born 4.15 pm on the 4th of November 1841 at 55 Vine Street,Westminster. Her father John Bellchamber was a Labourer and mother was Sarah Bellchamber formerly Sopp. The birth was recorded on the 11th of November.

Death Certificate:
John and Sarah's daughter Mary Ann Belchamber died of Paralysis in the Union Workhouse,Leytonstone on July 13th,1895 she was aged 53.her sister Louisa Brazell was in attendance and informant,Louisa`s address was given has 71 Fisher Street.

ii   Jane Belchamber was born on the 4th February,1844 in 5 Carpenter,Street, Westminster. She died on the 27th May,1845 at the same address.

Birth Certificate:
Jane Bellchamber was born 11am at No.5 Carpenter Street,Westminister on the 4th of February 1844. Parents were John Bellchamber a Labourer and Sarah Bellchamber formerly Sopp. George Pearse the Registrar for Westminster registered the birth on the 9th February.

Death Certificate:
Jane Bellchamber aged 17 months died on the 27th May,1845 at 5 Carpenter Street,Westminster. She was the daughter of John Bellchamber a Carman.Cause of

death was Pneumonia(2 weeks). Her mother Sarah Bellchamber was informant and present at the death. The death was registered on the 29th May in Westminster.

iii   Louisa Bellchambers was born on the 22nd December,1846 in 5 Carpenter Street,Westminster. She married Alfred Brazell on the 16th February,1869 in St.Stephens,Westminster.

Birth Certificate:
On the 22nd of December 1846 Louisa Bellchamber was born at 6 am at 5 Carpenter Street,Westminister. Her parents were John Bellchamber and Sarah Bellchamber.John was a Labourer. George Pearse recorded the birth on the 29 of January.

Marriage Certificate:
Louisa Bellchambers aged 23 and a spinster married Alfred Brazell a bachelor aged 22 and a Barman by trade at the parish church of St.Stephens,Westminster by banns on the 16th of February 1869. The service was taken by curate Frederick Shepherd and witness's were William Cutliff and Frances Brazell.Louisa and Alfred gave their abode as 22 Francis Street. Their fathers were John Bellchambers a Foreman and Richard Brazell a Plasterer.

iv   Sarah Ann Belchamber was born on the 4th September,1848. She died on the 1st July,1851 in 27 Market Street,Westminster.

Birth Certificate;
Sarah Bellchambers was born on the 4th of September 1848 at No.5 Carpenter Street,Westminster. Her father was John Bellchambers a Labourer and her mother was Sarah Bellchambers formerly Sopp both of 5 Carpenter Street. The birth was registered on the 5th of October by W G Hearse the registrar for Westminster. Sarah was baptized at St Marys, St. Marylebone Road Westminster on the 22nd of October.

Death Certificate:
Sarah Ann Belchamber aged 2 years died on the 1st of July,1851 at 27 Market Street,Westminister,London. Cause of death was Convulsions.Sarah Belchamber her mother was informant and present at death. The death was registered on the 3rd of July for Westminister.

v   John Belchamber was born on the 5th June,1851 in 27 Market Street, Westminster. He died on the 30th October,1902 in 4 Norman Street, East Ham. He married Emma Elizabeth Maxwell on the 31st May,1874 in St. Marys,Westminster. She died on the 25th September,1878 in 20 High Street, East Ham. He then remarried to Louisa Winchcombe on the 11th June,1879 in St.Margarets,Westminster. She died on the 21st May,1928 in 1 Old Church Road,Romford,Essex.

vi   Fanny Belchamber was born on the 29th September,1853 in 53 Carpenter Street,Westminster. She died on the 23rd February,1855 in 23 Tufton Street, Westminster.

Birth Certificate:

Fanny Bellchambers the daughter of John and Sarah was born at 35 Carpenter Street,Westminster on the 29th of September 1853. W G Hearse the registrar for Westminster recorded the birth on the 27th of October. Her father John Bellchambers was a Carman,and her mother was Sarah formerly Sopp.

Death Certificate:
17 month old Fanny Bellchamber died on the 23rd of February,1855 at 23 Tufton Street,Westminister cause of death was Pertussis 1.1\2 months,Convulsions 17 hours certified. The death was registered on the 24th February by registrar George Pearse. John Bellchamber was informant and present at death he signed with his mark.

vii   Charlotte Belchamber was born on the 28th December,1855 in 23 Tufton Street,Westminster. She married George David Alfred Darby on the 2rd April, 1876 in St.Marys,Lambeth.

Birth Certificate:
Charlotte Bellchamber was born on the 28th of December,1855 at 23 Tufton Street,Westminister. Her parents were John and Sarah Bellchamber formerly Sopp. John was a Carman. George Pearse the registrar recorded the birth on the 21st January,1856.

Marriage Certificate:
On April 2nd 1876 George David Alfred Darby a bachelor aged 19 and a Waiter married Charlotte Belchamber a spinster aged 20 both gave their address as Bond Street. Their witness's were Henry Darby and Jane Clark. J Tipper the Curate of St.Marys,Lambeth performed the service. Their fathers Henry Darby was a Coachman and John Bellchamber a Carman.

viii   Rapsey Patience Belchamber was born on the 26th June,1859 in 23 Tufton Street,Westminster. She married William Sellar on the 8th October,1877 at The Registry Office,Poplar.

Birth Certificate:
Rapsey Patience Bellchamber came into this world on the 26th of June,1859 at 23 Tufton Street,Westminister. Her father John Bellchamber was a Carman and her mother was Sarah Bellchamber formerly Sopp. Registrar George Pearse recorded the birth on the 10th of August.

Marriage Certificate:
William Sellar a bachelor and Furnace Liner aged 22 of 10 Elizabeth Terrace, Canning Town the son of William Sellar a gas fitter. Rosa a spinster was aged 18 and living at 13 Barchester Street,Bromley. They married by license at the registry Office, Poplar, on the 8th of October 1877. Their witness's were Alfred and Louisa Brazell.

William Belchamber
(James9,William8,Edward7,Edward6,John5,Thomas4,Robert3,Robert2,John1) was born on the 18th May,1814 in Wisborough Green,Sussex. He died on the 28th August,1872 in Ovingdean,Sussex. He married Barbara Hannah Westgate on the 21st August,1846 in The Parish Church,Sheffield,Yorkshire. She was born about the 15th

September,1822 in Patcham,Sussex. She died on the 19th April,1895 in Brighton,Sussex.

Marriage Certificate:
26 year old Soldier William Belchamber married 22 year old spinster Hannah Barbara Westgate on the 21st of August,1846 at the parish Church,Sheffield,Yorkshire. Witness's were Edward and Ann Dent?. Both fathers were Farmers,James Belchamber and William Westgate. William Harris,vicar performed the ceremony
Census:

To date I have been unable to find William and Hannah in the 1851 census.

In the 1861 census William and Hannah Barbara were in Ovingdean,Sussex with son William Thomas aged 2. William was a Gardener aged 46 and Hannah aged 38.

In 1871 William aged 56 and Hannah aged 48 were living in Ovingdean with their children William 12,Mary B 8 and Harry J 7

Widow Hannah Belchamber and her two sons were living ar 38 Quebec Street,Brighton,Sussex in 1881. Hannah was aged 58 with no occupation listed. Her eldest son William 22 was a Police Constable and youngest son Harry J aged 17 was a Labourer.

Widowed Hannah Barbara aged 68 and "living on her own means" was living at 41 Quebec Street,Brighton,Sussex,in the 1891 census.

Death Certificates:
58 year old William Belchamber died at Ovingdean,Sussex on the 28th of August 1872. Cause of death was"unknown not certified",his wife Hannah Barbara Belchamber was informant and present at death. William Verrall the registrar for Lewes recorded the death on the 17th of September.

Hannah Barbara Belchamber died on the 19th of April 1895 aged 72,cause of death was Senile Decay which was certified by Ernest Burchall MRCS. Henry James Belchamber her son was informant and present at death,his address was 29 Lennox Street,Brighton. J Francis the Registrar for Brighton recorded the death on the 23rd of April.

William Belchamber and Barbara Hannah Westgate had the following children:

i   William Thomas Belchamber was born on the 22nd April,1858 in Ovingdean,Sussex. He died on the 26th October,1927 in 250 Elm Grove,Brighton.He married Annie Kimpton on the 20th July,1887 in St.Lukes Church,Brighton. She was born in North Finchley,Middlesex. She died on the 6th July,1923 in the Royal Sussex County Hospital,Brighton.

ii   Mary Barbara Hannah Belchamber was born on the 1st August,1862 in Ovingdean,Sussex. She married Henry John Blundell on the 27th October,1888 in St.Lukes Church,Brighton.

Birth Certificate:
Mary Barbara Hannah Bellchamber was born in Ovingdean,Sussex on the 1st of August,1862. Her father William was a Gardener Journeyman and her mother was Hannah Barbara Bellchamber formerly Westgate. The birth was registered on the 4th of September by William Gobden the registrar for Lewes,Sussex.

Marriage Certificate:
Mary Barbara Hannah Belchamber a spinster aged 26 of 41 Quebec Street,Brighton married 26 year old bachelor and Marchantman Henry John Arthur Blundell on the 27th of October,1888. The fathers were Alfred Blundell a deceased Ships Officer and William Thomas Belchamber a deceased Gardener. The curate Edward King took the service.

iii   Henry James Belchamber was born on the 25th December,1868 in Ovingdean, Sussex. He died on the 28th August,1905 in 22 Cobden Road,Brighton,Sussex. He married Mary Ann Diggens on the 13th September,1890 in The registry Office,Brighton. She was born about 1857. She died on the 2ndDecember,1937 in 34 Windover Crescent,Lewes,Sussex.

Henry James Belchamber and Mary Ann Diggens had the following children:

i   Henry Belchamber was born on the 27th of July,1892. He died in France on the 11th December,1915.

Birth Certificate:
Henry Belchamber was born in Brighton on the 27th of July,1892 at 17 Quebec Street the family home. His Father Henry James Belchamber was a Hotel Porter and his Mary Ann Belchamber was listed as late Diggens,formerly Morley. The birth was registered on the 13th of August in St.Peters,Brighton.

Death Certificate:
Corporal Henry Belchamber service No.59107 of the11th Bty. Royal Field Artillery died in France on the 11th of Dec,1915 aged 22. Henry is buried in the Mazargues War Cemetry,Marseilles.

Census:
In 1911 Henry aged 19 was in the army in South Africa.Listed as a Gunner and born 1893 in Brighton,Sussex.

ii   Florence Belchamber born in Brighton,Sussex on the 20th of January,1891.

Birth Certificate:
Florence Belchamber was born at 42 Quebec Street,Brighton on the 20th of January,1891. Harry James her father was a Laundry Keeper and her mother was

Mary Ann Belchamber formerly Diggens. F Thorncroft the registrar for Brighton recorded the birth on the 24th of February.

Marriage Certificate:
Henry John Pierce aged 23 a batchelor and Electrical Fitter married 23 year old Florence Belchamber aged 23 and a spinster by banns on the 20th of June,1914 at St.Saviors Church,Preston,Brighton both were living at Winchester Street at the time of the marriage. Their witness's were Cecil B Pierce and Evelyn Belchamber. The fathers were Henry Pierce a Shop Fitter and Henry James Belchamber a deceased Soldier. The ceremony was performed by J A W Bell the vicar.

iii   Evelyn Belchamber born in Brighton,Sussex on the 6th September,1894.

Birth Certificate:
Evelyn Belchamber was born at 17 Quebec Street,Brighton on the 6th of September,1894. Henry James Belchamber was listed as a Laundry Keeper and her Mother Mary Ann Belchamber was Diggens,formerly Morley. J Thorncroft the registrar for Brighton registered the birth on the 13th of October.

Marriage Certificate:
Bachelor William Horace Noel a Carriage Trimmer aged 24 married Evelyn Belchamber a 21 year old spinster on the 28th of August,1915 at St.Lukes Church,Brighton by banns. Their residence at the time of the marriage was 327 Queens Park Road,Brighton. Witness's were Robert and Edith Noel. The fathers were Robert Noel a Ex.Police Officer and Henry James Belchamber deceased. Assist Curate C F D Trimming took the service.

Census:
In the 1891 census Harry James and Mary Ann Belchamber were living at 42 Quebec Street,Brighton. Harry James aged 27 was a Laundary Keeper and Mary Ann was a Laundress,living with them were Florence Belchamber aged 3 months ,also Eliza Diggens aged 13,Mary Diggens aged 11,Jane Diggens aged 8 and Elizabeth Diggens aged 2 all were step daughters and Scholars.Harry James was from Ovingdean,while the remainder were all from Brighton.

Henry James and Mary Ann are living at 22 Cobden Road,Brighton in 1901.Henry James aged 37 is a Soldier and Mary Ann a Laundress aged 43 and an employer. Florence is 10,there are two more children now born to Henry James and Mary Ann they are,Henry 8 and Evelyn 6,two remaining Diggens children of Mary Ann are still at home Mary A Diggens aged 21 and a Laundress(wash) and Elizabeth Diggens aged 12.

In the 1911 census William T and Annie Belchamber were living in Brighton at 22 Kemp Street with their daughter Edith Flora aged 17.Edith was a Shop Assistant and William T a Park Keeper aged 52,Annie was aged 49.

John Belchamber
(Edward9,William8,Edward7,Edward6,John5,Thomas,4,Robert3,Robert2,John1) was born About 22nd November,1835. He died on the 10th December,1883 in Kirdford,Sussex. He married Sophia Older on the 3rd October,1865 in Kirdford the

daughter of William Whittick Older and Sophia Southerton. She was born about 1st March,1840 in Wisborough Green,Sussex. She died on the 13th April,1920 in The Village,Kirdford,Sussex.

Marriage Certificate:
John Belchamber and Sophia Older both of full age married in the parish Church,Kirdford on the 3rd October 1865. Witness's were Thomas Bachelor and Fanny Older. John was a bachelor and Sophia a spinster. John's father Edward was a labourer and William Older,Sophia's father was a Farmer. The Rev.Cole performed the ceremony.

Death Certificates:
John Belchamber aged 48 died of Peritonitis Liver Disease on the 10th of December,1883 death was certified by Reginald Humphery MRCS.Informant and present at death was his daughter Ada Belchamber of Kirdford. The death was registered by George Brookfield on the 13th of December for Petworth. John Belchamber's occupation was Hostler. John was buried in Kirdford Churchyard on the 13th December,1883.

81 year old Sophie Belchamber died in the Village,Kirdford on the 13th of April,1920. Cause of death was (1) Endocarditis(2)Syncope certified by R B Heygate MRCS. Informant and present at death was her grandson E Belchamber,J W Pugley registered the death on the 13th for Petworth.

Census:
In the 1871 census John and Sophia were in Kirdford living at Pound Common. John was a Engine Driver aged 35,Sophia was 30. Their daughtes Alice aged 4 was a Scholar and Ada was aged 1. Also living with them was Agricultural Labourer George Ford a Lodger aged 28 from Kirdford.

In 1881 John and Sophia were living at 6 South Street,Kirdford,Sussex with their children. John was 43 and a Gardener,Sophia 42 and born in Wisborough Green,Ada 9 and a Scholar and John 2

In the 1891 census Sophia and her son John were in living in Kirdford,Sussex at Pound Common. Sophia 50 was listed as a Charwoman(Domestic),John 12 was a Scholar.

In the 1901 census 57 year old Sophia and two children were living in Wisborough Green,Sussex at Pound Common.Sophia was listed as a Housekeeper(not domestic) and the children Alice aged 30 was a General Servant(Domestic) and John aged 21 a Groom(Domestic).

In the 1911 census Sophia aged 71 was living in Kirdford in The Village.Living with Sophia was her daughter Alice aged 40 a domestic Housemaid,Alice's son Edgar a Grocer's errand boy aged 14 and Leslie Field a boarder aged 2.

John Belchamber and Sophia Older had the following children:

i   Alice Belchamber was born on the 29th August,1866 in Kirdford,Sussex. She died on the 13th October,1933 in The Village,Kirdford. Baptised on the 14th October,1866.

ii   Sophia Belchamber was born on the 3rd December,1869 in Kirdford,Sussex. She married Charles Henry Bagley on the 19th December,1891 in the parish church,Kirdford. Baptised Ada Sophia on the 23rd January, 1870.

iii   John William Belchamber was born on the 3rd February,1879 in Kirdford,Sussex. He died on the 27th of February,1971 in Barnes Hospital,Mortlake. He married Jane Elizabeth Pearson on the 4th April,1909 in St.Marys,Gunnersbury,Middlesex. She was born on the 18th November,1880 in Marylebone,Middlesex and died on the 12th September,1971 in Kingston Hospital,Kingston.Surrey. Baptised 20th April, 1879.

William Belchamber
(John9,William8,Edward7,Edward6,John5,Thomas4,Robert3,Robert2,John1) was born about 20th August,1820 in Shalford,Surrey. He married Mary Welch on the 23rd March,1846 in the parish church,Putney. She died on the 1st November,1880 in 49 Lower Park Street,Grenwich,Kent.

Marriage Certificate:
William Belchamber and Mary Welch married in the parish church Putney on the 23rd of March 1846. Witness's were George Bolder and Eliza Robinson. William was a bachelor and a Carpenter by trade Mary was a spinster with no occupation,both were of full age(over21).The fathers were John Belchamber a Carrier and Benjiman Welch a Carpenter.

Census:
In the census of 1851 William and Mary were living at 71 Ponsonby Road,Westminster with their daughters Martha aged 3 and Mary Jane 1. William aged 30 was a Joiner and Mary was 29.

In 1861 Mary was living at 71 Ponsonby Road,Westminster with her daughters Martha aged 13 and Mary Jane aged 10. Mary was 39 and a Laundress,theres no mention of husband William.
Also living at the same address is a Anne Welch aged 37 and her children, Anne was also a Laundress and both were from Pitstone,Dorset.Mary and Anne were most probably sisters in law.

Death Certificate:
56 year old Mary Belchamber died on the 1st of November,1880 at 49 Lower Park Street,Greenwich,Kent. Cause of death was Bronchitis(certified by H C Perceval LRCP). M J Simmons her daughter was informant and present at death. H K Lewis recorded the death on the 1st November.

There is no information for William death to date.He must have died prior to 1867,both daughters list him deceased on their marriage certificates.

William Belchamber and Mary Welch had the following children:

i   Martha Belchamber was born on the 13th January,1848 in Shalford,Surrey. She married Charles Frederick Murphy on the 14th July,1867 in St.Marys,Lambeth.

ii   Mary Jane Belchamber was born on the 2nd September,1850 in Westminster,Middlesex. She married William Henry Simmons on the 10th November,1867 in St.Marys,Lambeth,Surrey.

Birth Certificate:
Mary Jane Belchamber was born in Westminster on the 2nd September 1850. Her father William was a Carpenter by trade,Mary Janes's mother Mary signed her mark and gave the address as Great Tufton Street. The birth was registered by H G Pearse Registrar on the 27th of September.

Marriage Certificate:
William Henry Simmons a bachelor and minor married Mary Jane Belchamber also a minor and spinster in St.Marys parish church,Lambeth on the 10th of November 1867. Witness's were W Simmons and Edward Powell,J E Codlington MA performed the ceremony. Fathers William Simmons was a Painter and William Bellchamber(deceased) a Carpenter. Belvidere Road was their residence at the time of marriage.

iii   Alice Belchamber was born on the 23rd March,1857 in Westminster,Middlesex. She Died on the 12th April,1858 in 71 Ponsonby Place,Millbank,Westminster.

Birth Certificate:
Alice Belchamber was born in 71 Ponsonby Place,Millbank on the 23rd of March 1857. William the father was a Carpenter Journeyman and Mary her mother gave the home address as 71 Ponsonby Place,Millbank,Westminster. The birth was registered on the 27th of April by W E G Pearse,Registrar.

Death Certificate:
Alice Belchamber the daughter of William and Mary died on the 12th of April 1858.Alice died of Psoas Abscess(Muscle) 4 months and Phithitis 3 months. Alice's mother Mary was informant and present at death. W E G Pearse the Registrar registered the death on the 13th of April.

John Belchamber
(William9,James8,Edward7,Edward6,John5,Thomas4,Robert,3Robert2,John1) was born on the 27th August,1818 in Kirdford,Sussex. He died on the 2nd December,1900 in Cray Hill Pulborough,Sussex. He married Harriet Sheppard on the 5th May,1840 in Wisborough Green,Sussex. She died on the 4th February,1901 in Cray Hill Cottages,Pulborough.

Census:
In the 1841 census John and Harriet Belchamber were living in Wisborough

Green,Sussex. John Belchamber aged 20 was a Shoemaker and Harriet was 25.

In the 1851 Census John aged 32 and Harriet 36 were in the village of Wisborough Green with their daughter Mary Ann aged 4. John Belchamber was a Cordwainer.

In the 1861 census John Belchamber and his wife Harriet were listed as living in Wisborough Green,Sussex. John was a Shoemaker aged 43,Harriet 47 and daughter Mary Ann 14.

In the 1871 Census John and Harriet were living in Wisborough Green,Sussex in a Cottage. John was a Shoemaker aged 52 and Harriet was aged 56.

Living next door to John and Harriet again in a cottage were their daughter and son-in-law Mary Ann and Amos Streeter.
Amos was a Postman aged 29,Harriet was 24 and their children were Rosa 7,Frederick W 6,Mary Ann 4,Amos 2 and Frank 1 month.

In 1881 John and Harriet and their children were living in Belchambers Row,Wisborough Green,Sussex.
John a Shoemaker was 62 and Harriet a Shoe Binder was 68 ,living with them were their widowed Daughter Mary Ann Streeter aged 33 a Seamster and her children,Amos Streeter a Plough Boy aged 12,Frank Streeter 10,Frederick Streeter a Shoemaker 16 and Emma Streeter 6.

In the 1891 Census the family are living in Wisborough Green Village John is a Shoemaker aged 72,Harriet is 75,their grandson Frederick Streeter is living with them,he is aged 26 and a Postman.

Marriage Certificate:
John Belchamber of full age and a bachelor married Harriet Sheppard a spinster also of full age by banns. Witness's were Luke Towse brother-in-law and Sally Belchamber his sister. The ceremony was performed by the vicar John Thornton.John signed the licence and Harriet left a mark. The fathers were William Belchamber and William Sheppard both Labourers.

Death Certificates:
John Belchamber aged 82 and a Shoemaker by profession died on the 2nd of December,1900. The death took place at Cray Hill,Pulborough,Sussex,cause of death Was a cerebral heamorage and exhaustion certified by Ernest Foot MBCP. His son-in-law John Burberry was informant and present at the death. S A Comper the registrar for Thakeham recorded the death on the 2nd December.

87 year old Harriet Bellchamber died on the 4th of February 1901 at Cray Hill cottages,Pulborough,Sussex. Cause of death was heart failure from shock resulting from injuries sustained by accidentally falling out of her chair on the 30th of January. Certificate received from Frederick W Butler Coroner for Sussex. An inquest was held on the 5th February. The death recorded by S A Comper the registrar for Thakeham on the 7th of February. Harriet was listed as the widow of John Bellchamber a Shoemaker.

The will of John Belchamber Shoemaker of Wisborough Green

This is the last will and testament of me John Belchamber of Wisborough Green in the county of Sussex,Shoemaker made this 26th day of February 1892.As follows after all my just debts,funeral and testamentary expenses shall have been paid and satisfied I give,bequeath and devise unto my dear wife Harriot all and every of my property,both rear and personal,to and for her own sole and also like use and benefit.And I appoint my said wife sole excutive and trustee of this my will.Provided never the less should my said wife die before me.I then devise all my personal estate and effects to George Drinkald Hammond of Amblehurst Farm Wisborough Green afore said upon trust to divide the same as soon as convenient may be after my death,between my grandchildren and my son-in-law John Burberry share and share alike and I devise the house and premises belonging to the situate at Wisborough Green afore said also upon trust to the said George Drinkald Hammond to pay thereout yearly and every year the rent and profits arising there from,to my daughter Mary Ann and wife of John Burberry afore said and after the decease of my said daughter ,direct my said house and premises to be sold and the money arising there fom to be divided between my grandchildren and my son-in-law John Burberry share and share alike.In witness whereof I have set my hand the day and year above written.

John Belchamber……………………………………………..Signed and Published and declared by the testator as and for his last will and testament in the presence of us who in his presence at his request and in the presence of each other have subscribed our names as witness.

Walter Weale   Wisborough Green

Hy Hemmings   Wisborough Green

On the 18th day of March 1901 Adminstration with this of the estate of the testator was granted at Chichester to Mary Ann Burberry(Wife of John Burberry) the administrative of the estate of Harriet(in the will written Harriot)Belchamber deceased whilst living the widow,the sole executrix and pesidary legalee

Harriet Belchamber died intestate on the 4th of February 1901 below is a transcript of the administration:

BE IT KNOWN that Harriet Belchamber
Of Crayhill Pulborough in the county of
Sussex   widow
Who at the time of her death had a fixed place of abode at
Crayhill,Pulborough aforesaid within the District

AND BE IT FURTHER KNOWN that at the date hereunder written Letters
Of administration of all the estate which by law devolves to and vests in the personal
Representative of the said intestate were granted by His Majesty's High Court of

Justice at the District Probate Registry thereof at   Chichester
To Mary Ann Burberry of Crayhill
Pulborough aforesaid(wife of John Burberry,Bricklayer) the natural and lawful and
Only daughter and only next of kin
Of the said intestate

Dated the 14th day of March 1901
Gross value of estate...£ 13.0.0
Net Value of Personal Estate £
Extracted by   Brydone & Titfield
          Solicitors   Petworth
This is a true record
Sureties John Butler of Codmore Hill,Pulborough,Sussex Builder

John Belchamber and Harriet Sheppard he the following child:

i   Mary Ann Belchamber was born in Wisborough Green,Sussex on the 7th
          September,1846. She married Amos Streeter on the 21st October,1863 in
          Wisborough Green.

Birth Certificate:
Mary Ann Belchamber was born in Wisborough Green on the 7th of September
1846. The daughter of John Belchamber a Shoemaker and Harriet Belchamber nee
Sheppard. The birth was registered on the 16th of September by Henry Boxall the
registrar for Petworth Union.

Marriage Certificate:
Mary Ann Belchamber and Amos Streeter married on the 21st October 1863 at the
parish church,Wisborough Green,Sussex by banns. Both were of full age and living in
Wisborough Green,Amos a bachelor and Mary Ann a spinster.Amos was a Tailor by
trade. The fathers were William Streeter a Farmer and John Belchamber a
Cordwainer(Shoemaker). Their witness's were John Belchamber and Ruth
Streeter.John Thornton performed the service.

Amos Streeter died in 1880 and Mary Ann remarried to John Burberry in the June
Quarter of 1881 in Petworth,Sussex.

Sally Belchamber
(William9,James8,Edward7,Edward6,John5,Thomas4,Robert3,Robert2,John1) was
born obout the 14th Janury,1821 in Kirdford,Sussex. She died on the 2nd Febuary,1849
in Wisborough Green.

Death Certificate:
Sally now known as Sarah Belchamber aged 28 died in Wisborough Green,Sussex on
the 2nd February,1849. Listed as a Domestic Servant she died of Comsumption which
was certified,Lucy Vern was informant and present at the death.Henry Boxall the
registrar for Petworth Union recorded the death on the 6th February.

Census:
In the 1841 census Sally Belchamber was a Female Servant living with Henry Napper

and family.Also living their was Walter Napper,Henry's son and the future father of Sally's daughter Sarah Belchamber.

Sally Belchamber had the following child:

i   Sarah Belchamber was born on the 8th December,1844 in St.Marys Newington,Surrey. She died on the 13th June,1864 in St.Bartholomews Hospital,London.

Birth Certificate;
Sarah's birth was registered on the 3rd of January 1845 by Registrar William Seagrave in the county of Surrey. The father was registered as Walter Napper a Gentleman. Sally the mother was living in 2 Cole Street,Great Doves Street,Stoke Newington. Sarah was born on the 8th of December,1844.

Death Certificate:
Sarah was 19 years of age when she died of Diphpheria(11 Days Certified) on the 13th June,1864. The informant was Mark Morris the Occupier of St Bartholomews Hospital,London. Registrar William Fortescue registered the death on the 24 of June West London District.

Generation 11

Sarah Belchamber

(Edward10,Edward9,Edward8,Edward7,Edward6,John5,Thomas4,Robert3,Robert2, John1) was born about the 3rd September,1815 in Horsham,Sussex. She died on the 24th Janury,1851 in East Dulwich Grove,Camberwell.

Death Certificate:
Sarah Belchamber died at East Dulwich Grove,Camberwell on the 24th of July 1851 she was 36 years of age and a domestic servant. Father Edward was informant and in attendance. William Searle registrar,registered the death on the 28th January in Camberwell.

Sarah Belchamber had the following child

i   William Belchamber was born on the 5th October,1845 in North Street,Horsham,Sussex. He died on 6th September,1878 in Camberwell Infirmary.

Birth Certificate:
William Belchamber the son of Sarah Belchamber was born in North Street,Horsham,Sussex on the 5th of October,1845. No fathers name was given the birth was recorded in Horsham by the registrar J Lawman on the 11th of November.

Death Certificate:
32 year old William Belchamber died in the Camberwell Infirmary on the 6th of September,1878. Death was certified by H Chabot MRCS.Informant was Ann Bourne The Steward of the Infirmary Camberwell. The death was registered by C W Gregory

the registrar for Camberwell. William was listed as a Clerk from Peckham.

David Belchamber
(Edward10,Edward9,Edward8,Edward7,Edward6,John5,Thomas,4,Robert3,Robert2, John1) was born about the 9th December,1821 in Horsham,Sussex. He died on the 25th February,1902 in 46 Archbishop Place,Brixton. He married Jane Elliott in Amberley, Sussex on the 25th October,1845. She was born in Pulborough,Sussex. She died on the 17th October,1897 in 46 Archbishop Place.

Census:
In the 1851 census David and Jane were living in Mill Lane,Streatham with two of their children Mary A aged 4 and Edward 2 months. David aged 30 was a Gardener and Jane was also 30.

In the 1861 census David aged 40 and a Gardener lived with his wife Jane aged 40 with daughter Mary Ann 14 and Edward 10. They now lived in Lambeth at 21 Archbishops Place.

In the 1871 census the family were still in 21 Archbishops Place,Lambeth. David now 49 was still a Gardener,Jane 49 was a Laundress as was her daughter Mary Ann aged 23 and finally son Edward 20 like his father was a Gardener.

David and Jane were living in No.29 Archbishops Place, Lambeth in the 1881 census. Living with them were their daughter Mary Ann aged 34 born in Woolbeding, Sussex. a Laundress and Peter Wilson a Dairyman aged 39 from Benacre, Suffolk.

In 1891 David and Jane were living in Lambeth at 50 Archbishop Place,David was aged 69 and a Gardener ,Jane was also 69,their daughter Mary Ann was 44 and a Laundress,living with them was Peter Wilson a 50 year old boarder.

In the 1911 census David and his 54 year old daughter Mary Ann were living in Lambeth at 44 Archbishop Place. David was a Gardener aged 79 and Mary Ann was a Laundress(Wash).

Marriage Certificate:
David Belchamber and Jane Elliot were married by banns on the 25th October 1845 at Amberley,Sussex. They were both aged 24 and resided in Rackham not far from Amberley. George A. Clarkson performed the marriage and Henry Webb was their witness. Jane`s father Thomas Elliot was a Carpenter by Trade and Edward Belchamber Snr.was a Gardener like his son David.

Death Certificates:
David Belchamber aged 80 died at 46 Archbishop Place,Brixton Hill on the 25th of February,1902 . Cause of death was Influenza and Pulmonary Conjestion certified by S D Ashley MRCS.Informant and present at death was his Daughter Mary Ann of the same address. The death was registered on the 25th of Febuary by the Lambeth Deputy Registrar Robert Wassley. David was a retired Gardener(Domestic Servant).

Jane Belchamber aged 73 died of "White Softening of the Brain" on the 17th of December 1897. Cause of death was certified by J Karman MRCS Eng. and was recorded by deputy registrar Robert Classley for Lambeth on the 18th of December. Jane's husband,David Belchamber was informant and present at death. David's occupation was a Jobbing Gardener

David Belchamber and Jane Elliott had the following children:

i   Mary Ann Belchamber was on the 21st August,1846 in Woolbeding,Sussex. She died on the 12th November,1903 in Archbishops Place,Brixton.

Birth Certificate;
Their daughter Mary Ann Belchamber was born at Woolbeding,Sussex on the 21st of August 1846. Her father David was a Gardener,Jane Belchamber formerly Elliott was her mother. Daniel Moore the registrar for Midhurst recorded the birth on the 25th September

Death Certificate;
Mary Ann Bellchamber a Laundress aged 56 died on the 12th of November,1903 of a Rupture of an Aneurysm of wall of Heart and Syncope. The certificate was received from George Percival Wyatt the coroner for the counties of Surrey and London. The inquest was held on the 17th of November and the death was registered the same day by Registrar Nathaniel Chanley. Mary Ann never married.

ii   Edward Belchamber was born on the 12th January,1851 in Wandsworth. He died on the 15th May,1885 in 46 Archbishops Place,Brixton Hill. He married Amelia Ellen Heath on the 21st October,1877 in The Parish Church,St.Marys,Lambeth. She died on the 2nd November,1936 in 10 Percy Road,Southsea,Portsmouth,Hampshire.

Birth Certificate:
Their son Edward Belchamber was born at Creaseys Cottage,Mill Lane,Bristow Hill,Streatham on the 12th of January,1851. David his father was a Gardener and Jane Belchamber formerly Elliott was living at the same address as the birth. Registrar for Wandsworth & Clapham Union Henry Withall recorded the birth on the 4th of February.

Marriage Certificate;
Edward Belchamber a bachelor aged 27 and a Gardener by trade married 26 year old spinster Amelia Ellen Heath at the parish church,St Marys,Lambeth on the 21st of October,1877 the curate J G Tipper performed the ceremony. Their witness's were David Belchamber the father and Edward's sister Mary Ann Belchamber. The fathers were George Heath a deceased Gas Fitter and David Belchamber a Gardener. Edward and Amelia were both living in Archbishop Place,Lambeth the Belchamber family home.

Census:
Edward and Amelia both aged 29 were living in Lambeth at 39 Archbishop Place in the 1881 census. Edward was a Gardener(Non Domestic).

In the 1891 census Amelia Ellen was living with her sister in Islington at 1Marriot Road. Amelia was a widow aged 37.

In 1901 Amelia aged 54 was listed as a visitor to Joseph Nearn aged 79 a retired Civil Service Officer living at Clyde Park Cottages,Sudbury,Suffolk.

Amelia was living at Heathfield,Clarence Road,Sudbury,Suffolk in 1911 with 15 year old Servant Agnes Sowman. Amelia was 58 years old and "living on private means".

Death Certificates;
Edward Belchamber aged 34 died on the 18th of May.1885 at 46 Archbishop Place,Brixton Hill. Cause of death was Rheurmatism Serous Apoplexy 13 days exhaustion which was certified by J W Williams MRC and registered by Robert Chaisley deputy Registrar of Lambeth on the 19th of May. Father David Belchamber was informant and present at the death.

Amelia Ellen Belchamber died aged 85 of Senile Decay on the 2nd of November,1936. The place of death was 10 Percy Road,Southsea,Portsmouth. The death was certified by James Malpas MRCS and recorded for Portsmouth by W H Beale on the 3rd of November. The informant was Ellen Woolgar of 10 Percy Road,causing the body to be buried.

Amelia Ellen Belchamber's will
THIS IS THE LAST WILL and Testament
Of me Amelia Ellen Belchamber of GoudhurstSouthwater Way Hunston Chichester in the county of Sussex widow made this 26th day of January one thousand nine hundred and thirty one--
I HEREBY revoking all former wills and Testamentary instruments DEVISE BEQEATH AND APPOINT all the real and personal estate to which I may be entitled or over which I have any power of appointment at my death unto my friend ELLEN WOOLGAR now residing with me her executors administrators and assign absolutely--------AND I APPOINT the said Ellen Woolgar SOLE EXECUTRIX of this my will.
IN WITNESS whereof I have hereunto set my hand the day and year first above written

Signed by the said Amelia}
Ellen Belchamber in the}
Presence of us present at}
The same time whi in her}   Amelia Ellen Belchamber(signed)
Sight and presence do}

John Belchamber
(Edward10,Edward9,Edward8,Edward7,Edward6,John5,Thomas,4,Robert3,Robert2, John1) was born about the 2nd September,1827 in Horsham,Sussex. He died on the 6th October,1913 in 126 St.James Road,Bermondsey. He married Sarah Ann Darby on the 21st August,1860 in The Registry Office,St.Georges,Southwark. She died on the 5thNovember,1895 in 83 New Church Street,Jamica Road,Bermondsey. He married Susannah Mansfield on the 8th June,1898 in St.James,Bermondsey. She died on the 3rd January,1914 in 26 Barry Road,East Dulwich.

At some point John had possibly married an Amelia Farge?,although no Marriage certificate can be found.She died on the 27th August,1855 in 12 Charles Street,Newington. Farge may not have been Amelia's surname it is hard to decipher on Caroline's birth certificate.

There were two daughters Ellen and Caroline,I cannot find a birth for Ellen or Helen but Caroline was born in 1852.

Birth Certificate:Caroline Belchamber
Caroline Belchamber who was born in Charles Street, St.Marys,Newington on the 6th of August 1852. The birth was registered on the 8th of August. Father John Belchamber was a porter also living at 12 Charles Street. The mother was Amelia Belchamber formerly what looks like Farge.This needs further investigation.

Marriage Certificate:
William John Chapman and Caroline Belchamber married in the parish church,Covent Garden on the 10th of August,1879 by banns. William John was a Bachelor and carpenter by trade aged 30 living at 17 Maidin Lane,Covent Garden. Caroline was aged 26 and a spinster living at 83 New Church Street,Spa Road,Bermondsey. The Witness were Ellen Belchamber and Henry Chapman. Fathers William Chapman was a deceased Tailor and John Belchamber a chemists assistant.

Death Certificate:
Amelia Belchamber died at 12 Charles Street,Newington on the 27th of August 1855.Informant and present at death was her Husband John Belchamber a porter also of 12 Charles Street. The death was registered on the 29th of August by registrar Charles Linton Alexander.

Death Certificate:
Ellen Belchamber aged 85 died on the 19th of December,1935 at 48 Vanbrugh Hill,Greenwich. Cause of death was Myocardiac degeneration and Senility certified by H Summers. Her informant was C Chapman her sister of Grove Vale,East Dulwich. P C Wales the registrar for Greenwich recorded the death on the 19th of December.

Marriage Certificate:Sarah Ann Darby
John Belchamber and Sarah Ann Darby married at the registry Office,St.Georges,Southwark on the 21st of August 1860. John was a 33 year old druggists Assisant of Great Guildford Street and Sarah Ann was aged 35 and a widow her abode was Great Suffolk Street. Frederick Clarkes Fritch was the Registrar. Their witness's were A Beard and N Toombs(The Assistant to the Registrar). Fathers Edward was a gardener and Samuel Wright,Sarah's father was a coal Dealer(deceased)

Death Certificate:Sarah Ann Belchamber
Sarah Ann Belchamber aged 73 died of Pneumonia on the 5th of November,1895 the death took place at 83 New Church Street,Jamaica Road,Southwark. Cause of death was certified by D G Kennedy MB and registered on the 6th of November by G Hurst the registrar. Informant and present at the death was J Gold a daughter she gave her

address as 28 Eveline Road,Camberwell. Sarah Ann was the wife of John Belchamber a Drugist's assistant.

Marriage Certificate: Susannah Mansfield.
John Belchamber a 70 year old widower and druggists assistant of 20 Collet Road Bermondsey and widow Susannah Mansfield aged 63 of St.Martins Seambelsley,Lincolnshire were married by banns at St.James Church,Bermondsey on the 8th of June 1898. Witness's were Elizabeth and Alice Belchamber. Hammond B Bidshopp performed the ceremony. The fathers were both deceased Edward being a gardener and George York a fish salesman.

Census:
In the 1911 census John and Susannah Belchamber were living at 126 St.James Road,Bermondsey. John was an 85 year old Packer,Susannah was aged 66. With them were Helen Belchamber daughter single aged 51 and a servant,John Belchamber married aged 55 a Porter and Edward Belchamber aged 55 a Cellarman,also living with the family was Caroline Chapman aged 57 their widowed daughter who was a Corporation Attendant.

Death Certificates:
John Belchamber aged 86 and formerly a Druggist's Packer died of Senile Decay on the 6th of October 1913. The death took place at 126 St.James Road,Bermondsey,present at the death and informant was S Belchamber the widow of the same address. Cause of death was certified by D G Kennedy and was recorded on the 7th of October by registrar C H Hurst.

Susannah Belchamber aged 69 died at 26 Barry Road,East Dulwich on the 3rd of January,1914,after acidentaly falling down the stairs on the 1st of January causing a Cerebral Haemorrhage. A death certificate was received from G P Wyatt the Coroner of Surrey after the inquest which was held on the 5th of January. Listed as the widow of John Belchamber a Wholesale Chemist the death was recorded on the 5th of January by W.L.Churchill the registrar for Camberwell.

John Belchamber and Sarah Ann Darby had the following children:

i   John Belchamber was born on the 5th June,1857 in 1 Hearnes Buildings Locks Field,Walworth. He died on the 11th December,1949 in Sunnycliffe,May Avenue,Canvey Island,Essex. He married Elizabeth Ann Mansfield on the 22nd September,1878 in Newington. She was the daughter of Richard and Eliza Mansfield nee Holloway. She died on the 4th March,1941 in Orsett Lodge,Orsett,Thurrock,Essex.

Census:
John and Elizabeth were living in Bermondsey at 5 Longley Street in the 1881 census. John was a Grocer's Porter aged 23 and Elizabeth was 21

In 1891 John and Elizabeth were living at 47 Reverdy Road,Bermondsey,London. John was a Warehouseman aged 33,Elizabeth was 31 and the children were John 5 and Maud 2.

In the 1901 census John and Elizabeth were still in Bermondsey livin at 89 Southwark Park Road. John aged 42 was a Grocers Assistant,Elizabeth was 40 John R was 15 and a Music Setters Assistant and Maud was age 12.

John and Elizabeth were living in the City of London at 85 Aldergate Street in the 1911 census. John was a Grocers Assistant aged 53 and Elizabeth was aged 33.Their daughter Maud Louise was 22 and a Drapers Assistant

.

ii   Edward Belchamber was born on the 10th August,1858 in 1 Hearnes Buildings. He died on the 31st May,1924 in 48 Vanburgh Hill,Greenwich. He married Alice Saunders on the 25th December,1882 in St.Saviour,Newington. She died on the 17th Febuary,1919 in 37 Beauval Road,Camberwell.

iii   Charles John Belchamber was born on the 10th August,1862 in Hearnes Buildings. He died on the 9th January,1948 in Mile End Hospital,Stepney. He married Elizabeth Phyliss Potter on the 23rd July,1882 in The Parish Church,Shoreditch. She died on the 19th October,1926 in 204 Hoxton Street,Shoreditch.

Samuel Belchamber
(Edward10,Edward9,Edward8,Edward7,Edward6,John5,Thomas4,Robert3,Robert2,John1)Was born about the 13th September,1830 in Horsham,Sussex. He died on the 11th June,1896 in 19 Barland Road,Fulham. He married Ann Worman on the 15th March,1853 in St.Nicholas,Deptford,Kent. She died on the 13th January,1886 in 56 Beauchamp Place,Kensington.

Marriage Certificate:
Bachelor and gardener Samuel Belchamber of full age and Ann Worman a spinster also of full age married on the 15th of March,1853 in St.Nicholas,Deptford,Kent both gave Deptford as their residence. Their witness's were Charles Young and Ann Sargina. The fathers were Edward Belchamber Gardener and Samuel Worman a labourer.

Census:
In 1861 Samuel 30 and Ann 29 were living at 59 Grove Road,Brompton in the home of Edward Smith as lodgers. Neither had occupations listed.

In the 1871 census Samuel 40 and Ann 39 are still at 59 Grove Road,Brompton now Samuel is the head. It looks like Samuel is Foreman of a stone yard and Ann is a Housekeeper

In the 1881 census they lived in Middlesex, London at No.59 Grove Place with their son Frederick born in Middlesex aged 19 professor of Music, Caroline Bowden a Lodger aged 40 born in Middlesex and listed as a Needlewoman, Elizabeth Fordes aged 40 from Dublin, Ireland and a Governess and finally Guila Soldi aged 42 a Domestic Maid from Italy.

Death Certificates:

Samuel Belchamber aged 66 and a Police Constable died at 19 Darlan Road,Fulham on the 11th of June,1896. Frederick William Belchamber was the informant and in attendance,Frederick William's address was given as 5 Fulham Park Road,Fulham. David Sheppard the registrar for Fulham registered the death on the 12th of June. Cause of death was Asthma Chronic 5 Years and heart failure 2 hours which was certified by G H Pellen MRCS.

Ann Belchamber aged 55 died on the 13th of January,1886 of Heart Disease and Bronchitis certified by W Higden MRCS. Samuel Belchamber widower of the deceased was informant and present at the death. James L Hume deputy registrar recorded the death on the 14th of January for Kensington.

Police Record:
Samuel Belchamber joined the Metropolitan Police force on the 4th of March 1850 at Rochester Row first he was on street duty up until the 1st of March,1859,after that he was promoted to sergeant until he retired with a pension on the 6th of July,1869 at the age of 39.He was described as 5ft 11inches tall ,dark brown hair,blue eyes and a fresh complexsion,Samuel had no particular marks or defects,he gave his address as 59 Grove Place,Brompton.He gave his birthday as the 25th of April,1831 and his father was Edward Belchamber,his mother was listed as dead.He left the police force on the 6th of July,his pension of £36.8s per annum commenced on the 4th of July,1869.

Samuel Belchamber and Ann Worman had the following child:

i   Frederick William Belchamber was born on the 15th April,1861 in 59 Grove Place,Brompton. He died on the 8th May,1944 in 1 Elmer Gardens,Edgware, Middlesex. He married Charlotte Ethel Hunt on the 26th June,1890 in All Saints Church,Knightsbridge. She died on the 3rd July,1964 in 6 Fairfield Road Burgess Hill,Sussex.

Ann Belchamber
(James10,James9,William8,Edward7,Edward6,John5,Thomas4,Robert3,Robert2,John 1)
Was born on the 15th January,1837 In Kirdford,Sussex. She married Frederick Phillips on the 10th November,1855 in Kirdford. He was the son of James and Ann Phillips born on the 13th March,1836.

Census:
In the 1851 Census Ann Belchamber aged 14 was a Housemaid to the family of John and Henrietta Childs at Waphurst House,Kirdford.

Marriage Certificate:
Frederick Phillips a bachelor and Labourer by trade married spinster Ann Belchamber on the 10th of November,1855 both were minors. The marriage took place in the parish church,Kirdford. Their witness's were Thomas Bentley and Sarah Phillips,Sarah signed her mark on the certificate,as did both the bride and groom. Their fathers were James Phillips and James Belchamber both Labourers. The Rev.Coles performed the service.

Ann Belchamber had the following child:

i   Rhoda Belchamber was born on the August,1853 in Kirdford,Sussex. She married Henry John Russell on the 30th September,1873 in Kirdford. Baptised 7th August, 1853.

Birth Certificate:
Rhoda Belchamber was born in Plaistow,Sussex on the 22nd of June 1853,she was the child of Ann Belchamber. There was no father recorded,George Wells registered the birth on the 4th of July for Petworth District.
Rhoda Belchamber was baptised at Kirdford on the 7th of August,1853

Marriage Certificate:
Henry Joseph Russell and Rhoda Belchamber were married in Kirdford on the 30th of August 1873 by banns,the service was performed by J F Coles. Witness's were Israel Cooper and Julia Phillips.Henry Joseph was a bachelor of full age and a Gardener by trade,Rhoda a spinster and a minor. Both gave their residence as Kirdford. Only one father was listed,that was George Russell a Cordwainer.

James Belchamber 2nd Great Grandparents
(James10,James9,William8,Edward7,Edward6,John5,Thomas4,Robert3,Robert2,John 1)
Was born on the 14th November,1839 in Foxbridge,Kirdford,Sussex. He died on the 8th November,1905 in Golden Cross Cottage,Plaistow,Sussex. He married Abigail Pennicard on the 1st June,1864 in St.John the Baptist,Kirdford. She was the daughter of Robert and Ruth Pennicard born on the 15th June,1845. She died on the 18th December,1903 in Plaistow,Sussex in Golden Cross,Cottage.

Birth Certificate:
James Belchamber was born in Foxbridge,Kirdford,Sussex on the 14th of November,1839. The birth was registered in Petworth by George Wells on the 25th of November. His father James Belchamber was a Labourer.

Marriage Certificate:
James Belchamber and Abigail Pennicard were married on the 1st June 1864,James was of full age and Abigail a minor,both signed the register with their mark. The witness`s were George Pennicard and Hannah Pennicard. J.F Cole the vicar performed the marriage.

Death Certificates:
James Belchamber of Plaistow,Sussex died on the 8th of November,1905. Cause of death was Brights disease certified by F Heygate MRCS. Elizabeth Belchamber his daughte of Plaistow, was informant and present at death. Charles Randall recorded the death on the 8th of November at Petworth.

Abigail Belchamber died aged 58 in Plaistow,Sussex on the 18th of December,1903. Her son William Belchamber was informant and present at the death. Abigail died of Acute Pnuemonia(10 days). Charles Randall the Petworth registrar recorded the death on the 19th of December.

Census:

In the 1871 census James aged 31 and Abigail aged 25,were living in Durfold Cottage,Dunsfold,Surrey with three of their children Frederick 6,George 3 and William 1.James was listed as a Labourer and Abigail a Labourer's wife.

James and Abigail were living in Plaistow Street,Plaistow in the 1881 census with their children. James was 41,Abigail 35,Frederick 16,George 13,William 11,Emma 9,John 7,Annie 3 and finally Harriet 8 months. James was a Agricultural Labourer,Abigail a Agricultural Labourer's wife. Frederick and George were also Agricultural Labourers.

In the 1891 census James and Abigail were living in Plaistow,Sussex in Rickmans Lane with Alice Beaty and Elizabeth their daughters.James was aFarm Labourer aged 51,Abigail was 45,Alice Beaty 8 Scholar,and Elizabeth 4.

In 1901 James and Abigail were in Plaistow,Sussex,probably living at Golden Cross Cottage. James 62,Abigail 56 and son William aged 31. Also living with them was Frederick Baker a boarder aged 64. James and Abigail were listed as paupers,William was a farm worker.

James Belchamber and Abigail Pennicard had the following children:

i   Frederick Belchamber was born on the 28th March,1865 in Petworth,Sussex. He died on the 19th September,1931 in 3 Lion Mead,Shottermill,Surrey. He married Jane Baker on the 24th July,1895 in Kirdford. She was born in 1857. She died on the 13th October,1926 in The Infirmary,Hale Road,Farnham, Surrey.

Birth Certificate:
Frederick Belchamber was born in Plaistow,Sussex on the 28th of March,1865. His father James was a Hewer and Abigail his mother signed her mark. The birth was recorded on the 27th of April by registrar for Petworth George Wells.
Frederick was baptised in Kirdford on the 16th April, 1865

Marriage Certificate:
Frederick Belchamber who spent some of his life as a military man married Jane Baker at Kirdford on the 24th July 1895 by banns,witness`s were Annie and Frederick Baker(signed with a cross) the ceremony was performed by Erskin A Birrell. Frederick and Jane Belchamber only had one son Charles Fredereick born in Chuter Cottages,Shottermill on the 19th of May,1896 the birth was registered in Farnham,Surrey on the 29th May.

Census:
In the 1891 census Frederick Belchamber aged 25 was a Guard at the Calvary and Artillery Barracks in Colchester,Essex.

In the 1901 census Frederick aged 36 and Jane 41 are living in Lion Lane,Shottermill with their son Charles Frederick aged 4. Frederick's occupation is a Gunner RHA reserves. They have a boarder by the name of Walter Jaques a General Labourer aged 18 from Whitmore Bottom,Surrey.

In the 1911 census Frederick Belchamber a Labourer aged 46 was living in Lion Lane,Shottermill,Haslemere,Surrey with his wife Jane Belchamber aged 52 and their 14 year old son Charles Frederick Belchamber.Jane Belchamber was a Household Worker.

Death Certificates:

Jane Belchamber aged 67 died at The Infirmary,Hale Road,Farnham on the 13th of October 1926. Cause of death was cerebral Vascular Desease and Bronchitis which was certified by T Brockington MD. Registrar R Balchin registered the death on the 16th October. Charles Frederick Belchamber of 3 Chuter Cottages her son was informant. Jane's husband Frederick was a domestic gardener. Jane is buried in St.Stephens churchyard,Shottermill.

Frederick Belchamber died at 3 Lion Mead,Shottermill on the 19th of September,1931 of cardiac failure his son Charles was the informant of the same address,Fredericks age was 66 and a domestic gardener,the death was registered on the 25th September,he is buried in St Stephens,churchyard Shottermill on the 23rd of September. E G Clifford Frend performed the service.

ii   George Belchamber was born on the 24th May,1867 in Petworth,Sussex.
        He died on the 11th January,1953 in Burcot,Woodside Road,Chiddingfold,
        Surrey. He married Kate Horn on the 14th October,1893 in Petworth. She was
        the daughter of Silas Horn and Harriet Thayre,born on 1874 in Kirdford. She
        died on the 25th November,1939 in Burcot.
        George was baptised on the 11th July, 1867 in Kirdford

iii   William Belchamber was born on the 13th June,1869 in Durfold Cottage,
        Dunsfold,Surrey. He died on the 3rd August,1941 in Golden Cross Cottage,
        Plaistow,Sussex. He married Louisa Jane Remnant on the 17th February,1906
        in Petworth,Sussex,the daughter of Thomas Remnant and Charlotte Cooper.
        She was born on the 30th March,1879 in Chiddingfold,Surrey. She died on the
        4th November,1957 in Southlands Hospital,Shoreham by sea,Sussex.

iv   Emma Belchamber was born on the 15th October,1871 in Hambledon,Surrey.
        She married William Edward Philps on the 11th September,1897 in Portsea,
        Hampshire,the son of William George Philps and Elizabeth King. He was born
        on the 28th April,1869 in 47 Maitland Street,Portsea,Hampshire.
        Baptised on the 15th October, 1871.

v   Jehu Belchamber was born on the 5th December,1873 in Dunsfold,Surrey.
        He died on the 21st August,1953 in St.Lukes Hospital,Guildford,Surrey.
        He married Rosina Voice on the 27th October,1947 in Midhurst,Sussex. She
        was born in 1879 and died in The Southlands Hospital,Shoreham by sea on the
        31st January,1959.
        Baptised on the 4th January, 1874.

Birth Certicate:

Jehu Belchamber was born in Durfold,Dunsfold,Surrey on the 5th of December,1873. His father James Belchamber was a Farm Labourer. The birth was recorded for Hambledon,Surrey on the 2nd January,1874.
Jehu was baptisted in Kirdford on the 4th January,1874.

Census:
In 1891 Jehu was living as a 17 year old Lodger in the home of William Durrant and family in the High Street,Kirdford,Sussex. Jehu was listed as an Agricultural Labourer.

Marriage Certificate:
Jehu Belchamber married late he was 73 when he married a widow Rosina Voice age 61 at Midhurst registry office on the 27th October 1947. Both Jehu and Rosina were living at Foresters Cottage,Kirdford.Witness's were G.Trussler and G.H Luff the ceremony was performed by A.F.Werry the Registrar. Both fathers were deceased James Belchamber and William Wooding.

Death Certificates:
Rosina Belchamber aged 80 died at Southlands Hospital,Shoreham by Sea on the 31st of January 1959. Cause of death was Bronchial Carcinoma which was certified by J F Varley MB. The informant was G M Baker her daughter of 20 Council Cottages,Kirdford. Rosina was listed as the widow of Jehu Belchamber a Forestry Worker,her address at the time of death was Forresters Cottages,Kirdford.
Rosina Belchamber is buried in plot 24 in Kirdford Churchyard(No Headstone)

Jehu Belchamber of Foresters Cottage,Kirdford,Sussex died on the 21st of August,1953 at St.Lukes Hospital,Guildford aged 79. Cause of death was Haematemesis & Melaena,Chronic Duodenal Ulcer and Gross Arteriosclerosis PM certified by R Benson MB. The registrar for Surrey South Western H J Simmonds. registered the death on the 25th of August.G M Baker of 20 Council Cottages,Kirdford his step daughter was informant

Notes For Jehu Belchamber:
After a short term in the Sussex Militia. Jehu joined the army on the 21st of February, 1893, when he enlisted in the Royal Sussex Regiment in Chichester. As a Private No 4305 and the age of 21 years 1 month he was 5ft 3 inches tall, weighed 132 Lbs. With a fresh complexsion, brown eyes and hair and no distinctive marks on his body. After passing a medical examination he was attested.
He was posted to India on the 3rd of April 1894 where he stayed for over 20 years, returning home on the 3rd April,1914 where he was discharged medically unfit(too old) on the 28th April at Netley,serving a total of 21 years 61 days. He gained two certificates of education 3rd class in 16th of September, 1896 and 2nd class on the 16th of July, 1896. He passed two classes of instruction Pushtu (LS) on the 1ST April 1901 and Supply Duties on the 31st July 1903.
On the 27th of September at Camp Thobba he agreed to extend his military service to 12 years for which he received the sum of 150 rupee and an additional gratuity of 247-5-0 in lieu of furlough to England. He was in the Tirah Campaign for which he received a medal.

The Tirah Campaign was an India Frontier War in 1897-98. The Afridis tribesmen had for 16 years received a subsidy from the government of British India for safeguarding the Khyber Pass. This was carried out by a regiment of Afridis who rose up in revolt.

Jehu Belchamber also received the India Medal with clasps for the Punjab Frontier and the GB Medal for long service. After leaving the army he returned to Kirdford where he lived out the rest of his days.

(Pushtu, is the language of the Pathan races of Afghanistan and the North-West Frontier province of India.)

Census:

Jehu Belchamber aged 27 was serving in the military in India in the 1911 census. He was a private in the 1st Royal Sussex Regiment.

vi   Ruth Mary Belchamber was born on the 16th November,1874 in Durfold, Dunsfold,Surrey. She died three weeks later on the 8th December.

Birth Certificate;

The birth of Ruth Mary Belchamber took place in Durfold Wood,Dunsfold on the 16th of November,1874. James Matthew George Walder recorded the birth on the 4th of December at Hambledon. James Belchamber her father was a Agricultural Labourer.

Death Certificate:

Ruth Mary Belchamber aged 3 weeks died on the 8th of December,1874 at Durfold Wood,Dunsfold,Surrey. Cause of death was Convulsions she had been ill from birth. Her father James Belchamber was present at the death and informant. The death was registered on the 11th of December by James Matthew George Walder registrar for Hambledon.

vii   Ann Belchamber was born on the 4th June,1877 in Petworth,Sussex. She married George Frederick Ede on the 1st August,1903 in Petworth,Sussex. He was the son of Caleb Ede and Elizabeth.
Ann was baptised on the 12th July, 1877

viii   Harriet Belchamber was born on the 16th August,1880 in Plaistow,Sussex. She died on the 10th January,1882 in Plaistow.
Baptised on the 17th October, 1880

Birth Certificate:

Harriet Belchamber was born on the 16th of August,1880 in Plaistow,Sussex. Her father James Belchamber was a Farm Labourer. George Brookfield registered the birth on the 1st of August in Petworth,Sussex.

Death Certificate:

Harriet Belchamber aged 16 months died in Plaistow,Sussex on the 10th of January,1882. James Belchamber her father was informant of Plaistow. Cause of death was Pneumonia(By Post Mortem by order of the Coroner) certified by Reginald

Humphrys MRCS. George Brookfield recorded the death for Petworth on the 14th of January.

ix   Alice Beatrice Belchamber was born on the 8th April,1883 in Plaistow,Sussex. She married John Edwin Birch on the 5th July,1902 in Leek,Staffordshire,the son of James Birch and Emily Finney.
Alice B was baptised on the 24th May, 1883

.

x   Elizabeth Belchamber was born on the 27th March,1887 in Plaistow,Sussex. She married Percy Wooldridge on the 30th March,1907 in Shamley Green, Surrey. Percy was the son of Joshua Wooldridge and Alice Georgina Elliot.
Baptised on the 1st May, 1887

Jane Belchamber

(James10,James9,William8,Edward7,Edward6,John5,Thomas4,Robert3,Robert2,John 1) was born on the 22nd May,1842 in Lyons Farm,Kirdford,Sussex. She married Israel Cooper on the 17th November,1860 in Kirdford. He was born on the 15th March,1840 in Kirdford.

Birth Certificate:
Jane Belchamber was born at Lyons Farm,Kirdford on the 22nd of May,1842. James her father was a Labourer her mother Mary formerly Denyer made her mark. The birth was registered by George Wells registrar for Petworth.

Marriage Certificate:
Jane Belchamber was the next to wed when she married Israel Cooper in Kirdford in 1860 on the 17th of November,they were both minors. J.F Cole performed the ceremony,neither Israel or Jane could write because they both left their marks on the register. The witness`s were James Belchamber and Jane Elliot.

Israel Cooper and Jane Belchamber had the following children:

i   Harriet Cooper born 1867
ii   William Cooper born 1868
iii   Joseph Cooper born 1871
iv   Henry Cooper born 1873
v   James Cooper born 1875
vi   Peter Cooper born 1882
vii   Edith Cooper birth not known

William Belchamber

(James10,James9,William8,Edward7,Edward6,John5,Thomas4,Robert3,Robert2,John 1) was born on the 20th October,1844 in Plaistow,Sussex. He died on the 14th May,1923 in Rose Cottage,Plaistow,Sussex. He married Eliza Greenfield on the 30th June,1866 in Kirdford. She was the daughter of William Greenfield and Susannah

Remnant. Eliza was born about the 18th April,1847 in Kirdford. She died on the 29th April,1930 also in Rose Cottage,Rickmans Lane,Plaistow.

Birth Certificate:
William Belchamber was born in Plaistow,Sussex on the 16th of September,1844,Mary his mother signed with a cross and his father James was a Labourer. George Wells recorded the birth in Petworth on the 26th of September.

Marriage Certificate:
William Belchamber and Elizabeth Greenfield married in 1866 in Kirdford on the 30th of June. William was of full age while Elizabeth was a minor. J.F Cole was vicar and performed the wedding ceremony. The witnesss` were William Greenfield and Fanny Belchamber William`s sister. Both William and Elizabeth signed a cross as their mark on the register.

Census:
In the 1871 Census William is aged 26 and a Farm Labourer,Eliza is 24,their son Thomas is 3 and Alfred 7 months.Their abode is the Hamlet of Plaistow.

In the 1881 census they were living at No 8 Rickmans Lane Kirdford with sons Thomas age 13 a farm servant,Alfred age 10 a scholar and Walter C age 3. William aged 36 is a Farm Labourer and Eliza is 34.

In the 1891 Census William and Eliza are living in Chapel Road,Kirdford with their chidren Alfred 20 a Farm Servant,Charles 13 also a Farm Servant and 9 year old James. William is a AgriculturalLabourer aged 46 and Eliza is 43

In the 1901 census William is 56 and still a Ag.Lab.,Eliza is now 54,William is now the only child left at home aged 19 and a Postman.

In the 1911 Census finds William and Eliza Belchamber living in Plaistow,Sussex.William is a Labourer aged 66 and Eliza is 64

Death Certificates:
William Belchamber aged 78 and a general labourer died of Gangrene of the foot and blood poisoning on the 14th of May,1923. His son William James was the informant and was present at death. The death was registered on the 15th of May by M Pugsley Registra. William was living at Rose Cottage,Plaistow.

Eliza Belchamber Aged 83 died at Rose Cottage,Rickmans Lane,Plaistow on the 29th of April 1930. She was the widow of William Belchamber a Farm Labourer and the cause of death was Apoplexy and Arteris Sclerosis certified by R B Heygate MRCS.R Belchamber(possibly her son Reginald) was informant and present at the death of Rose Cottage Wisborough Green. M F Graville the registrar for Petworth recorded the death on the 1st of May.

Eliza Belchamber left a will which is transcribed below

THIS IS THE LAST WILL AND TESTAMENT of me ELIZA BELCHAMBER of Rose Cottage Rickman Lane Plaistow in the Parish of Kirdford in the County of

Sussex made this eighteenth day of August in the year of our Lord one thousand nine hundred and twenty three I hereby revoke all wills by me made at any time heretofore I appoint Harry Garman of Tenfold House Loxwood near Horsham in the County of Sussex to be my

EXECUTOR and I direct that all my just debts and funeral expenses be paid as soon as possible after my decease I hereby give and bequeath equally unto my four sons Alfred Thomas Charles and James Belcnamber all that I die possessed of or am entitled to or in, the event of either of my sons deceasing previous to myself I direct their fathers portion be equally devided amongst his children - ELIZA BLLCHAMBER - Signed publised and declared by the said testatrix as and for her last will and testament in presence of us who at her request in her preseace and in presence of

Each other have hereunto subscribed our names as witnesses   HARRIET STEER 13 Grange road,Hove,Sussex   ARTHUR FREDERICK WOOLDRIDGE Rickman Lane Plaistow Horsham Sussex

Proved 10th July 1930

William Belchamber and Eliza Greenfield had the following children:

i   Thomas Belchamber was born on the 5th April,1867 in Plaistow,Sussex.
He died on the 26th April,1951 in Chalkdell Hospital,Hitchin,Hertfordshire.
He married Mary Ann Hook on the 18th May,1898 in The Church of St.John Greenwich,she was the daughter of James Hook and Mary Ann. She was born in 1868 in Stratten Strawless,Norfolk. She died on the 13th November,1941 in 17 Wellhouse Lane,Barnett,Hertfordshire.
Baptised 19th May, 1867

Birth Certificate:
Thomas Belchamber was born on the 5th of April,1867 and bapt.May 19th.His father William was a Farm Labourer the birth was registered by George Wells on the 16th of May in Petworth.

Marriage Certificate;
Thomas Belchamber and Mary Ann Hook married on May 18,1898 by Banns in the Church of St.John in the parish of Greenwich he was a 30 year old bachelor and Labourer and Mary Ann a 29 year old spinster with no occupation listed, they were both living at 12 Coulhurst Road,witness`s were E A Bale and N U Balls. Fathers William was a Labourer and James Hook was deceased.The curate was J A Anderson.

Death Certificates:
Mary Ann Belchamber aged 73 died of Mycardial Degeneration and Senility on the 13th of November,1941(certified by Roland Segar MB) the death took place at 17 Wellhouse Lane,Barnet,Hertfordshire. Mary Ann was listed as the widow of T Belchamber of 86 High Street,Codicote,Hertfordshire who was the informnant. O Timpson the registrar for Barnet recorded the death on the 14th of November.

Thomas Belchamber died on the 26th of April 1951 at the Chalkdell Hospital,Hitchin. The registrar Alan Wearmouth registered the death on the 30th of April.Cause of death was Syncope(Fainting/Passing Out) and Senility. He was a General Labourer(Retired) aged 85 his address was 86 High Street,Cudicote,Hitchin. The informant was R I Lapage of Chalkdell Hospital.

Census:
In the 1901 census Thomas and Mary Ann were living in Dunsfold,Surrey at The Common . Thomas was a 33 year old Bricklayer and Mary Ann was also aged 33.

Thomas and Mary Ann were living at WestWood Lodge,Windlesham,Surrey in 1911. Thomas was aged 42 and a Domestic Coachman,Mary Ann was aged 40 with no occupation listed

Thomas Belchamber and Mary Ann Hook had no children.

ii   Alfred Belchamber was born on the 23rd October,1870 in Petworth,Sussex. He died on the 2nd January,1955 in 50 Victoria Street,Englefield Green,Surrey. He married Sarah Jane Hawkins on the 7th September,1895 in The Parish Church,Hascombe,Surrey. Sarah Jane was born about the 7th July,1872 in Wisborough Green,Sussex the daughter of John and Mary Hawkins. She died on the 20th January,1961 in The Grange,St.Anne's Hill,Chertsey, Surrey.
Baptised 23rd October, 1870

iii   Walter Charles Belchamber was born on the 15th July,1877 in Plaistow,Sussex.He died on the 7th October,1946 in St.James Place,Cranleigh,Surrey. He Married Alice Winifred Carpenter on the 12th April,1904 in The Registry Office,Guildford,Surrey.She was born in 1885. She died on the 24th October, 1965 in Cranleigh Village Hospital,Cranleigh,Surrey.
Baptised 9th September, 1877

iv   William James Belchamber was born on the 19th April,1881 in Petworth, Sussex. He died on the 28th November,1945 in Ivy Cottage,Wisborough Green, Sussex. He married Kate Pennicard on the 2nd April,1904 in Kirdford,Sussex. Kate was the daughter of James Pennicard and Jane Stemp,born 1879. She died on the 5th February,1961 in 8 Butts Mead,Wisborough Green
Baptised on the 26th June, 1881

Fanny Belchamber
(James10,James9,William8,Edward7,Edward6,John5,Thomas4,Robert3,Robert2,John 1) was born on the 28th May,1848 in Kirdford,Sussex. She married Alfred Cooper in Kirdford on the 23rd November,1867 in Kirdford,the son of Clement Cooper and

Emma Rapley,he was born about the 20th June,1847. Fanny Cooper died on the
30thJune,1905 in Kirdford.

Birth Certificate:
Fanny Belchamber was born in Plaistow,Sussex on the 28th of May,1848. James
Belchamber her father was a Labourer and her mother Mary formerly Denyer signed
her mark. George Wells recorded the birth in Petworth on the 14th of June.

Marriage Certificate:
Fanny Belchamber a minor and spinster and Alfred Cooper a minor and bachelor
were married at Kirdford,Sussex on the 23rd of November,1867. Alfred was a
Labourer. Their Witness's were James and Harriet Pannell,the ceremony was
performed by J F Coles. Alfred signed the register with his cross. The fathers were
Clement Cooper a Farmer and James Belchamber a Labourer

Alfred Cooper and Fanny Belchamber had the following childen:

i   Albert Thomas Cooper born 1871
ii   Harriet Cooper born 1873
iii   Emma Mary Cooper born 1876.

John Belchamber
(John10,James9,William8,Edward7,Edward6,John5,Thomas,4,Robert3,Robert2,John1
) John Belchamber was born on the 5th June,1851 in 27 Market Street,Westminster.
He died on the 30th October,1902 in 4 Norman Street,East Ham. He married Emma
Elizabeth Maxwell on the 31st May,1874 in St.Marys,Westminster. She died on the
25th September,1878 in 20 High Street,East Ham.He then remarried to Louisa
Winchcombe on the 11th June,1879 inSt.Margarets,Westminster. She died on the 21st
May,1928 in 1 Old Church Road,Romford,Essex.

Birth Certificate:
On the 5th of June 1851 at 27 Market Street,Westminister John Belchamber was born
to John and Sarah Belchamber formerly Sopp. John's occupation was a Carman.
George Pearse the registrar for Westminister recorded the birth on the 3rd of July.

Marriage Certicate:Emma Elizabeth Maxwell
John Belchamber married Emma Elizabeth Maxwell on the 31st of May, 1874.at
Sy.Marys, Westminster by banns. John aged 23 of 36 Great Smith Street the son of
John a Carman.Emma Elizabeth aged 20 was the daughter of Edward Maxwell a
Coach painter of 50 Marsham Street. Their witness's were John Belchamber and Eliza
Maxwell. The service was taken by A C D Ryden

Death Certificate:Emma Elizabeth Belchamber.
Emma Elizabeth Belchamber aged 23 wife of John a plasterer, died of Placenta Previa
and Puerperal Fever on the 25th September 1878 at 20 High Street, East Ham,
husband John was informant and present at death.

Marriage Certificate:Louisa Winchcombe.

Now a widower John Belchamber aged 30 and a Labourer remarried on the 11th of June 1879 to Louisa Winchcombe aged 30 of 13 Buckingham Cottages. Louisa was the daughter of Henry Winchcombe a Traveller.John and Louisa married by banns at St.Margarets, Westminster their witness's were Louisa Brazell and George Darby The marriage was taken by H H Montgomery the Curate. John Bellchamber the father was a Carman.

Death Certificate:Louisa Bellchambers.
Louisa Bellchambers aged 84 died on the 21st of May,1928 at 1 Old Church Road,Romford,Essex,Louisa was the widow of John Bellchambers a Gas Works Labourer of 339 Ley Street,Ilford. Cause of death was Peritonitis Perforation of common bile duct and Carcinorma of Pancreas which was certified by C Edgar Lewis the coroner for Essex after a post mortum without inquest.Informant was J H Wheeler of 339 Ley Street,Ilford causing the body to be buried. J S Nicoll registrar for Romford recorded the death on the 5th June.

Death Certificate:John Belchambers.
John Belchambers Jnr. Aged 52 died on the 30th of October 1902,at 4 Plowman Terrace,West Ham.Cause of death was Syncope and the death was recorded on the 1st of November by E R Elliott of registrar for West Ham.

John Belchamber's Adminstration 1923

Administration

DEATH ON OR AFTER 1st JANUARY,1898

LET IT BE KNOWN that John Bellchambers of 4 Norman Terrace,High Street south,East Ham in the county of Essex

Died there on the 30th day of October 1902 at 22 Cobden Road aforesaid

Intestate

AND BE IT FURTHER KNOWN that at the date hereunder written
Letters of Administration of all the Estate which by law devolves to and vests in the personal representative of the said intestate were granted by His Majesty's High Court Of Justice at the Principal Probate Registry thereof to
Clara Emily Moore of 9 Caledon Road,East Ham aforesaid (Wife of George Arthur Moore) the natural and lawful daughter and me of the next of kin

Of the said intestate

Dated 25th day of September 1923
By registrars order dated the 27th day of July,1923
Cross value of estate £186.0.0

John Belchamber and Emma Elizabeth Maxwell had the following children:

i   Edward John Belchamber was born on the 26th February,1875 in 38 Johnson, Street,Westminister. He died on the 12th February,1878 in 3 Edward Street, Plaistow,Essex.

Birth Certificate:
Edward John Bellchambers was born on the 25th of February 1875 at 38 Johnson Street,Westminster. W G Pearse the registrar recorded the birth on the 1st of April. Her parents were John Bellchambers a Contractors Foreman and Emma Elizabeth formerly Maxwell.

Death Certificate:
Edward John Bellchambers died on the 12th of February 1878 aged 2,Edward John died of Acute Laryngitis(2 days) which was certified by R Carey MRCS. The death was registered by the registrar for West Ham Union on the 21st of February. J Bellchambers was informant and present at the death

ii   Clara Emily Belchamber was born on the 5th November,1876 in 31 Tufton Street,Westminister. She married George Arthur Moore on the 2nd November, 1914 in All Saints,Forest Gate,West Ham.

Birth Certificate:
Clara Emily Bellchambers was born at 31 Tufton Street,Westminster on the 5th of November 1876. Her parents were John Bellchambers a Contractors Foreman and Emma formerly Maxwell. The birth was registered on the 11th of December by W G Pearse the registrar for St.George Hanover Square.

Marriage Certificate:
Clara Emily Bellchamber and George Arthur Moore married on the 2nd of November at All Saints Church,Forest Gate,West Ham. George Arthur was aged 28 a bachelor and a Traveller and Clara Emily was aged 37 and a spinster,both gave their address as 23 Shrewsbury Road.Witness's were Mary Price,William Henry Grove,J Bellchamber and K Moore. Their fathers were Frederick Moore a Traveller and John Bellchamber a Inn Keeper?

John Belchamber and Louisa Winchcombe had the following children:

i   Female Belchamber was born on the 18th March,1880 in 13 Fisher Street, Plaistow,Essex. She died there on the 20th March,1880.

Birth Certificate:
A female was born to John and Louisa at 13 Fisher Street,Plaistow,Essex on the 18th of March 1880. Father John Bellchambers was a Dock Labourer and her mother was Louisa formerly Winchcombe. R March the registrar for West Ham recorded the birth on the 22nd of March.

Death Certificate:

John and Louisa Bellchamber's female child died on the 20th of March 1880,cause of death was Debility form premature birth which was certified by R Carey MRCS. J Bellchambers was informant and present at death. The registrar for West Ham,R March recorded the death on the 22nd of March.

ii   Elizabeth Gwenllian Belchamber was born on the 14th September,1881 in 5 Charles Street,Plaistow,Essex. She married James Alfred Jones on the 29th September,1912 in Forest Gate,West Ham.

Birth Certificate:
Elizabeth Gwenllian Bellchambers was born on the 14th of September 1881 at 5 Charles Street,Plaistow,Essex. Her father John Bellchambers was a Dock Worker and her mother was Louisa formerly Winchcombe. Registrar R March recorded the birth on the 22nd of October for West Ham.

Marriage Certificate:
Gwenllian Elizabeth Bellchamber and James Alfred Jones married at the Emmanuel Church,Forest Gate,West Ham on the 29th of October 1912 by banns. Witness's were H W Jones and C E Bellchambers. Their fathers were Henry Charles Jones a Harbour Man and John Bellchambers now deceased.Both were living in 60 Chaucer Road,James Alfred was a 28 year old bachelor and Clerk and Gwenllian was a spinster aged 30. The ceremony was performed by the curate Adelphe Hadley.

iii   Male Belchamber was born on the 29th April,1883 in 58 Winsor Terrace, Beckton. He died on the same day.

Birth Certificate:
A Boy was born to John and Louisa on the 29th of April 1883 at 58 Winser Terrace,Beckton,West Ham,Essex. John Bellchamber was a Gas Labourer and Louisa his mother was formerly Winchcombe. The birth was registered on the 1st of May by Registrar R March for West Ham.

Death Certificate:
The male child died on the 29th of April 1883 of Debility he only lasted 7 hours after the birth certified by R Carey MRCS. J Bellchamber was informant and present at death the death was at 58 Winser Terrace,Beckton,Essex. The death was recorded by R March the registrar for West Ham.

William Thomas Belchamber
(William10,James9,William8,Edward7,Edward6,John5,Thomas4,Robert3,Robert2, John1) was born on the 22nd April,1858 in Ovingdean,Sussex. He died on the 26th October,1927 in 250 Elm Grove,Brighton,Sussex. He married Annie Kimpton on the 20th July,1887 in St.Lukes Church,Brighton. She was born in North Finchley,Middlesex. She died on the 6th July,1923 in The Royal Sussex County Hospital,Brighton.

Birth Certificate:
William Thomas Belchamber was born in Ovingdean,Sussex on the 22nd of April,1858. William Belchamber the father was a Domestic Servant,Hannah Barbara

Belchamber formerly Westgate was his mother. William Cobden the registrar for Lewes recorded the birth on the 1st of May.

Marriage Certificate:
Police Constable William Thomas Belchamber aged 29 married 25 year old Annie Kimpton in St.Lukes Church,Brighton,Sussex on the 20th of July,1887. Witness's were Mary Barbara Hannah Belchamber and Henry John Blundell.Both were living at 41 Quebec Street,Brighton. Fathers James Kimpton was a Carpenter and William Belchamber a Gardener. W A Smith the vicar performed the service.

Death Certificates:
Annie Belchamber died aged 60 at the Royal Sussex County Hospital on the 6th of July,1923. The cause of death was Chronic Nephritis and Pulmonary Oedema which was certified by J F Knight LRCS. Annies husband William Thomas Belchamber was informant of 22 Newmarket Road,Brighton. C J Webb the registrar for Brighton recorded the death on the 7th July.Recorded on the death certificate William Thomas was a Park Keeper.

William Thomas Belchamber passed away at 22 Newmarket Road,Brighton,Sussex on the 26th of October,1924 aged 69. The cause of death was Arteris Sclerosis which was certified by J McCurrick MRCS. The informant was his daughter Edith Green also of 22 Newmarket Road.William Thomas was a Borough Police Constable(Pensioned). C J Webb the registrar for Brighton recorded the death on the 27th of October.

Census:
Police Constable William T and Anne were in Brighton,Sussex in 1891 living at 17 Quebec Street. William was aged 32 and Anne 28

William and Annie were living in Brighton,Sussex at 49 Grosvenor Street in 1901. William was a General Labourer aged 42 and Annie was aged 39. Their daughter Edith F was aged 7.

In the 1911 census William T and Annie Belchamber were living in Brighton at 25 Kemp Street with their daughter Edith Flora aged 17. Edith was a Shop Assistant and William T a Park Keeper aged 52,Annie was aged 49.

William Thomas Belchamber and Annie Kimpton had the following children:

i	Nellie Annie Belchamber was born on the 3rd December,1890 in NapoleanCottages,North Finchley,Middlesex. She died aged 9 months on the 21st September,1890 in 17 Quebec Street,Brighton,Sussex.

Birth Certificate:
Nellie Annie Belchamber was born on the 3rd of December,1889 at Napolean Cottages,North Finchley. Her father William Belchamber was a Police Constable. Annie Belchamber formerly Kimpton was the mother and the informant was James

Kimpton of Napolean Cottages. Charles Plowman recorded the birth on the 7th of December for Barnet.

Death Certificate:
Nellie Annie Belchamber aged 9 months died at 17 Quebec Street,Brighton on the 21st of September,1890.Cause of death was Diarrhea(Choleraic) which was certified by Herbert Mckeon LRCP. Her mother Annie Belchamber was informant and present at the death,which was recorded for Brighton district by the Registrar

ii   Edith Flora Belchamber was born on the 29th January,1894 in 7 Grant Street, Brighton. She married Max Ernest Green on the 24th December,1924 in The Registry Office,Brighton.

Birth Certificate:
Edith Flora Belchamber was born on the 29th of January,1894 at No.7 Grant Street,Brighton. Her father was William Thomas Belchamber a Stableman and her mother is Annie Belchamber formerly Kimpton.J Thorncroft the registrar for Brighton recorded the birth on the 2nd of March.

Marriage Certificate:
Edith Belchamber and Max Ernest Green were married on the 24th of December at the registry office, Brighton. Max was aged 21 a bachelor and an Hotel Waitor,Edith aged 26 was a spinster and Clerk in a Motor Company. They both gave their address as 22 Newmarket Road,Brighton. The witness's were A W Stanswick and W J Maskell. The fathers were Henry William Green a deceased Coachman and William Thomas Belchamber a Police Constable. The registrar G A Morrison performed the ceremony with Horace Burfield the Supt.Registrar.

Henry James Belchamber
(William10,James9,William8,Edward7,Edward6,John5,Thomas4,Robert3,Robert2, John1) was born on Christmas Day,1868 in Ovingdean,Sussex. He died on the 28th August,1905 in 22 Cobden Road,Brighton,Sussex. He married Mary Ann Diggens on the 13th September,1890 in The Registry Office,Brighton. She was born about 1857. She died on the 2nd December,1937 in 34 Windover Crescent,Lewes,Sussex.

Birth Certificate:
Henry James Bellchamber was born in Ovingdean,Sussex on December the 25th,1863. His father William Belchamber was a Journeyman Gardener and the mother was Hannah Barbara formerly Westgate. William Gobden the registrar for Lewes record the birth on the 27th of January,1864.

Marriage Certificate:
26 year old bachelor Harry James Belchamber a Labourer married Mary Ann Diggens a Widow aged 33 at the Registry Office,Brighton,Sussex on the 13th of September,1890. Harry James was living at 41 Quebec Street and Mary Ann at no 42. Witness;s were Louisa Morley and Ellen Bowles who signed with a cross. The fathers were William Belchamber a Gardener and George Morley a deceased Sail Maker. Benjamin Burfield Registrar took the service.

Death Certificate:

Henry James Belchamber aged 40 died on the 28th of August 1905 at 22 Cobden Road,Brighton,Sussex. Cause of death was natural causes namely Vascular disease of the heart. The certificate was received from J E Bush the coroner for Brighton an inquest was held on the 29th of August,Stephen Holman registrar recorded the death on the 30th of August. Henry James was a Laundry Porter.

An excerpt from the inquest of Henry James Belchamber dated 29th of August 1905 The death of Henry James Belchamber aged 40 who died suddenly at 10.am Monday 28th at No 22 Cobden Road.
Mary Ann Belchamber No 22 Cobden Road states:The deceased Henry James Belchamber aged 40 was my husband and was a Laundry Porter.
On Monday 28th at about 9.45am the deceased was sitting in a chair in the kitchen reading a newspaper when he was suddenly taken ill. I asked him to have a little brandy but he refused saying he would be alright. I sent for some brandy and also a neighbour named Mary Ann Knight No 27 Cobden Road,but in the meantime the deceased had fell forward from the chair against the table.
Mrs Knight came in and was pulling him back in his chair when he suddenly expired. I had sent for Dr Watson No 1 Gladstone Terrace and he came and examined the deceased and stated that he was dead. The deceased had been in bad health for about 12 months and had been an out patient for 6 months at the county hospital where he was told that his heart was weak Dr.Shaw No 2 Hanover Place also attended the decease about 3 weeks ago for a bad leg.

Mary Ann Knight No 27 Cobden Road states: I was called on Monday 28th by the last witness about 9.45am. And on going into the kitchen I saw the deceased seated in a chair but the upper part of his body was resting on a table. I lifted up his head and he then expired.
Dr.Watson came shortly after and pronounced life extinct.
The deceased had been in bad health for several months.

Dr Soloman George Watson No 1 Gladstone Terrace states: I was called to No.22 Cobden Road on Monday the 28th August at 11am to the deceased. On my arrival I found life extinct.
The inquest took place at the Town Hall,Brighton on the 29th of August 1905 the conclusion was Henry James Belchamber a 40 year old Laundry Porter of 22 Cobden Road,Brighton had died of natural causes namely vascular disease of the heart. The coroner was J G Bush.

Henry James died intestate and below is a transcription of the administration of his will:

Administration
                    DEATH ON OR AFTER 1st January 1898
BE IT KNOWN that Henry James Belchamber of
22 Cobden Road Brighton in the County of
Sussex
Died on the 28th Day of August 1905
At 22 Cobden Road aforesaid
Intestate

AND BE IT FURTHER KNOWN that at the date hereunder written
Letters of Administration of all the estate which by law devolves to and
Vests in the personal representative of the said intestate were granted by
His Majesty's High Court of Justice at the Prinicipal Probate Registry thereof
To Mary Ann Belchamber of 22 Cobden Road aforesaid the lawful widow and
Relict

Of the said intestate

Dated 4th day of December 1905
Gross value of Estate....£ 34.13.4
~~Net value of Personal Estate..£~~

Death Certificate:
Mary Ann Belchamber died on the 2nd of December,1937 at 34 Windover
Crescent,Lewes,Sussex.Cause of death was Senility which was certified by R S Tooth
MRCS.Mary Ann was aged 80 and the widow of Harry Belchamber a Laundary
Worker.The informant was G C Earl listed as son-in-law of Rosemary,Park
Road,Coldean,Stanmer.The death was registered on the 3rd of December by H H
Green registrar for Lewes.

Census:
In the 1891 census Harry James and Mary Ann Belchamber were living at 42 Quebec
Street,Brighton.Harry James aged 27 was a Laundary Keeper and Mary Ann was a
Laundress,living with them were Florence Belchamber aged 3 months ,also Eliza
Diggens aged 13 and step daughter,Mary Diggens aged 11,Jane Diggens aged 8 and
Elizabeth Diggens aged 2 all were step daughters and Scholars.Harry James was from
Ovingdean,while the remainder were all from Brighton.

Henry James and Mary Ann are living at 22 Cobden Road,Brighton in 1901.Henry
James aged 37 is a Soldier and Mary Ann a Laundress aged 43 and an
employer.Florence is 10,there are two more children now born to Henry James and
Mary Ann they are,Henry 8 and Evelyn 6,two remaining Diggens children of Mary
Ann are still at home Mary A Diggens aged 21 and a Laundress(wash) and Elizabeth
Diggens aged 12.

Henry James Belchamber and Mary Ann Diggens had the following children:

i   Henry Belchamber was born on the 27th July,1892 in 17 Quebec Street,
         Brighton,Sussex. He died on the 11th December,1915 in France.

Birth Certificate:
Henry Belchamber was born in Brighton on the 27th of July,1892 at 17 Quebec Street
the family home. His Father Henry James Belchamber was a Hotel Porter and Mary
Ann Belchamber was listed as late Diggens,formerly Morley. The birth was registered
on the 13th of August in St.Peters,Brighton.

Death Certificate:

Corporal Henry Belchamber service No.59107 of the11th Bty. Royal Field Artillery died in France on the 11th of Dec,1915 aged 22. Henry is buried in the Mazargues War Cemetry,Marseilles.

ii   Florence Belchamber was born on the 20th January,1891 in 42 Quebec Street, Brighton,Sussex. She married Henry John Pierce on the 20th June,1914 in St. Saviours,Preston,Brighton.

Birth Certificate:
Florence Belchamber was born at 42 Quebec Street,Brighton on the 20th of January,1891. Harry James her father was a Laundry Keeper and her mother was Mary Ann Belchamber formerly Diggens. F Thorncroft the registrar for Brighton recorded the birth on the 24th of February.

Marriage Certificate:
Henry John Pierce aged 23 a bachelor and Electrical Fitter married 23 year old Florence Belchamber aged 23 and a spinster by banns on the 20th of June,1914 at St.Saviors Church,Preston,Brighton both were living at Winchester Street at the time of the marriage. Their witness's were Cecil B Pierce and Evelyn Belchamber. The fathers were Henry Pierce a Shop Fitter and Henry James Belchamber a deceased Soldier. The ceremony was performed by J A W Bell the vicar.

iii   Evelyn Belchamber was born on the 6th September,1894 in 17 Quebec Street, Brighton,Sussex. She married William Horace Noel on the 28th August,1915 in St.Lukes,Brighton.

Birth Certificate:
Evelyn Belchamber was born at 17 Quebec Street,Brighton on the 6th of September,1894. Henry James Belchamber was listed as a Laundry Keeper and her Mother Mary Ann Belchamber was Diggens,formerly Morley. J Thorncroft the registrar for Brighton registered the birth on the 13th of October.

Marriage Certificate:
Bachelor William Horace Noel a Carriage Trimmer aged 24 married Evelyn Belchamber a 21 year old spinster on the 28th of August,1915 at St.Lukes Church,Brighton by banns. Their residence at the time of the marriage was 327 Queens Park Road,Brighton. Witness's were Robert and Edith Noel. The fathers were Robert Noel a Ex.Police Officer and Henry James Belchamber deceased. Assist Curate C F D Trimming took the service.

Alice Belchamber
(John10,Edward9,William8,Edward7,Edward6,John5,Thomas4,Robert3,Robert2,John 1) was born on the 29th August,1866 in Kirdford,Sussex. She died on the 13th October,1935 in The Village,Kirdford.

Birth Certificate:
Alice Belchamber was born on the 29th of August,1866 in Kirdford,Sussex. John Belchamber her father was a Engine Driver of Steam Thrashing Machine,Sophia her mother was listed formerly Older. George Wells the registrar for Petworth registered the birth on the 4th of October.

Death Certificate:
Alice Belchamber aged 70 died in Kirdford on the 17th of October 1936. She was the spinster daughter of John Belchamber(deceased). The informant was her son E R Belchamber of Creamery Cottage,Kirdford. The death was registered on the 14th of October for Midhurst and Petworth.

Alice Belchamber's Will 1925
I Alice Belchamber of the village of Kirdford Sussex declare this to be my last will and testament and revoke all previous wills or codicils by me.
I appoint my sister Ada Bagley (now living with me) and widow of Charles Bagley deceased together with my brother John Belchamber of Garage Cottage,Old Palace Road,Richmond,Surrey to be my Executors jointly.
I give and bequeath to Edgar Belchamber of Creamery Cottage,Kirdford,Sussex the sum of twelve pounds
I give and bequeath to Leslie Field of Pound Common,Kirdford,Sussex the sum of ten pounds.
To my sister Ada Bagley as aforesaid,all my goods and chattels,wearing apparel,furniture,linen which I did forward of her use as long as she may live-At her death the same to go to my Brother John Belchamber of Richmond,Surrey absolutely.
I declare it to my wish to be buried at Kirdford in a respectable manner.Expenses of which together with all any just debts,to be paid by my Executors from the residue of my estate.
As to the residue,money or anything not mentioned in the foregoing.I give to my sister Ada Bagley and John Belchamber to be equally divided between them.
Should my sister Ada Bagley die before me then the same to my brother John Belchamber absolutely.
Signed in the presence of all of us present at the same time on the eighteenth of May nineteen hundred and twenty five.
Signature of}
The testatrix}   Alice Belchamber
Witness to the]
Signature of Testatrix]   Mercy Enticknap.Boot
Witness to the}   Warehouse,Kirdford.
Signature of Testatrix}   Percy Fosl Independent
Witness to the}   Park View,Wisborough Green.
Signature of Testatrix}

Alice Belchamber never married but she had the following child:

i   Edgar Reginald Belchamber was born on the 26th November,1896 in 8
         Meadow Brook Road,Dorking,Surrey. He died on the 9th August,1963 in 44
         Hale Road,Farnham,Surrey. He married Mary Jane Wakeford on the 6th
         September,1922 in Kirdford,Sussex. She was born on the 2nd September,1901
         in Petworth,Sussex. She died on the 16th April,1980 in The Spinney,Reading
         Road South,Church Crookham,Hampshire.

Census:
In the 1891 census Alice was a Servant aged 24 in the Petworth Police Station for Inspector of police Thomas Cooper aged 34 and his wife Rose Cooper aged 29

Sophia (Ada) Belchamber
(John10,Edward9,William8,Edward7,Edward6,John5,Thomas4,Robert3,Robert2,John 1) was born on the 3rd December,1869 in Kirdford,Sussex. She married Charles Henry Bagley on the 19th December,1891 in Kirdford,Sussex.

Birth Certificate:
Sophia Belchamber was born on the 3rd of December,1869 in Kirdford,Sussex. Father John Belchamber was a Agricultural Labouer and her mother Sophia made her mark as listed herself as Sophia Belchamber formerly Older. Henry Boxall the registrar for Petworth registered the birth on the 14th of January 1870. Later Sophia added Ada as a christian name.

Marriage Certificate:
Ada Sophia Belchamber,23 a spinster with no occupation married Charles Henry Bagley,22 a bachelor and Farmer at the parish church,Kirdford on the 19th of December,1891. Witness's were Edward Tribe and Alice Belchamber. Erskine A Burrell performed the marriage. The fathers were James Bagley a Farmer and John Belchamber deceased.

Census:
Ada Belchamber aged 21 was living in Petworth in North Street as a Nursemaid to the RT.Hon Henry Baron Leconfield and family.

In the 1911 census Charles Henry and Ada Sophia Bagley were living at The Village,Kirdford with their children Edgar Charles 17,James 15 and Reginald aged 14. Also living with them was Ada's brother John William Belchamber aged 32 and married. John William was a Motor Cleaner and Driver for the Creamery. Charles Henry was a farmer. Edgar Charles was a Milk Float Driver and James Bagley a Farm Labourer.

John William Belchamber
(John10,Edward9,William8,Edward7,Edward6,John5,Thomas4,Robert3,Robert2,John 1) was born on the 3rd February,1879 in Kirdford,Sussex. He died on the 27th February,1971 in Barnes Hospital,Mortlake,Surrey. He married Jane Elizabeth Pearson on the 4th April,1909 in St.James,Gunnersbury,Middlesex. She was born on the 18th November,1880 in Marylebone,Middlesex. She died on the 12th September,1971 in Kingston Hospital,Kingston,Surrey.

Birth Certificate:
John William Belchamber was born in Kirdford,Sussex on the 3rd of February 1879. Father John was a Farm Labourer. Sophia was listed as formerly Older . George Brookfield recorded the birth on the 20th of March at Petworth,Sussex.

Marriage Certificate:
John William Belchamber a 30 year old and Chaffeur married Jane Elizabeth Pearson aged 28 and a widow with no occupation listed on the 4th of April,1909 in St.James church Gunnersbury,Middlesex by banns. Their abode was listed as 37 Surrey

Crescent,Gunnersbury. Witness's were Arthur Edgar Brown and Rose Nunn.Both fathers were deceased,John William SNR was a farmer and Frederick Cornelius a tradesman. The ceremony was performed by Charles Whitfield,Vicar.

Death Certificates:
John William Belchamber died on the 27th of February 1971 at Barnes Hospital,Mortlake. He was a retired Chauffeur of Garage Cottage,Old Palace Lane,Richmond. His son Bernard J H Belchamber of 56 Craneford Way,Twickenham was informant. Cause of death was 1) a Bronchopneumonia,b Carcinoma of Prostate c Metastases which was certified by Dorothy P L Chua NB. The death was registered on the 1st of March by Jean Gavin,Deputy Registrar for Richmond and Barnes.

Jane Elizabeth Belchamber aged 90 died at the Kingston Hospital,Kingston on the 12th of September,1971 cause of death was Right Upper Lobe Pueumonia and Inner Alised Arteriosilerosis which was certified by D L Child MB. Jane Elizabeth was listed as the widow of John William Belchamber,Chauffeur of Garage Cottage,Twickenhan,Middlesex. The informant was her son Bernard John Hugh Belchamber of 56 Craneford Way,Twickenham. B F Ridgway the registrar for Kingston upon thames recorded the death on the 21st of September.

Census:
In the 1911 census Jane Elizabeth was living in Chiswick at 11 Brooks Road she was aged 30 and listed herself as married 2 years.

John William Belchamber service no.202923 RASC enlisted on the 17th August,1916 has part of The British Expeditionary Force he was aged 37. Listed as married and a Motor Driver he was reliable,intelligent with a good sobriety. His wife was listed as Jane Elizabeth Pearson married on the 4th April,1904 they had three children Grace Elizabeth born 14th April,1905,Bernard John 18th June,1912 and Gladys Margaret 25th September,1916 all born in Kirdford,Sussex. John William also spent some time in Mesopotamia.

John William Belchamber and Jane Elizabeth Pearson had the following children:

i   Bernard John Hugh Belchamber was born on the 13th June,1912 in 11 Brooks Road,Chiswick. He died on the 4th January,1996 in Richmond Upon Thames. He married Ethel Marjory Guy on the 3rd July,1937 in The Parish Church ,Twickenham,Middlesex. She was born on the 20th November,1913 in Twickenham,Middlesex. She died on the 11th January,1997 in West Middlesex Hospital,Isleworth.

ii   Gladys Marguerite Belchamber was born on the 25th July,1916 in Cardigan House,Richmond Hill,Richmond,Surrey. She died on the 11th February,2010 in Looe,Cornwall.

Birth Certificate:
Gladys Marguerite Belchamber was born on the 25th of July 1916 at the family home,Cardigan House,Richmond Hill,Richmond. Father John William was a

Domestic Chauffeur and mother Jane Elizabeth was listed as,late Pearson,formerly Nunn. The Registrar Charles L Fenn recorded the birth on the 17th of August for Richmond.

Death Information:
Gladys Marguerite Belchamber died on the 11th of February 2010 in Looe,Cornwall. She was cremated on the 25th of February at the Glyn Crematorium,service took place at 10.30.

Martha Belchamber
(William10,John9,William8,Edward7,Edward6,John5,Thomas4,Robert3,Robert2,John) was born on the 13th January,1848 in Shalford,Surrey. She married Charles Frederick Murphy on the 14th July,1867 in St.Marys,Lambeth,London.

Birth Certificate:
Martha Belchamber was born in Shalford,Surrey on the 13th of January 1848.William Belchamber,Martha's father was a Carpenter. Mary the mother signed the certificate with her mark. The registrar James Arnold registered the birth on the 15th of January.

Marriage Certificate:
Charles Frederick Murphy and Martha Bellchamber both of full age(over 21) married at St.Marys,Lambeth in the county of Surrey on the 14th of July 1867. Spinster Martha had no occupation listed,while Charles Frederick was a bachelor and Railway Clerk. Their residence at the time of marriage was Paris Street. Their witness's were Edward Powell and Anne Miles. The ceremony was performed by J E Codlington MA. Fathers James Murphy was a Soldier and William Belchamber(deceased) a Carpenter.

Charles Frederick Murphy and Martha Belchamber had the following children:

i   Charles James Murphy born about the 13th June,1869 in Millbank,London.

ii   Walter John Murphy born about the 22nd September,1871 in Pimlico,London.

Iii   Emer Fanny Murphy born about the 7th March,1875 in Pimlico,London.
         She died on the 1st October,1875 in Pimlico.

Generation 12

John Belchamber
(John11,Edward10,Edward9,Edward8,Edward7,Edward6,John5,Thomas4,Robert3,Robert2,John1) was born on the 5th June,1857 in 1 Hearnes Building,Locks Field,Walworth. He died on the 11th December,1949 in Sunnycliffe,May Avenue,Canvey Island,Essex. He married Elizabeth Ann Mansfield on the 22nd September,1878 in Newington,she was the daughter of Richard Mansfield and Eliza Holloway. She died on the 4th March,1941 in Orsett Lodge,Orsett,Thurrock,Essex.

Birth Certificate:
John Belchamber came into this world on the 5th of June,1857,place of birth was 1 Heares Buildings,Lock Field,Walworth. His father also John Belchamber was a

Chemists Labourer Sarah Ann Belchamber his mother was listed late Darby,formerly Wright. Frances Thornton the registrar for Newington registered the birth on the 8th of June.

Marriage Certificate:
At St.Pauls Church in the parish of St.Marys,Newington John Belchamber aged 21 a bachelor and Grocer married 19 year old spinster Elizabeth Ann Mansfield on the 22nd of September,1878 by banns. John was living at 10 Lorrimore Street and Elizabeth Ann at no 31. Witness were Alfred Joseph Mansfield and Eliza Mansfield.Edward J Frere performed the service. Their fathers were John Belchamber a Druggist and Richard Mansfield a Fish Salesman.

Census:
In 1881 John and Elizabeth were living at 5 Longley Street.John was listed as a Grocers Porter aged 23 and from Walworth,Surrey. Elizabeth aged 21 was from Bermondsey,Surrey no occupation listed.

In 1891 John and Elizabeth were living at 47 Reverdy Road,Bermondsey,London.John was a Warehouseman aged 33,Elizabeth was 31 and the children were John 5 and Maud was 2.

In the 1901 census John and Elizabeth were still in Bermondsey living at 89 Southwark Park Road. John aged 42 was a Grocers Assistant,Elizabeth was 40,John R was 15 and a Music Setters Assistant and Maud was age 12.

1911 saw the family living at 85 Aldergate Street,Bermondsey with their daughter Maud Louise. John was 53 and a Grocer's Assistant,Elizabeth was 51 no occupation listed and daughter Maud Louise 22 a Draper's Assistant.

Death Certificates:
92 year old John Belchamber died on the 11th of December 1949 at Sunnycliffe,May Avenue,Canvey Island,Essex. John died of Myacardia Degeneration which was certified by J H Styles MB. S J Kingsley his son-in-law was informant who was living at the same address. The death was registered on the 14th of December.

Elizabeth Belchamber of Sunnycliffe,May Avenue,Canvey Island aged 80 died on the 4th of March,1941 at Orsett Lodge,Orsett,Essex. Cause of death was Hypostatic Pneumonia and Malignant Hypertension. The informant was A H White the occupier of Orsett Lodge. G H James the registrar for Thurrock recorded the death on the 6th of March.

John Belchamber and Elizabeth Ann Mansfield had the following children:

i   Florence Ellen Belchamber was born the 28th May,1883 in St.Olave. She died on the 20th September,1887 in Stockwell Fever Hospital,Lambeth.

Birth Certificate;
Florence Ellen Belchamber was born on the 28th of May,1883 at 54 Southwark Park Road,Bermondsey. Her father was John Belchamber a Porter and her mother was

Elizabeth Ann formerly Mansfield. J Hurst the registrar for St.Olave,Southwark registered the birth on the 9th of July.

Death Certificate:
Florence Ellen Belchamber died of Scarlett Fever(7 days) on the 20th of September,1887 aged 4. Cause of death was certified by D A Cresswell MB. The family were living in 83 New Church Road,Bermondsey. Informant was N Ingrams who was Attendant and Inmate at the Stockwell Fever Hospital. Robert Chastley deputy registrar for Lambeth registered the death on the 26th of September.

ii   George Edward Belchamber was born on the 24th July,1885 in 83 New Church Street,Bermondsey,London. He died on the 20th December,1885 at the same address.

Birth Certificate:
George Edward Belchamber was born at 83 New Church St.Bermondsey on the 24th of July,1885. His Father John Belchamber was a Grocer's Porter and his mother was Elizabeth Ann Belchamber formerly Mansfield. The deputy registrar for Southwark G J H Iveson registered the birth on the 13th of August.

Death Certificate:
Sadly George Edward Bellchamber died on the 20th of December,1885 aged 5 months at 83 New Church Street,Bermondsey. His father John Bellchamber was a Grocer,his mother E Bellchamber was informant and present at death,cause of death was Bronchitis and Tonsilitis which was certified by R W Foster MRC. The death was recorded by N J Hurst the registrar for St.Olave,Southwark on the 22nd of December

iii   John Richard Belchamber was born on the 24th July,1885 in 83 New Church Street,Bermondsey,London. He died on the 21st May,1963 in Wokingham Hospital,Wokingham,Berkshire. He married Amy Nellie Allen on Christmas Day 1910 in The Parish Church,Aldersgate. She died on the 12th May,1927 in Charing Cross Hospital,London. He later married Phyliss Louise Holloway on the 4th July,1931 in St.Johns,Walthamstow. She was born on the 15th January, 1893 in Stoke Newington,London. She died on the 20th February,1888 in Weald House Nursing Home,St.Neots,Huntingdon.

Birth Certicate:
John Richard Belchamber came into this world on the 24th of July,1885 in 83 New Church St.Bermondsey. John Belchamber his father was a Grocer's Porter and Elizabeth Ann his mother was formerly Mansfield. W G Hurst Registrar for Southwark recorded the birth on the 13th Of August,George Edward Belchamber and John Richard Belchamber were twins.

Marriage Certificate;Amy Nellie Allen
John Richard Belchamber a 25 year old bachelor and Shop Assistant married Amy Nellie Allen Wilkie a 21 year old spinster on the 25th of December,1910 at the parish church,Aldersgate,Witness's were Samuel Carver and Margaret Cox and Maud Belchamber.C O Becker performed the service. Both were living in 85 Aldergate Street. Their fathers were John Belchamber a Tea Merchant and Thomas William Allen

deceased.

Census:
In the 1911 census John Richard aged 25 and Amy Nellie aged 21 were living at 36 Gladsmuir Road,Upper Holloay,Highgate North. John Richard as a Commisionaire Theatre Attendant.

Marriage Certificate:Phyliss Louise Holloway.
John Richard Belchamber and Phyliss Louise Holloway married at the parish church St.Johns Walthamstow on the 4th of July 1931 by banns. John Richard was aged 46 a widower and Telephone Operator. Phyliss Louise was a spinster aged 38 with no occupation.Both gave their abode as 12 Walthamstow Avenue,Walthamstow. Witness's were Alfred H Holloway and Sidney John Kingsley. The fathers were John Richard Belchamber,retired and Harry Holloway(Deceased) a Glass Driller. The curate Fred.E Lownds performed the marriage.

Death Certificates:
John Richard Belchamber age 77 died on the 21st May 1963 at Wokingham Hospital, Wokingham. Cause of death was (1) Recurrent Cerebro Vascular Accidents (2) Cerebral Arteries Valerious which was certified by Ian W Kerr MB. John Richard was a retired Glass Writer of 55 Barkham Ride,Wokingham. P L Belchamber his widow was informant. K Pointon the registrar recorded the death for Wokingham on the 22nd May.

Amy Nellie Belchamber aged 38 died at Charing Cross,Hospital on the 12th of March 1927. Cause of death was Cancer of the breast. She was listed as the wife of John Richard Belchamber of 13 Suffolk Street,Pall Mall a Housekeeper. The death was recorded at St.Martins,The Strand on the 13th of March by W Parkhouse the registrar.

Amy Nellie died intestate,I have transcribed the administration below:

In His Majesty's High Court Of Justice
The Principal Probate Registry
Be it known that   Amy Nellie Belchamber of
13 Suffolk Street Pall Mall East in
The county of London
Died on the 12th Day of March 1927
At Charing Cross Hospital in the same
County
Intestate

AND BE IT FURTHER KNOWN that at the date hereunder written letters of administration of all the
Estate which by law devolves to and vests in the personal representative of the said intestate were
Granted by His Majesty's High Court Of Justice at the Principal Probate Registry thereof to
John Richard Belchamber of 75 Dale
View Avenue Chingford in the

County of Essex Glass Writer the
Lawful husband of the said
Intestate
And it is hereby certified that an Affidavit for Inland Revenue has been delivered
wherein it is shewn that the cross value
Of the said Estate in Great Britain
(exclusive of what the said deceased may have been possessed of or entitled to as a
Trustee
And not beneficially) amounts to £ 143.17.9   and that the net value of the personal
estate
Amounts to £ 143.17.9
And it is further certified that it appears by a receipt signed by an Inland Revenue
Officer on the said Affidavit that £ 2.0.4 on account of Estate Duty and Interest on
such duty has been paid
Dated the   21st day of January 1939
N Lang
Registrar

Extracted by W G Singleton
        37 Essex Street Strand London WC 2

Death Certificate;
Phyliss Louisa Belchamber died on the 20th of February,1988 at Weald House
Nursing Home,St.Neots,Huntingdon of Coronary Thrombosis,Arterio Soleroris and
Rheumatiod Arthritis which was certified by T Lyle LRCPvS. The informant was her
daughter-in-law Laurie Eleanor Constance Belchamber of The White House,Hatfield
Heath,Bishops Stortford,Herts. Listed as the widow of John Richard Belchamber a
Signwriter her death was registered on the 22nd of February at Huntingdon,Cambs.

iv   Maud Louise Belchamber was born on the 16th April,1888 in 3 Dockley Road,
        Bermondsey,London. She married Sidney John Kingsley on the 29th April,
        1922 in St.Mary Magdalene,Bermondsey.

Birth Certificate:
Maud Louise Belchamber was born at 3 Dockley Road,Bermondsey on the 16th of
April,1888. Her father John Belchamber was a Grocer's Porter,and her mother was
Elizabeth Ann formerly Mansfield. The birth was registered by W Hurst the registrar
for St.Olaves,Southwick.

Marriage Certificate;
Maud Louise Belchamber married Sidney John Kingsley at St.Mary Magdalene
Bermondsey on the 29th April 1922 by banns. Maud Louise was a spinster aged 34
and a Draper's Assistant by trade and Sidney John was aged 38 a widower and a
Traveller. Sidney John lived at 16 Moray Road,Finsbury and Maud Louise at The
Shelter,The Grange. Father's were Charles Kingsley a Farmer and John Richard a
Caretaker. The witness's were J Belchamber,J G Kingsley,E Belchamber and A
Claydon. H H Gillingham the rector performed the ceremony.

Edward Belchamber

(John11,Edward10,Edward9,Edward8,Edward7,Edward6,John5,Thomas4,Robert3,Robert2,John1) was born on the 10th August,1858 in 1 Hearnes Buildings,Locks Field,Walworth. He died on the 31st May,1924 in 48 Vanburgh Hill,Greenwich. He married Alice Saunders on Christmas Day,1882 in St.Saviour,Newington. She died on the 17th February,1919 in 37 Beauval Road,Camberwell.

Birth Certificate:
Edward Belchamber was born on the 10th of August,1858 at 1 Hearnes Buildings,Locks Fields,Walworth. His father was John Belchamber a General Porter and Sarah Ann his mother was formerly Wright. Francis Thorton the Registrar for Newington registered the birth on the 17th of September.

Marriage Certificate:
Edward Belchamber and Alice Saunders were married on Christmas Day,1882 by banns at the parish church in the parish of St.Marys,Newington. Edward was 25 a bachelor and Cellarman of 35 Carter Street.Alice was aged 22 and a spinster of 70 Lorrimore Road. Their witness's were Richard and Harriet Saunders. Fathers were John Belchamber a Druggist and Richard Saunders an Engineer. The curate Samuel F Hooper performed the marriage.

Census:
Edward and Alice were living in Bermondsey at 17 Collett Road in the 1891 census.Edward was a Cellarman aged 31,Alice was aged 30. Their children were Edward 7,Alice 6 and William 2
.

In the 1901 census Edward and Alice were living in Bermondsey at 21 Collett Road.Edward aged 41 was a Cellarman and Alice was aged 41. Their children Edward 17 a Stationers Assisitant and Alice H aged 16 a Dressmaker. Also living at the same address were boarders father and son,widower William S Masters a Warehouseman aged 31 and William E Masters aged 7.

Edward and Alice were living at 8 Colwell Road,East Dulwich in the 1911 census. Edward was aged 52,Alice 51 their son Edward was 27,daughter Alice was 26 and finally son William 22.Edward's occupation was a Cellarman,son Edward was a Sailor RN AB,William was a Compositer and Alice a Dressmaker.

Death Certificates:
Alice Belchamber aged 58 died on the 17th of February,1919 at 37 Beauval Road,Camberwell. Present at death and informant was her husband Edward Belchamber a Cellarman. Cause of death was Chronic Bronchitis which was certified by J E Boon LRCP. The death was registered on the 18th of Febraury by A Lucas the registrar for Camberwell.
Alice was buried aged 58 in Nunhead Cemetry plot no.10179 sqr.23 on the 21st February,1919.

Edward Belchamber aged 65 died on the 31st of May,1924 of Senile Decay and a Cerebral Haemorage which was certified by W D Wiggins MRCS. The death was registered on the 2nd of June in Greenwich by P C Wates Registrar. The informant was his son William Robert Belchamber of 56 Upper Brockley Road,Brockley the address given has Edwards,who's occupation was a Wine Merchants Cellarman

Edward Belchamber and Alice Saunders had the following children:

i   Edward Belchamber was born on the 14th October,1883 in
Bermondsey,London. He died on the 5th June,1916 in Scapa Flow,Scotland.

Birth Certificate:
Edward Belchamber born 14th of October 1883 and was baptized in Bermondsey at
St.Mary Magdalen on the 23rd December 1883.
Edward Belchamber was born at 21 Collett Road,Bermondsey on the 14th of
October,1883. His father Edward Belchamber was a Cellarman and his mother Alice
was formerly Saunders. The registrar for St.Olave,Southwark N G Hurst registered
the birth on the 19th of November.

Employment:
Railway Employee:Edward Belchamber no 459 was employed by the railway as a
Cleaner with a wage of 2/2 on the 18th 0f April 1901 at New Cross Station.
Ref:UK Railway Employment Records 1833-1963.

Edward Belchamber aged 20 joined the Royal Navy around about April 1903 when he
was aboard HMS Nelson from April until December that year as a Stoker.13 different
ships later he sailed with HMS Hampshire on the 15th of December 1915.His
character all through his service was always Very Good. He joined on the 24th of
April 1903 signing on for 12 years. He was 5 foot 5 inches tall with brown hair,blue
eyes and a fresh complexion,his occupation was a Engine Driver. He gained badges
G/D&R.
He served on 13 different ships during his period with the Royal Navy from HMS
Nelson 27th April to the 11th of December 1903 he was a Stoker,(16a5/764)
probably training,as the ship was a Stoker Training Ship. 12th of December 1903 until
the 17th of January 1904 he was with HMS Firequeen a Special Service Vessel and a
Steam Yacht again as a Stoker(15a4/436). Next he served on HMS Ceasar a Majestic
Class Battleship from the 2nd to the 10th of February 1904(5a/98) Stoker. He was
back onboard HMS Firequeen 11th of February to the 24th
1904,Stoker(15a4/547).From 25th of February 1904 until the 31st May 1907 he
served as a Stoker(5a/115) onboard HMS Crescent an Edgar Class Battleship at which
he made Leading Stoker. Next he was at a Land Base HMS Victory 2 in Portsmouth a
Stoker Training base Edward had 4 stints here from June 1907 through to September
1911.Between his first and second time with Victory he served aboard HMS Hecla a
Destroyer Depot ship as Leading Stoker(1215/71). Next between his 2nd and 3rd time
at Victory he served with HMS Spanker as Leading Stoker(5a2/58),HMS Spanker
was a Torpedo Gunboat . He was aboard two more ship between his 3rd and last stint
at Victory,first was HMS Indefatiable a Battle Cruiser of the Indefatiatable Class
Leading Stoker(5a2/61),14th of April 1909 till 10th January 1910 and then HMS
Melponene 11th January 1910 till 30th June 1911 again as Leading Stoker(5a1/51)
After HMS Victory he served on HMS Vernon a land based Torpedo School in
Portsmouth(5a2/110) from 15th September 1911 until 17th April 1912. He was
Leading Stoker(15a2/71) aboard HMS Spartaite a Dibden Class Protector Cruiser
from 18th April to 24th May 1912. He served aboard HMS Minotaur a Minotaur
Class Armoured Cruiser as Leading Stoker(5a2/71) from 25th May 1912 through to
the 7th May 1915. Finally the ill fated HMS Hampshire in which he served from 8th

of May 1915 until the 5th of June 1916 again as a Leading Stoker(5a2/193).HMS Hampshire was a Devonshire Class Armoured Cruiser,which at the time of Edward's death was transporting Lord Kitchener to Archangel. Edward's body was never recovered from the sea. His name is engraved on the seamens memorial in Southsea. Edward Belchamber an Acting Leading Stoke Service no.303849 won the Star,Victory Medal and British War Medal in the WW1 conflict.

Death Certificate:
Edward Belchamber died on the 5th of June 1916 when HMS Hampshire hit a German mine.
The death certificate confirms service number and date of death unfortunately cause of death is not stated it just says "on war service"

NB:The figures in brackets refer to his List and number refer to his entry in the Ship's Book in simple terms it was his pay number
The 'badges' entries refer to Good Conduct Badges, which can be granted 'G', deprived 'D' or restored 'R' according to punishments awarded.
The NP reference is to a letter with that number from the Naval Personnel Division of the Admiralty.

Belchamber Edward of 37 Beauval Road,Dulwich,Surrey died 5 June 1916 at sea on HMS Hampshire on active service. Administration London 21 October to Edward Belchamber cellarman the natural and lawful father and next of kin
Effects £ 135 18s 10d.

ii   Alice Harriet Belchamber was born on the 8th January,1885 in 21 Collet Road,Bermondsey. She married Sidney Reuben Rittman on the 25th September,1915 in St.Mary Magdelane,Peckham.

Birth Certificate:
Alice Harriet Belchamber was born at 21 Collett Road,Bermondsey on the 8th of January,1885. Her father Edward Belchamber was a Cellarman and her mother was Alice Belchamber formerly Saunders. W J Hurst the registrar for St.Olave,Southwick recorded the birth on the 12th of January.
Baptized on the 8th of March 1885 at St.Mary Magdalen,Bermondsey

Alice Belchamber aged 30 a spinster and Waitress married Sidney Reuben Rittman a bachelor aged 29 and a Motor Tyre Examiner both lived in Hollydale Road Sidney at no. 93,Alice at no. 92. They married on the 25th of September 1915 at the parish church St.Mary Magdelane,Peckham. Witness's were Ada Rittman and Albert Edwards. The fathers were Edward Belchamber a Cellarman and William John Rittman a Retired Policeman.

iii   William Robert Belchamber was born on the 31st March,1889 in 21 Collet Road,Bermondsey. He died on the 13th October,1976 in 32 Ullswater Road,Sompting,Sussex.He married Jessie Morris on the 3rd August,1913 in St.Alban,Holborn. She was born on the 27th November,1892 and died on the 29th March,1979 in Torbay Hospital,Torquay,Devon.

Birth Certificate:

Born on the 31st of March 1889 at 21 Collett Road,Bermondsey,William Robert Belchamber was the son of Edward and Alice Belchamber nee Saunders. Edward Belchamber the father was a Cellarman of 21 Collett Road. The birth was recorded on the 29th of April at St.Olave,Southwark by W J Hurst the registrar.

Marriage Certificate:
William Robert Belchamber and Jessie Morris married by banns on the 3rd of August 1913 at the parish church of St.Alban,Holborn,London. They were both 24 years of age. William Robert was a bachelor and Compositer by trade of 69 Cavendish Buildings. Jessie Morris had no occuption she lived at 49 Grays Inn Buildings. Witness' were Robert and Elizabeth Morris. Their parents were Edward Belchamber a Wine Merchant and Robert Morris a Tailor. The service was performed by the curate E F Russell.

Death Certificates:
Jessie Belchamber aged 86 died of Congestive heart failure and Myocardial Infarction and Right femur neck which was certified by Ya Tsai Hsing MB on the 29th of March,1979 at Torbay Hospital,Torquay,Devon.Jessie was listed as the widow of William Robert Belchamber a retired Compositor of 32 Ullswater Road,Lancing,Sussex. The informant was her daughter Phyliss Jessica Daniel of Greynote,Daddyhole Road,Torquay,Devon. W M Wotton the deputy registrar for Torbay,Devon recorded the death on the 30th of March.

William Robert Belchamber a retired Compositer aged 87 died at 32 Ullswater Road,Sompting,Sussex on the 13th of October 1976. Cause of death was Coronary Occlusion,Athero Sclerosis and Osteo Arthritis which was certified by J O Peskett MB. His son Ronald Edward Charles Belchamber was informant of 39 Rowan Way,Rottingdean,Sussex. The registrar E D M Tidmarsh recorded the death on the 13th of October in Worthing,Sussex.

Charles John Belchamber
(John11,Edward10,Edward9,Edward8,Edward7,Edward6,John5,Thomas4,Robert3,Robert2,John1) was born on the 10th August,1862 in Hearnes Buildings,Walworth. He died on the 9th January,1948 in Mile End Hospital,Stepney. He married Elizabeth Phyliss Potter on the 23 July,1882 in The Parish Church,Shoreditch. She died on the 19th October,1926 in 204 Hoxton Street,Shoreditch.

Birth Certificate:
Charles John Bellchamber was born in Hearns Buildings,Walworth on the 10 of August 1862. His father John Bellchamber was a General Porter and his mother was Sarah Ann Bellchamber formerly Wright of Hearn Buildings. The birth was registered by Registrar of Newington Francis Thornton on the 16th September.

Charles John Belchamber and Elizabeth Phillis Potter were married by banns on the 23rd of July 1882 at the parish church Shoreditch. Bachelor Charles John aged 19 was a Wine Bottler of 9 Branch Place,Hyde Road.Elizabeth Phillis aged 20 and a spinster with occupation was living at 7 Branch Place,Hyde Road. Witness's were William and Emily Potter.Fathers John Belchamber was a Carpenter and William Potter a Paper Marbler. The vicar Michael Puttock performed the service.

Census:
Charles John and Elizabeth Phyliss were in Shoreditch living at 290 Kingsland
Road in 1891. Charles John aged 28 was a Wine Porter,Elizabeth Phyliss was aged 29
and their children were Charles J aged 7,William H 4 and Elizabeth P 1.

In the 1901 census Charles and Elizabeth were living in Shoreditch at 1 Hearn
Buildings with their children.Charles was a Glass Packer aged 38,Elizabeth was 39
their son William was a Telegraph Messenger aged 14 and daughters Elizabeth 12 and
Grace 7.

Charles John Belchamber 48 and his wife Elizabeth Phylis 49 were living at 38 Hyde
Road,Hoxton in the 1911 census with their children Elizabeth Phylis aged 21 Grace
Maud 17 and Henry John 9 all single. Charles John was a Plate Glass Packer his
daughter Elizabeth Phylis was a Tea Packer and Grace Maud a Artificial
Florist. Henry John was at school.

Death Certificates:
Charles John Belchamber aged 85 died at the Mile End Hospital,Stepney on the 9th of
January,1948. Cause of death was Myocardial Degeneration,Senility and Gangrene of
the toe which was certified by W Gordon Sears MB. Elizabeth Phillis Belchamber his
daughter of 18 Hyde Road,Shoreditch the family home was informant. John Sullivan
the registrar for Stepney recorded the death on the 10th of January.

Elizabeth Phillis Belchamber aged 64 of 38 Hyde Road,Shoreditch on the 19th 0f
October,1926. Cause of death was Carcinoma Descending Colon which was certified
by C H Williams MB. Informant was Charles John Belchamber the widower of the
deceased a Vanman by trade,living at 38 Hyde Road,Shoreditch. The death was
recorded by Ernest Sibley registrar for Shoreditch on the 20th of October.

Charles John Belchamber and Elizabeth Phyliss Potter had the following children:

i   Charles John Belchamber was born on the 21st May,1883 in 62 Newton Street,
         Old Hoxton Town,Shoreditch. He died on the 9th February,1949 in 20 Hope
         Street,Halifax,Yorkshire. He married Annie Elizabeth Walker on the 2nd
         October,1915 in The Registry Office,Halifax,Yorkshire. She was born on the
         6th February,1887 and died in The Royal Infirmary,Halifax on the 7th
         March,1961.

Birth Certificate:
At 62 Newton Street,Old Hoxton Town,Shoreditch Elizabeth Phillis Belchamber gave
birth to Charles John Belchamber on the 21st of May,1883,Charles John's father also
Charles John Belchamber was a Wine Porter. George Pearce the registrar for
Shoreditch recorded the birth on the 25th of June.

Charles John was baptised on the 1st July,1883 at Hoxton St.Savior,Vicar William
Goddard performed the service. His father Charles John was a Wine Bottler of 62
Newton Street,Hoxton.
He was admitted to Virginia Road School in the borough of Tower Hamlets on the
27th August,1894 aged 11. The school opened in 1875 and was renamed Virginia
School in 1951.

Marriage Certificate:
On the 2nd of October,1915 at the Registry Office in Halifax,Yorkshire Charles Belchamber and Annie Elizabeth Walker were married.Charles(He had dropped the John) was a 32 year old bachelor and Clerk Warehouseman,Annie Elizabeth was a spinster aged 28 and a Worsted Spinner both were living at 4 Nelson Street,Halifax. Their witness's were George J Verity and Catherine O'Shea.The father's were Charles John Belchamber a Plate Glass Warehouseman and Harry Walker a General Labourer(Deceased). Registrar Fred Jagger performed the wedding.

Death Certificates:
Charles Belchamber jnr aged 62 died at 20 Hope Street,Halifax,Yorkshire on the 9th of February,1946. J McCowan certified cause of death as Syncope,Congestive Heart Failure and Acute Bronchitis.Annie E Belchamber his wife was present at death and informant. The death was registered in Halifax by P P Mitchell Interim Registrar on the 9th February. Charles occupation was a Wool Warehouseman. Again Charles has dropped the John as he did when he married

On the 7th of March,1961 at the Royal Halifax Informary,Halifax Annie Elizabeth Belchamber passed away,cause of death was Carcinoma Colon and Broncho Pueumonia,which was certified by Sued Iftikhar Ali M.B. Annie Elizabeth was 75 years of age and the widow of Charles Belchamber a Woollen Percher,home address was 10 Vickerman Street,Halifax. The informant was a daughter E M Hartley of 20 Hammond Street,Halifax. The death was registered in Halifax by Frank Mallinson the registrar on the 7th of March.

Census:
Charles and Annie were living at 16 Swan Street,Crossfield,Halifax. Charles was 26 and listed as a Licenced Hawker and Annie was aged 23 in the 1911 census.

ii   William Henry Belchamber was born on the 20th August,1886 in 309 Kingland Road,West Hackney. He died on the 27th January,1945 in Mackayville,Quebec,Canada. He married Marie Therrien on the 23rd Jun,1906 in St.Damien,Bedford,Comte Missisquoi,Quebec,Canada. She was the daughter of Louis Henri Therrien and Edwidge Chausse. He later married Marie Alice Marguerite Guillet on the 2nd April,1918 in St.Elizabeth De Portuga. She was the daughter of Phiias Guillette and Alphonsine Rheaume.

Birth Certificate;
William Henry Belchamber was born on the 20th of August,1886 in 309 Kingsland,West Hackney. His father Charles John Belchamber was a Wine Porter and his mother Elizabeth Phillis formerly Potter. The birth was registered on the 11th October by the registrar G R Thepioay

iii   Elizabeth Phillis Belchamber was born on the 24th April,1889 in 290 Kingsland Road,Haggerton. She died on the 23rd March,1967 in The Royal Halifax Infirmary,Halifax,Yorkshire.

Birth Certificate:

On the 24th of April,1889 at 290 Kingsland Road,Haggerton,Shoreditch district the birth took place of Elizabeth Phillis Belchamber the daughter of Charles John and Elizabeth Phillis Belchamber nee Potter. Charles John Belchamber her father was a Wine Porter. Registrar A A Gough recorded the birth on the 3rd of June.

Death Certificate:
Spinster Elizabeth Phillis Belchamber aged 76 died in the Royal Halifax Infirmary,Halifax on the 23rd of March 1967. Cause of death was Heart Failure,Myccardial Infarction and Atheroma which was certified by B W Little Corona for the county borough of Halifax after a postmortem without an inquest. Her nephew Donald Hartley was informant of 20 Eldon Place,Hopwood Lane,Halifax. GK Butler the registrar for Halifax recorded the death on the 1st of April. Elizabeth Phillis died while visiting family in Halifax,her address at the time of death was Flat 3 Hilliard House,Station Road,Cowley,Middlesex. She was listed as retired.

iv   Grace Emily Belchamber was born on the 26th April,1891 in 290 Kingsland Road,Haggerton. She died on the 12th December,1891.

Birth Certificate:
Grace Emily Belchamber was born at 290 Kingsland Road,Haggerton,Shoreditch on the 26th of April,1891. Charles John Belchamber her father was a Wine Bottler and her mother was Elizabeth Phillis Belchamber formerly Potter. The Shoreditch deputy registrar R Tyrrell recorded the birth on the 8th of June.

Death Certificate:
Sadly Grace Emily Belchamber passed away on the 12th of December,1891 at 290 Kingsland Road. Cause of death was Bronchitis(4 days) which was certified by Robert George Watts MB. The death was registered by A A Lough the Registrar for 18th of December. Elizabeth Belchamber her mother was informant and present at the death.

v   Grace Maud Belchamber was born on the 10th October,1893 in 47 Abbott Street,Kingsland,Hackney. She married John Watson on the 25th October,1913 in St.Saviours Church,Hoxton,Shoreditch.

Birth Certificate:
Grace Maud Belchamber was born on the 10th of October,1893 the birth took place at 47 Abbott Street,Kingsland,Hackney. Charles John Belchamber his father was a Wine Bottler while his mother was E P Belchamber formerly Potter. C Haynes the registrar for Hackney registered the birth on the 20th of November.

Marriage Certificate:
22 year old John Frances Watson a bachelor and Cardboard Box Cutter of 40 Hemsworth Street married Grace Maud Belchamber spinster aged 20 of 38 Hyde Road and a Artificial Florist at St.Saviours Church in the parish of Hoxton on the 25th of October1913 by banns. Witness's were Benjiman George Watson and Elizabeth Phillis Belchamber. The vicar C C Milburn performed the ceremony. Their fathers were Arthur William Chetwynd Watson a Boot Checker and Charles John Belchamber a Plate Glass Packer.

vi   Albert Edward Belchamber was born on the 2nd October,1897 in 123 Crondall Street,Old Hoxton Town. He died on the 6th May,1899 in 1 Hoxton Market(Residences) Hoxton Old Town.

Birth Certificate:
Albert Edward Belchamber was born on the 2nd of October 1897 in 123 Crondall Street,Hoxton Old Town. E J Pearce the registrar for Shoreditch on the 13th of November. Charles John Belchamber the father was a Wine Bottler and Elizabeth Phillis his mother was formerly Potter.

Death Certificate;
Albert Edward Belchamber aged 19 months died of Pneumonia and Convulsions on the 6th May 1899. The cause of death was certified by H Sinclair MB. His mother Elizabeth Belchamber of 1 Hoxton Market(Residences),Hoxton Old Town was the informant and present at the death. E J Pearce the registrar for Shoreditch registered the death on the 9th of May.

vii   Henry John Belchamber was born on the 6th September,1901 in 1 Henson House,Hoxton New Town. He died on the 9th September,1926 in St.Bartholomews Hospital,London.

Birth Certificate:
Henry John Belchamber was born in number 1 Henson House,Hoxton,New Town on the 6th of September 1901. His father Charles John Belchamber was a General Labourer and his mother was Elizabeth Phillis formerly Potter. A E Davies deputy registrar for Shoreditch recorded the birth on the 5th November.

Death Certificate:
Henry John Belchamber died at St.Bartholomew's Hospital on the 9th of September,1926. He was aged 25 and a Slater's Labourer by trade. The cause of death was Vesical Calculus which was certified by H J Seddon MRCS. The death was recorded on the 11th of September by the registrar of London City. His sister Elizabeth Phillis Belchamber was the informant and gave her address as 32 Hyde Road,Hoxton the same address that Henry John had given.

Frederick William Belchamber
(Samuel11,Edward10,Edward9,Edward8,Edward7,Edward6,John5,Thomas4,Robert3, Robert2,John1) was born in 59 Grove Place,Brompton on the 15th April,1861. He died on the 8th May,1944 in 1 Elmer Gardens,Edgware,Middlesex. He married Charlotte Ethel Hunt on the 26th June,1890 in All Saints Church,Knightsbridge,London. She died on the 3rd July,1964 in 6 Fairfield Road,Burgess Hill,Sussex.

Notes for Frederick William Belchamber
A Professor of Music,he was a organist of some repute,giving recitals mainly in places of worship.

Birth Certificate:
Frederick William Belchamber was born at 56 Grove Place,Brompton on the 15th Of April,1861. His father Samuel Belchamber was a Police Constable,Ann Belchamber his mother was formerly Worman. The birth was recorded in Kensington

on the 10th of May by registrar James Hone.

Marriage Certificate:
On the 26th of June 1890 at All saints church in the parish of Knightsbridge Frederick William Belchamber a bachelor aged 29 and a Professor of Music married spinster Charlotte Ethel at 9 Ethelden Road,Shepherds Bush. Samuel Belchamber the father of Frederick was a Teacher of Music and Charlotte Ethel's father was a Gentleman. Witness's were Emily Ann Cooper,Edith M Hunt,William Charles Marson and Charles J Hunt. The vicar Ravenscroft Stewart performed the ceremony.

Death Certificates:
Professor of Music Frederick William Belchamber aged 83 died at home on the 8th of May,1944,home was 1Elmer Gardens,Edgware,Hendon. He died of Cerebral Thrombosis and softening and Myocardial degeneration which was certified by H S Faber M R C S. Informant and present at death was his daughter A B Rudge. Joan M Reynolds recorded the death on the 9th of May for Hendon.

Frederick William Belchamber's will
THIS IS THE LAST WILL AND TESTAMENT of me Frederick William Belchamber of 53 Cranhurst Road,Cricklewood,London,NW2   I revoke all prior wills made by me .   I appoint my dear wife Charlotte Ethel Belchamber sole Executrix of this my will and I give and bequeath to her absolutely all my rear and personal property.
In witness whereof I have hereunto set my hand this third day of July One thousand nine hundred and thirty-six.

Signed by the said Frederick}
William Belchamber the}
Testator in the presence of}   Frederick W Belchamber(signed)
us present at the same time}
who in his presence at his}
request have hereunto}
subscribed our names as}
witnesses.}

(Cannot read the 1st name or address
Below)

A C Allen
100 Marylebone Road
NW1
Civil Servant

Charlotte Ethel Belchamber aged 96 and the widow of Frederick William Belchamber a Professional Musician died on the 3rd of July 1964. She died of Coronary Thombosis and Arterio Sclerotic Heart Disease which was certified by R B Deering MB at the family home 6 Fairfield Road,Burgess Hill. Her daughter Audrey Rudge of 4 Fairfield Road was informant. G C Farley recorded the death on the 6th of July for Cuckfield.

Census:
In The 1891 census the family were living with Charlotte's parents Charles and Edith Hunt at 1 Crondace Road,Fulham. Frederick aged 29 was a Professor of Music,Charlotte Ethel was 28 and daughter Audrey Beatrice aged 3.Also living in the house was boarder Samuel Belchambers widow and a Teacher of Violins aged 61

In the 1901 census Frederick and Charlotte aged 32 were living in Hampstead,at 187 Fordwych Road with their children Audrey B 10,Olive M 8 and Thoedore H 7. Also living with them was Charlotte's sister Edith M Hunt who listed herself as a mothers help. Frederick was 39 and a Professor of music living on his own account.

In 1911 Frederick William and Ethel were living at 368 High Road,Brondesbury,Kilburn.NW.
Living with them were children Audrey Beatrice aged 20,Olive Maud 18 and Theodore Hugh aged 17. Frederick William was a Organist and Prof.of Music and son Theodore a Auctioneer's Clerk,neither daughters had occupations listed.

Frederick William Belchamber and Charlotte Ethel Hunt had the following children:

i   Audrey Beatrice Belchamber was born on the 11th December,1890 in 1 Crondace Road,Fulham. She married Arthur E Rudge on the 17th April,1926 in St.Gabriels Church,Willesden,Middlesex.

Birth Certificate:
Frederick and Charlotte's first daughter Audrey Beatrice Belchamber was born at No.1 Crondace Road,Fulham on the 11th of December,1890. Her father Frederick William Belchamber was a Professor Of Music and Charlotte Ethel Belchamber nee Hunt her mother. David Shopland the registrar for Fulham recorded the birth on the 14th of January,1891.

Marriage Certificate:
On the 17th of April,1926 at St.Gabriels Church,Willesden,Middlesex Audrey Beatrice Belchamber and Arthur Ernest Rudge got married by banns. Arthur Ernest was a bachelor aged 26 and a Clerk and Audrey Beatrice was aged 21 with no occupation listed and a spinster. Witness's were Ernest William Rudge and Frederick William Belchamber the fathers,their occupations were Ernest William Rudge an Architect and Frederick William Belchamber an Organist. At the time of the marriage Arthur Ernest was living at 8 Melrose Avenue and Audrey Beatrice at 64 Cranhurst Road. The vicar J Bradshaw performed the ceremony.

ii   Olive Maud Belchamber was born on the 9th December,1893 in 5 Fulham Park Road,Fulham. Unmarried she died on the 17th May,1978 in The Pouchlands Hospital,East Chiltington,Sussex.

Birth Certificate:
On the 31st of October,1892 Olive Maud Belchamber was born at 1 Crondace Road,Fulham she was the second daughter of Frederick William and Charlotte Ethel. Frederick William was a Professor of Music. The birth was registered by David Shopland on the 9th of November for Fulham registration district.

Death Certificate:
Olive Maud Belchamber aged 86 died on the 17th of May 1978 at the Pouchlands Hospital,East Chiltington,Sussex. She was living with her brother Theodore Hugh Belchamber at 6 Fairfield Road,Burgess Hill,Sussex who was the informant. Olive Maud was living by independant means,the cause of death was Parkinson's Disease and fractured neck of Femur rt which was certified by J R Caldwell MB. The death was registered by M Moth the registrar for Lewes,East Sussex on the 18th of May.Olive Maud never married.

iii   Theodore Hugh Belchamber was born on the 9th December,1893 in 5 Fulham Park Road,Fulham. He died on the 10th March,1987 in Prescot,Upper St.Johns Road,Burgess Hill,Sussex. He married Olive Marion Carter on the 24th December,1921 in St.Gabriels Church,Willesden,Middlesex. She was born on the 24th August,1896 and died on the 10th April,1969.
          Theodore Hugh later married Ivy May Allen on the 4th July,1942 in St.Asaph,Flintshire. She was born in 1902.

Birth Certificate:
The birth of Theodore Hugh Belchamber Frederick and Charlotte's first son took place at No.5 Fulham Park,Road,Fulham on the 9th of December,1893. The deputy registrar for Fulham A Busby recorded the birth on the 20th of January,1894. Frederick William Belchamber his father was a Professor of Music,his mother Charlotte Ethel Belchamber was formerly Hunt.

Marriage Certificate:Olive Marion Carter.
Theodore Hugh Belchamber and Olive Marion Carter married in St.Gabriels Parish Church Willesden on the 24th of December,1921. Bachelor Theodore Hugh aged 28 and a Clerk of 64 Penhurst Road and Olive Marion was a spinster aged 25 and a Dental Mechanic of 46 Christchurch Avenue,Bermondsey. Witness's were both fathers Frederick William Belchamber an Organist and Edwin Ryhton Carter an Electrical Engineer. J Gill vicar performed the ceremony.

Death Certificate:Olive Marion Belchamber.
Olive Marion Belchamber aged 72 died at The Sunbury Nursing Home,Sunbury,Surrey on the 10th of April,1969. Cause of death was multiple cerebral thombosis certified by A Allanshire MRCS. Listed as the former wife of Theodore Hugh Belchamber. The informant was her nephew Kenneth Hyde Dickinson of 7 Blackblake Close,Egham. The death was registered on the 11th of April for Surrey Northern.

Marriage Certificate:Ivy May Allen.
At some point Theodore Hugh and Olive Marion got divorced.
Divorcee's Theodore Hugh Belchamber and Ivy May Allen were married in the Registry Office St.Asaph,Flintshire on the 4th of July,1942. Theodore Hugh was aged 48 and a Civil Servant for the Ministry of Works and 40 year old Ivy May was a Clerk L.P.J.B she was living at 2 Avenue Mansions,St Paul Avenue,London N.W.2 and Theodore Hugh at 32 Lake Avenue,Rhyl. Witness's were E.Belchamber and H.R.Allen. Fathers were Frederick William Belchamber a Professor Of Music and Alfred James Chamberlain a Trolley Driver. The ceremony was performed by

registrar R Roberts for St.Asaph.

Death Certificate:
Theodore Hugh Belchamber died of Brunlis Puenomia at Prescott,Upper St.Johns Road,Burgess Hill,Sussex on the 10th of March,1987. Joan Mary Moss his cousin was informant,her address being 11 Pounsley Road,Dunton Green,Sevenoaks,Kent. Cause of death was certified by S Hussain MB and registered on the 11th of March for Haywards Heath. Theodore Hugh was a retired Civil Servant.

Marriage Certificate:
Ivy May Belchamber aged 78 and William George Pharo aged 83 married on the 11th of April,1980 at The Registry Office,Hitchin,Hertfordshire. William George was a widow and a retired Local Goverment Officer and Ivy May whose previous marriage had been dissolved had no occupation listed. William George gave his address as Ashley House,68 Heathfield,Royston and Ivy May as 16 Queens Road Royston. Witness's were G.W.Pharo and J.C.Chamberlain. Their fathers were Samuel Pharo a Journeyman Wheelwright and Albert James Chamberlain(Deceased) a Driver. The marriage was performed by Alan Wearmouth Superintendant Registrar and C.M Hogman Deputy Registrar.

Frederick Belchamber
(James11,James10,James9.William8,Edward7,Edward6,John5,Thomas4,Robert3, Robert2.John1) was born on the 28th of March,1865 in Plaistow,Sussex. He died at 3 Lion Mead,Shottermill,Surrey on the 19th of September,1931. He married Jane Baker on the 24th of July,1895 in Kirdford,Sussex. She was born in 1857 and died at The Infirmary,Hale Road,Farnham,Surrey.

Birth Certificate:
Frederick Belchamber was born in Plaistow,Sussex on the 28th of March,1865. His father James was a Hewer and Abigail his mother signed her mark. The birth was recorded on the 27th of April by registrar for Petworth George Wells.

Marriage Certificate:
Frederick Belchamber who spent some of his life as a military man married Jane Baker at Kirdford on the 24th July 1895 by banns,witness`s were Annie and Frederick Baker(signed a cross) the ceremony was performed by Erskin A Birrell. Frederick and Jane Belchamber only had one son Charles Frederick born in Chuter Cottages,Shottermill on the 19th of May,1896 the birth was registered in Farnham,Surrey on the 29th May.

Census:
In the 1891 census Frederick Belchamber aged 25 was a Guard at the Calvary and Artillery Barracks in Colchester,Essex.

In the 1901 census Frederick aged 36 and Jane 41 are living in Lion Lane,Shottermill with their son Charles Frederick aged 4.Frederick's occupation is a Gunner RHA reserves. They have a boarder by the name of Walter Jaques a General Labourer aged 18 from Whitmore Bottom,Surrey.

In the 1911 census Frederick Belchamber a Labourer aged 46 was living in Lion

Lane,Shottermill,Haslemere,Surrey with his wife Jane Belchamber aged 52 and their 14 year old son Charles Frederick Belchamber. Jane Belchamber was a Household Worker.

Death Certificates:
Jane Belchamber aged 67 died at The Infirmary,Hale Road,Farnham on the 13th of October 1926.Cause of death was cerebral Vascular Desease and Bronchitis which was certified by T Brockington MD. Registrar R Balchin registered the death on the 16th October. Charles Frederick Belchamber of 3 Chuter Cottages her son was informant. Jane's husband Frederick was a domestic gardener. Jane is buried in St.Stephens churchyard,Shottermill.

Frederick Belchamber died at 3 Lion Mead,Shottermill on the 19th of September,1931 of cardiac failure,his son Charles was the informant of the same address,Frederick's age was 66 and a domestic gardener,the death was registered on the 25th September,he is buried in St Stephens,churchyard Shottermill on the 23rd of September,E G Clifford Frend performed the service.

Frederick Belchamber and Jane Baker had the following child:

i   Charles Frederick Belchamber was born on the 19th May,1896 in Chuter Cottages,Lion Lane,Shottermill,Surrey. He died on the 4th December,1954 in 48 Selwood Road,Woking,Surrey. He married Elizabeth Bridget Power on the 21st January,1920 in Church of Aughrim Street,Dublin,Eire. She was born on the 25th October,1896 in Ireland the daughter of Patrick Power and Bridget Lynch. She died on the 6th July,1992 in St.Peters Hospital,Chertsey,Surrey.

Birth Certificate:
Frederick and Jane Belchamber's only son Charles Frederick Belchamber was born in Shottermill,Frensham,Surrey on the 19th of May 1896. His father Frederick Belchamber was a General Labourer. The birth was registered on the 29th of May in Farnham,Surrey. Jane Belchamber formerly Baker was the mother of Shottermill,Frensham.

In 1910 with the help of the Vicar of Shottermill Parish E P.C Frend(Vicar of Shottermill 1909-1933) and A.R Chandler the Headmaster of Shottermill School, Charles Frederick applied to go into The Gordon Boys Home in West End,Woking,Surrey. All forms were duly filled in by his parents Frederick and Jane Belchamber and he finally went to the school on the 2nd of January 1911 as number 2452. His height was 5.0ft,chest size 28inches and his weight was 8 stone.He was aged 14and a half and had been a Telegram Boy earning 6s 6d a week.
By his record Charles had an eventful time there, his punishment records show that in 1912 on the 14th of October he stole potatoes from the cookhouse his punishment was 4 Cuts and 14 days, 1913 on the 18th February he Improperly obtained leave to go to the latrine punishable with 10 days referral and finally March 24 he was caught smoking on the Brookwood Road of which his punishment was 3 cuts and 10 days referral.
After 2 years and 3 months at the age of 16 he left the Gordon Boys to join the 2nd Btn.Worcestershire Regiment.2452 Charles Frederick Belchamber was struck off the strength on the 26th March 1913 he was 5ft 3 inch tall, weight was 11st 2lbs with a

33inch chest. By then he had a trade of a Shoemaker and his proficiency was good. The commandant Report was good" An average kind of lad, inclined to be foolish- should do well in the Army where his silliness will be removed.

The 3rd Battalion Worcestershire Regiment was raised in Aldershot on the 14th of February, 1900. After postings to Ireland and South Africa the regiment was back in Ireland in 1919, it was probably where Charles Frederick met and fell in love with Elizabeth Power. By 1920 the regiment was back in England, but in 1921 Charles and Elizabeth were in Fyzabad, India where their first child was born.
Charles Frederick joined the Army on the 1st June, 1915 as a private no.13340. His theatre of war was France; he received the Victory Medal, British Medal and 15 Star Medal.

Marriage Certificate:
Charles Frederick Belchamber a bachelor married Elizabeth Power a spinster in Dublin, Ireland on the 21st January.1920 in the Catholic Church of Aughrim Street No 3 North City district. Witness`s were John Power and Annie Power. There was no occupation for Elizabeth and Charles was a Sergeant in the 3rd Btn.Worcestershire Regiment. Charles and Elizabeth were both of full age. Father's occupations were Frederick Belchamber a Gardener and Patrick Power was a Cattle Drover.

Patrick Power born about 1870 married Christine Lynch prior to 1896,they were possibly from County Meath.Patrick died in 1910 aged 27 when Elizabeth was 13 years old,Christine died aged 42 as a result of hanging curtains,she fell off a chair.After the parent's death the children were sent to live with family,Elizabeth came to the UK where she lived with her Aunt Ann in Coventry,later returning to Ireland. Aunt Ann could be the Ann who witnessed the marriage of Charles and Elizabeth. Patrick had a brother Edward,he was known as Ned,Ned was living in Fountain Place,Dublin from where Elizabeth went to her wedding.

George Belchamber Great Grandparents
(James11,James10,James9,William8,Edward7,Edward6,John5,Thomas4,Robert3,Robert2,John1) was born on the 24th May,1867 in Plaistow,Sussex. He died on the 11th January,1953 in Chiddingfold,Surrey. He married Kate Horn on the 14th October,1893 in Petworth,Sussex .She was the daughter of Silas and Harriet Horn born 1874. She died on the 25th November,1939 in Chiddingfold.

Birth Certificate:
George Belchamber was born Plaistow,Sussex on the 17th of May,1867,the birth was registered on the 14th of June. Father James was a Hewer and Farm Labourer.

Marriage Certificate:
George Belchamber age 25 married Kate Horn age 20 from Kirdford on the 14th October 1893, witnesss` were John Potter and Arthur King. Erkskine A.Birrell performed the ceremony by banns in the parish church, Kirdford. George was a Bachelor and Blacksmith by Trade and Kate with no occupation was a spinster. Kate's father Silas Horne was a Shoemaker and James Belchamber a Labourer.

Census:
In the 1891 census George Belchamber age 23 boarded with a Harriet Horn a

launderess age 63 in Kirdford,Sussex at The Cottage, he listed himself as a Blacksmith Journeyman from Plaistow Sussex. Harriet Horn recorded her place of abode as Thursley Surrey.

In the 1901 census George and Kate were living in Burningfold,Dunsfold with their children Ethel aged 7,Ivy aged 5,Basil 3 and Bob 1.George aged 34 was a Blacksmith and Kate was 29. George probably worked at Burningfold Manor in the Blacksmith shop.

In 1911 George and Kate Belchamber were living at Maple Tree Cottage,Dunsfold,living with them were Ethel 17 a Housemaid,Basil 13, Robert 11,Dennis 9,Gordon 7,James 5 and finally Ronald 3 Ivy had been entered but then crossed out. She was in Kensington a Nursery Maid.

Death Certificates:

George Belchamber died in Burcot,Woodside Road,Chiddingfold on the 11th of January,1953 aged 85,he was a Fitter Attendant Waterworks(Retired). Cause of death was Bronchopneumonia certified by R G R Gethen MRCS. The death was registered by G Kefales on the 13th of January for Surrey South Western.

Kate Belchamber aged 65 from Burcot,Woodside Road,Chiddingfold died on the 25th of November,1939.D Barber MB certified the cause of death as Coronary Thombosis,Cardio Vascular degeneration and Diabetes Mellitis. Hugh Gordon Belchamber her son was informant and present at the death. Charles Elford recorded the death on the 28th of November for Surrey South Western.

George Belchamber's Will

THIS IS THE LAST WILL AND TESTAMENT of me George Belchamber of Burcot,Chiddingfold in the county of Surrey.I revoke all previous Wills heretofore made by me and declare this to be my last Will whereof I appoint my son-in-law RONALD HERBERT SMITH to be my Executor

I give all my furniture and personal effects of which I may dic possessed to my Son JAMES O'BRIEN BELCHAMBER absolutely.

As to all the rest and residue of my property I give the same subject to the payment of my debts and funeral and testamentary expenses to my Executor to be equally divided into nine shares and direct that one ninth share shall be paid to each if my children namely:

Ethel Elizabeth May Cowlishall

Ivy Gladys Steeves

Frederick George Basil Belchamber

Robert Baden Powell Belchamber

Hugh Gordon Belchamber

James O'Brien Belchamber

Ronald Silas Belchamber

Kitty Faith Smith

And as the remaining one ninth share I direct that the same shall be paid into a joint account in the names of my Executor and of the two children of my deceased Son Arthur Dennis Belchamber namely: Evelyn Joyce Belchamber and George Belchamber in the Post Office Savings Bank to be held in such account until the said Evelyn Joyce Belchamber and George Belchamber shall respectively attain the age of Twenty One years.

In witness whereof I have hereunto set my hand this Seventh day of June One Thousand nine hundred and forty.

Signed by the Testator in the presence of us who in his presence and in the presence of each other have hereunto subscribed our names a witnesses:.

(George signed the will as did his witnesse's who unfortunately I cannot make out any names)

Census:
In the 1891 census George Belchamber age 23 boarded with a Harriet Horn a launderess age 63 in Kirdford,Sussex at The Cottage, he listed himself as a Blacksmith Journeyman from Plaistow Sussex. Harriet Horn recorded her place of abode as Thursley Surrey.

In the 1901 census George and Kate were living in Burningfold,Dunsfold with their children Ethel aged 7,Ivy aged 5,Basil 3 and Bob 1. George aged 34 was a Blacksmith and Kate was 29. George probably worked at Burningfold Manor in the Blacksmith shop.

In the 1911 census George and Kate were living at Maple Tree Cottage,Dunsfold,living with them were Ethel 17 a Housemaid,Basil 13, Robert 13,Dennis 9,Gordon 7,James 5 and finally Ronald 3 Ivy had been entered but then crossed out. She was in Kensington a Nursery Maid.

George Belchamber and Kate Horn had the following children:

i   Ethel Elizabeth May Belchamber was born on the 29TH January,1894 in Kirdford,Sussex. She died on the 2nd April,1977 in Brookwood Hospital,Surrey. She married Samuel Cowlishaw on the 9th August,1915 in The Wesleyan Methodist Church,Colwyn Bay,Conway,North Wales.

Birth Certificate:
Ethel Elizabeth May Belchamber was born 29th January,1894 in Kirdford,Sussex and registered on the 8th March that year in Petworth by registrar George Brookfield. Her mother was Kate Belchamber formerly Horn,George Belchamber her father was a Blacksmith Journeyman.
Ethel was baptised in Kirdford on the 1st January, 1894.

Marriage Certificate:
Ethel Elizabeth May Belchamber aged 21 spinster (A Housemaid) and Samuel
Cowlishaw aged 42 batchelor (A Gentlemens Valet) were married on the 9th August
in the Wesleyan Methodist Church,Colwyn Bay,Conway. Robert Sims Armsby
performed the ceremony and the witness`s were Thomas and Mary Grindley. Ethel's
address at the time of the wedding was Bryn-y-glyn,Nanty-glyn road,Colwyn Bay and
Samuel was living at Bella Vista,Park Road,Colwyn Bay.

Death Certificate:
Ethel Elizabeth May Cowlishaw died in the Brookwood Hospital,Woking on the 2nd
of April,1977. Cause of death was Cardiac failure,Senility,Senile dementia and a
fractured neck sustained in July,1976 certified by B Zaman MB. Informant was
Dorothy Annie Belchamber of 3 Coombe View,Chiddingfold,Surrey sister-in-
law. Ethel was listed as the widow of Samuel Cowlishaw a retired Gentlemens Valet.
The death was registered by the registrar at Brookwood Hospital on the 4th of April.

ii   Ivy Alice Belchamber was born on the 29th August,1895 in The High
        Street,Petworth,Sussex. She died on the 7th February,1973 aged 78 in
        Young,Saskatchwen,Canada.
        She married Roy Steeves on the 9th January,1918 in Chiddingfold,Surrey.
        He was born in Canada on the 19th September,1889. He also died in
        Young,Saskatchwen on the 13th April,1963.

Roy Steeves and Ivy Gladys Belchamber had the following children:

i   Douglas Roy Steeves born 1918 in London,England

ii   Hazel Ann Steeves born 1923 in Young,Sask.

iii   George Henry Keith Steeves born 1926 in Young,Sask.

iii   Frederick George Basil Belchamber was born on the 21st May,1897 in The
        High Street,Petworth,Sussex. He died on the 18th July,1981 in The Royal
        Surrey Hospital,Guildford,Surrey. He married Dorothy May Radley in The
        Registry Office,Guildord on the 15th February,1922. She was the daughter of
        Albert Henry Radley and Lilian Sarah Denyer,born on the 5th October,1900
        .She died on the 2nd February,1988 in St.Lukes Hospital,Guilford.

iv   Robert Leonard Powell Belchamber was born on the 24th March,1900 in
        Burningfold,Dunsfold,Surrey. He died on the 3rd February,1963 in 33 Warren
        Ridge,Frant,Sussex. He married Ivy Elizabeth Rabson on the 28th
        February,1928 in The Registry Office,Ticehurst,Sussex. She was born on the
        26th October,1904 in Wadhurst,Sussex. She died on the 23rd August,1974 in
        St.Helens Hospital,Hastings,Kent.

v   Arthur Dennis Belchamber was born on the 24th September,1901 in
        Burningfold,Dunsfold,Surrey. He died on the 11th October,1933 in The Royal
        Surrey County Hospital,Guildford,Surrey. He married Esther Ellen Jenner on

the 27th February,1926 in The Registry Office,Guildford,Surrey. She died on the 22nd August,1997.

vi   Hugh Gordon Belchamber was born on the 25th October,1903 in Burningfold,Dunsfold,Surrey. He died on the 6th March,1979 in 20 Queens Mead,Chiddingfold,Surrey. He married Lydia Alice Davis on the 17th February,1930 in The Registry Office,Guildford,Surrey. She was born on the 23rd December,1911 in Portsmouth,Hampshire. She died on the 25th March,1998.

vii   James O'brien Belchamber was born on the 14th March,1906 in Maple Tree Cottage,Dunsfold,Surrey. He died on the 28th November,1980 in 3 Coombe View,Chiddingfold,Surrey. He married Dorothy Annie Lawrence on the 11th October,1930 in Northchapel,Sussex. Dorothy Annie was the daughter of William George Lawrence and Rose Annie Streeter. She was born in Colhook,Northchapel on the 18th September,1909. She died on the 12th May,2008 in The Beechcroft Nursing Home,Eynsham,Oxfordshire.

viii   Ronald Silas Belchamber was born on the 22nd March,1908 in Maple Tree Cottage,Dunsfold,Surrey. He died on the 16th August,1976 in Pontrilas,Codette,Saskatchwen,Canada. He married Ellen Gooden. Ronald and Ellen divorced and he married Elizabeth Stensrud on the 28th October,1950 in Mayerthorpe,Alberta,Canada.

ix   Kitty Faith Belchamber was born on the 7th July,1911 in Maple Tree Cottage,Dunsfold,Surrey. She died on the 8th October,1993 in Maidstone,Kent. She married Ronald Herbert Smith on the 23rd October,1937 in St.Marys Church,Chiddingfold,Surrey. He was born on the 11th November,1911,he died on the 24th November,1993 also in Maidstone.

x   Roy Belchamber was born on the 15th April,1917 in 97 Woodside Road,Chiddingfold,Surrey. He died there on the 24th November.

Birth Certificate:
Roy Belchamber came into the world on the 15th of April.1917 at Woodside Road,Chiddingfold. His father George was an Engineer at Water Works. The birth was recorded by M N Ginders registrar for Hambledon,Surrey.

Death Certificate:
Roy Belchamber died aged 7 months at Woodside Road,Chiddingfold on the 24th of November,1917. Cause of death was Broncho Pneumonia(3 Days) certified by N F Kendall MRCS. Deputy registrar M N Ginder for Hambledon recorded the death on the 26th of November.

There was a family story that there was another son born to George and Kate,who also Died named Wilford or Wilfred but no evidence has come to light to prove this.There is a gap between the birth of Kitty Faith and Roy,so maybe he was born sometime then and because he died it was never registered. Illegal of coarse but it happened sometimes.

William Belchamber

(James11,James10,James9,William8,Edward7,Edward6,John5,Thomas4,Robert3,Robert2,John1) was born on the 13th June,1869 in Durfold Cottage,Plaistow,Sussex. He died on the 3rd August,1941 in Golden Cross Cottage,Plaistow,Sussex. He married Louisa Jane Remnant on the 17th February,1906 in Petworth,Sussex. She was the daughter of Thomas Remnant and Charlotte Cooper born on the 30th March,1879 in Chiddingfold,Surrey. She died on the 4th November,1957 in Southlands Hospital,Shoreham by sea,Sussex.

Birth Certificate:
William Belchamber was born in Durfold Cottage,Dunsfold,Surrey in the year 1869 on the 13th of June. James Belchamber his father was a Farm Labourer.Edward Davey the registrar for Hambledon,Surrey recorded the birth on the 29th of July.

William was privately baptisted on the 31st October,1869.

Marriage Certificate:
Louisa Jane Remnant aged 27 a spinster with no occupation and 36 year old Labourer William Belchamber married in the parish church,Kirdford by banns on the 17th February 1906 witness's were Elizabeth and James Remnant. The marriage was performed by Erskine A Birrel vicar. Louisa's father Thomas Remnant was a Labourer and James Belchamber, father of William was deceased.

Death Certificates:
72 year old retired Farm Labourer William Belchamber died at Golden Cross Cottage,Plaistow,Sussex on the 3rd of August,1941. Cause of death was Chronic Bronchitis and Paraplegia(Cerebral Heamorhage) certified by J Vine MB. The death was recorded on the 6th of August for Midhurst and Petworth.

Louisa Jane Belchamber aged 77 died at the Southlands Hospital,Shoreham by sea on the 4th of November 1957,the cause of death was Right Cerebral Trombosis and Ischaemic Heart disease,Congestive heart failure certified by A B Macintyre MB. She was listed as the widow of William Belchamber of Golden Cross Plaistow a Farm Worker. Louisa Jane's son in law A H Forrest was informant of 2 Stroud Lodge,Grayswood,Haslemere,Surrey. Registrar W E Savage recorded the death on the 5th of November for Worthing district.
Louisa Jane is buried in Kirdford Churchyard plot no 14(No Headstone)

Census:
In the 1911 census William and Louisa were living in Plaistow,Sussex with their childen Abigail aged 3,Annie 1,also living in the house were Louisa's Father Thomas Remnant and his children Frederick 29,Edith 20,Thomas 14 and Charlotte 13 all Farm Labourers as was William.

William Belchamber and Louisa Jane Remnant had the following children:

i   Abigail Charlotte Belchamber was born on the 13th March.1908 in Plaistow,Sussex. She died on the 10th August,1928 in The Royal Surrey County Hospital,Guildford,Surrey.

Birth Certificate:
Abigail Charlotte Belchamber was born in Plaistow,Kirdford,Sussex on the 13th of March 1908. William Belchamber her father was a General Labourer. Charles Randall the registrar for Petworth registered the birth on the 16th of April.

Death Certificate:
Abigail Charlotte Belchamber died aged 20 at the Royal Surrey County Hospital,Guildford,Surrey on the 10th of August 1928. Cause of death was Pueperal Eclampsia certified by B A Lampsell LRCP. Abigail Charlotte was a Domestic Servant living at Golden Cross Cottage,Plaistow,Sussex the family home. Her mother Louisa Jane was informant and present at the death. Walter R Harris Registrar for Guildford recorded the death on the 10th of August,

ii   Annie Elizabeth Belchamber was born on the 3rd February,1910 in Plaistow,Sussex. She married Alec Mitchell on the 6th November,1933 in The Registry Office,Swindon,Wiltshire.

iii   Bertha Florence Belchamber was born on the 4th September,1916 in Golden Cross Cottage,Plaistow,Sussex. She married Andrew Hamilton Forrest on the 19th February,1940 in Plaistow.

Emma Belchamber
(James11,James10,James9,William8,Edward7,Edward6,John5,Thomas4,Robert3,Robert2,John1) was born on the 24th August, 1871 in Durfold,Dunsfold,Surrey. She married William Edward Philps on the 11th September,1897 in Portsea,Hampshire. He was the son of William George Philps and Elizabeth King born on the 28th April,1869.

Birth Certificates:
Emma Belchamber's birth took place in Durfold,Dunsfold on the Surrey/Sussex border on the 24th of August 1871. James Belchamber her father was a Farm Labourer and her mother was Abigail formerly Pennicard. The birth was recorded in Hambledon on the 4th of October by registrar Edward Emery.

Census:
In the 1891 census Emma was a General Domestic Servant aged 19 living at the Coffee Tavern (Catteshall Hatch) in Meadrow, Farncombe,Surrey

William Edward Philp was born on the 28th of April,1869 at 47 Maitland Street,Portsea. His father was William George a dockyard labourer,his mother was Elizabeth formerly King the birth was registered by William Hatch the registrar for Kingston in the county of Southampton(Portsea Island).

Marriage Certificate:
Emma Belchamber a spinster with no occupation listed and aged 26 married William Edward Philp a 28 year old Driller on the 11th September 1897 by Banns, in the parish church,Portsea,Hampshire. Witness's were Emily Hill and Arthur Lush.

The Rev.Wallington performed the ceremony. James,Emma's father was a Labourer and William George Philps was a Driller like his son.

William Edward Philps and Emma Belchamber had the following children:
i   Annie Florence Beatrice Philps born 1898 in Portsmouth,Hampshire.

ii   Frederick Samuel James Philps born 1900 in Plaistow,Sussex.

Census;

In the 1891 census Emma Belchamber 19 was a General Domestic at the Coffee Tavern,Catteshall Lane,Godalming.

The 1911 Census sees William Edward and Emma Philp living in Aldershot in the Stanhope Lines,Barrack with them are two children Annie Florence Beatrice Philp born in the June qtr of 1898 and Frederick Samuel James Philp born 1900 in the December qtr.

Anne Belchamber
(James11,James10,James9,William8,Edward7,Edward6,John5,Thomas4,Robert3,Robert2,John1) was born on the 4th June,1877 in Plaistow,Sussex. She married George Frederick Ede on the 1st August,1903 in Kirdford,Sussex.

Birth Certificate:
Anne Belchamber came into this world on the 19th of June 1877 in Plaistow,Sussex. Her father James Belchamber was a Agricultural Labourer and her mother Abigail was formerly Pennicard. George Brookfield recorded the birth for Petworth on the 26th of July.

Marriage Certificate:
Ann Belchamber age 26 and a spinster married George Frederick Ede a Bricklayer aged 26 also by Banns in the parish Church, Kirdford on the 1st August 1903. Elizabeth and Frederick Belchamber,Ann's brother and sister were their witness's. Erskine A Burrels Vicar performed the marriage service. George's father Caleb Ede was a Police Pensioner and James Belchamber was a Labourer.

George Frederick Ede and Anne Belchamber had the following children:

i   Bertha Ede

ii   George Ede

Census:
The 1911 census saw George Frederick and Annie Ede living in Lion Lane,Shottermill with their daughter Bertha Ede aged 7, who was born in the March qtr of 1905. George Frederick was a Bricklayer by trade.

Alice Beatrice Belchamber
(James11,James10,James9,William8,Edward7,Edward6,John5,Thomas4,Robert3,Robert2,John1) was born on the 8th April,1883 in Plaistow,Sussex. She married John Edwin Birch on the 5th July,1902 in Leek,Staffordshire. He was the son of James Birch and Emily Finney,born on the 27th September,1870.

Birth Certificates:
The birth of Alice Beatrice Belchamber took place in Plaistow,Sussex on the 8th of April,1883. Her father James Belchamber was a Farm Labourer. The birth was registered on the 17th of May by George Brookfield the Petworth registrar.

John Edwin Birch was born in 51 Newport Lane,Burslem on the 27th of September,1870. His father James Birch was a Potter by trade and his mother was Emily Birch formerly Finney. James signed the certificate with his mark as informant. The birth was registered by J H Power the registrar of Wolstanton on the 3rd of October.

Marriage Certificate:
Alice Beatrice Belchamber married John Edwin Birch in All Saints Church in Leek, Staffordshire on the 5th July 1902 . Alice Beatrice was a spinster aged 19 and John Edwin was 31 years of age and a Joiner by trade. The ceremony by banns was performed by William Benson Wright the vicar. Tom and Fanny Markson were witness's.
Fathers James Birch was a deceased Labourer and James Belchamber a Gardener.

Census:
In the 1901 census Alice age 20 was a Housemaid in the home of Dorothy H Cruickshank in Alverstoke,Hampshire at 35 Crescent Road.
At the same time John Edwin aged 30 was a private in the Royal Garrison Artillery in Fort Gomer,Alverstoke,Hamphire. This could be how they met,later to marry.

In the census of 1911 Alice Beatrice Birch aged 27 was living with her son James Birch aged 7 in 3 High Lane,Chell,Stoke on Trent. James Birch was born in 1904 in the September qtr.There was no mention of John Edwin nor it was listed that Alice Beatrice was a widow. Taking a further look in 1911,I found John Edwin Birch aged 40 in the Cheddleton,Lunatic Asylum. He died December 1912.

Jennifer Bridget Gratrix nee Belchamber can remember Alice and James' son James visiting Lion Lane with his son William,possibly for her grandmother Jane's funeral(Jane Belchamber nee Baker)

Elizabeth Belchamber
(James11,James10,James9,William8,Edward7,Edward6,John5,Thomas4,Robert3,Robert2,John1) was born on the 27th March,1887 in Plaistow,Sussex. She married Percy Wooldridge on the 30th March,1907 in Shamley Green,Surrey. He was the son of Joshua Wooldridge and Alice Georgina Elliot.

Birth Certificate:
Elizabeth Belchamber was born in Plaistow,Sussex on the 27th of March,1887. James Belchamber her father was a Farm Labourer and her mother Abigail formerly

Pennicard signed her mark. The registrar for Petworth George Brookfield recorded the birth on the 5th of May.

Census:
In the 1901 census Elizabeth Belchamber aged 14 was a General Domestic in the household of George and Caroline Remnant in Plaistow Street,Plaistow

Marriage Certificate:
Elizabeth Belchamber and Percy Wooldridge were married in Christs Church, Shamley Green,Surrey by banns on April the 30th 1907. The witness`s were Charles and Lily Wooldridge and James Elson. The vicar C Eagles performed the ceremony. Percy Wooldridge was aged 20 and a Labourer and Elizabeth a spinster aged 20 also. The fathers Joshua Wooldridge was a Bricklayer and James Belchamber was deceased.

In 1911 Percy and Elizabeth were living in Back Lane,Plaistow with three children Abigail Alice 3,George 2 and Jehu 9 months. Percy was a Farm Labourer aged 25 and Elizabeth was 24

Alfred Belchamber

(William11,James10,James9,William8,Edward7,Edward6,John5,Thomas3,Robert3,Robert2,John1) was born on the 23rd October,1870 in Petworth. He died on the 2nd January,1955 in 50 Victoria Street,Englefield Green,Surrey. He married Sarah Jane Hawkins on the 7th September,1895 in The Parish Church,Hascombe,Surrey. She was born about 7th July,1872 in Wisborough Green,Sussex,the daughter of John and Mary Hawkins. She died on the 20th January,1961 in The Grange,St.Annes Hill,Chertsey.

Birth Certificate:
Alfred Belchamber bapt.Oct 23,1870 he was born on the 25th Of August in Plaistow the birth was registered on the 10th Of September by Henry Boxall Registrar. William Belchamber his father was a Agricultral Labourer and his mother was Eliza Belchamber of Plaistow Sussex.

Alfred Belchamber married Sarah Jane Hawkins in the parish church in Hascombe,Surrey on the 7th of September 1895 he was aged 25 and Sarah Jane was 23 a spinster from West Grinstead,Sussex and the daughter of John Hawkins a Woodman. Alfred`s father William was a Labourer and Alfred himself was a Gardener the witness`s were William Hawkins and Emma Warner.

Census:
In the 1901 census Alfred and Sarah Jane were living in Woodhay,Wiltshire at West Field Cottage with their children. John W A aged 4 and Reginald C L aged 3.Alfred aged 31 was a Gardener(Domestic) and Sarah Jane was aged 28.

In the Census of 1911 Alfred aged 40 and Sarah aged 38 were living in Northcroft Cottage,Englefield Green,Surrey with them were children John 14,Reginald 13,Stanley 6 and Cedric aged 3. Alfred was a Domestic Gardener as was his son John who was an Under Gardener(Domestic).

Death Certificates:

Alfred Belchamber died on the 2nd January, 1955 at 50 Victoria Street, Englefield Green, Surrey he was 84 years of age and a retired Gardener. He died of Coronary Thrombosis and Arteria Sclerosis which was certified by Dr.W G R Branch. The death was registered by registrar H Mayted on the 3rd of January. His son Reginald was informant of 25 Victoria Street, Englefield Green.

Sarah Jane Belchamber aged 88 of 50 Victoria Street,Englefield Green died on the 20th of January,1961.Cause of death was Cerebral Haemorhage certified by S A Williams MRCS. Sarah Jane was recorded as the widow of Alfred Belchamber a Gardener. She died at The Grange,St.Annes Hill,Chertsey,Surrey. A M Venton the occupier was informant. The registrar for Walton and Chertsey registered the death on the 20th of January.

Alfred Belchamber and Sarah Jane Hawkins had the following children:

i   John William Belchamber was born on the 24th June,1896 in The
         Common,Dunsfold,Surrey. He died on the 26th March,1916 in Egypt.

Birth Certificate:

John William Alfred Belchamber was born to Alfred and Sarah Jane on the 24th of June 1896 at"The Common"Dunsfold,Surrey the birth was registered on the 13th July by Charlotte Walder the Deputy Registrar for Hambledon in Surrey. Father Alfred was a Domestic Gardener by trade.

Death Certificate:

John William Alfred Belchamber died aged 20,he was"killed in action" in Egypt on the 26th of March 1917.
T/201121 Private John William Alfred Belchamber was aged 20 when he was killed in action. John W A of the Royal Sussex Regiment 4th Bn Commonwealth War Dead is buried in Jerusalem Memorial panels 26/27.

Private John W.A Belchamber of The Royal Sussex Regiment service no 4/3558,201121 was awarded the Victory Medal and The British War Medal.(Citation/roll e/2/101b15.PAGE 3177) during WW1

ii   Reginald Clonard Leslie Belchamber was born on the 3rd March,1898 in The
         Common,Dunsfold,Surrey. He died on the 10th November,1967 in Ashford
         Hospital,Stanwell. He married Elsie Caister Beauchamp on the 5th
         November,1921 in St.Marys Church,Staines,Middlesex. She was born on the
         17th July,1897 in Staines. She died on the 12th October,1970 in 26 Victoria
         Street,Englefield Green,Surrey.

iii   Stanley Aubrey Alec Belchamber was born on the 18th September,1904 in
         Northcroft Cottage,Englefield Green,Surrey. He died on the 2nd June,1999 in
         Westmorland General Hospital,Kendal,Cumbria. He married Marjorie Violet
         Crane on the 30th January,1932 in The Church of

St.Michaels,Highgate,Middlesex. She was born on the 13th April,1906 and died on the 27th January,1978 in 17 Torrington Road,Berkhamstead.

iv   Cedric Cecil Guy Belchamber was born on the 10th September,1907 in Northcroft Cottage,Englefield Green,Surrey. He died on the 18th May,1997 in Surbiton Hospital,Surbiton,Surrey. He married Marion Harris on the 1st August,1938 in The Baptist Church,Church Road,Teddington,Middlesex. She was born on the 7th September,1905 in Teddington. She died on the 13th May,1992 in Itchingfield,Sussex.

Walter Charles Belchamber
(William11,James10,James9,William8,Edward7,Edward6,John5,Thomas3,Robert3,Robert2,John1) was born on the 15th July,1877 in Plaistow,Sussex. He died on the 7th October,1946 in St.James Place,Cranleigh,Surrey. He married Alice Winifred Carpenter on the 12th April,1904 in The Registry Office,Guildford,Surrey. She was born in 1885 and died on the 24th October,1965 in Cranleigh Village Hospital, Cranleigh,Surrey.

Birth Certificate:
Walter Charles Belchamber was born in 1877 on July 15th in Plaistow,Sussex. Father William was a Agricultral Labourer. The birth was registered by George Brookfield Registrar on the 16th of August.

Marriage Certificate:
Alice Carpenter and Charles Belchamber(He did not use Walter on the marriage licence) married at the Registry Office Guildford on the 13th of April,1904. Bachelor Charles was listed as a Gardener aged 24 and Alice a spinster aged 19 with no occupation listed. Witness's were William H Emery and Edward Stent.

Death Certificates:
Charles Walter Belchamber a 69 year old retired Taxi Driver died at St.James Place,Cranleigh,Surrey on the 7th of October,1946. Cause of death was. Myocarditis, arteriosclerosis and a Chronis Septic Ulcer certified by M B Kettlewell MB. His son Victor C Belchamber was informant of Fernhurst,Mead Road,Cranleigh. Jack Elliott the registrar for Surrey South Western recorded the death on the 7th of October.

Alice Winifred Belchamber,80 of Elstow St.James Place,Cranleigh died at the Cranleigh Village Hospital on the 24th of October 1965. Cause of death was Cardio Vascular Degeneration,Arterio Silerosis and Severe Anaesnia which was certified by F B Knight MB. Alice Winifred was listed as the widow of Walter Charles Belchamber a Taxi Driver.Victor Charles Belchamber of 5 Glebe Road,Cranleigh her son was informant. The death was recorded on the 25th of October by G K Swabey the registrar for Surrey S W.

Census:
In 1911 Charles aged 32 and 28 year old Alice were living at Mill Cottage,Dunsfold,Surrey,Charles was a Gardener Domestic. With them were their children Nester 6,Victor 5 and Jack aged 2.

Walter Charles Belchamber and Alice Winifred Carpenter had the following children:

i   Lois Nesta Belchamber was born on the 1st September,1904 in 3 Dene Street,Dorking,Surrey. She married Thomas Joseph Peters on the 26th May,1928 in The Registry Office,Windsor,Berkshire.Lois and Thomas divorced at some point.
She married James Edward Goldfinch on the 26th May,1944 in The Registry Office,Lambeth.

Birth Certificate:
Lois Nesta Belchamber was born in No.3 Dene Street,Dorking on the 1st of September,1904. Father Charles Walter was a Domestic Gardener,he was living at The Mill,Dunsfold. The birth was registered on the 18th of October by William Alloway registrar for Dorking.

Marriage Certificate:
Thomas Joseph Peters aged 22 and a bachelor his occupation was as a Coal Carter married Lois Nesta Belchamber on the 26th of May,1928 at The Registry Office,Windsor. Lois Nesta was 23 years old and a spinster with no occupation of Wall House,Eton College her father Charles Walter was a Motor Driver. Charles Alfred Peters was a Labourer of 3 Merrit Meadows,Egham Hill. Witness were S K French and Charles A Peters. Registrar William Harvey Bennett performed the ceremony.

29 year old bachelor James Edward Goldfinch a corporal in The Duke of Cornwalls light infantry(Groom) service no 544225 married Lois Nesta Peters formerly Belchamber on the 26th of May,1944 at the registry office,Lambeth by licence. Both gave their abode as 309 Kennington Road,SE11.Lois Nesta aged 39 was listed as the divorced wife of Thomas Joseph Peters. Witness's were M Goldfinch and A Goldfinch. Fathers were John Thomas Goldfinch a General Labourer and Charles Walter Belchamber a Garage Proprietor. The ceremony was performed by Acting Registrar PJ Gunn and Superintendent Registrar W C Best.

ii   Victor Charles Belchamber was born on the 2nd January,1906 in Mill Cottage,Dunsfold,Surrey. He died on the 7th February,1995 in Cranleigh Village Hospital,Cranleigh,Surrey. He married Gwendolin Marjorie Killick on the 29th April,1933 in Ewhurst,Surrey. She was born on the 27th June,1908 in Sutton,Surrey. She died on the 13th January,1994 in 21 Parsonage Road,Cranleigh,Surrey.

iii   Jack Belchamber was born on the 26th July,1908 in Mill Cottage,Dunsfold,Surrey. He died on the 12th June,1943 in North Africa. He married Nellie Elizabeth Howick on the 17th November,1929 in The Registry Office,Guildford,Surrey. She was born on the 17th April,1909 in Ellens Green,Rudgwick,Sussex and died on the 20th April,2000 in Honeywood House,Rowhook,Horsham.

Jack Belchamber and Nellie Elizabeth Howick had two children one of whom is deseased and the other is living.

William James Belchamber
(William11,James10,James9,William8,Edward7,Edward6,John5,Thomas3,Robert3,Robert2,John1) was born on the 19th April,1881 in Plaistow,Sussex. He died on the 28th November,1945 in Ivy Cottage,Wisborough Green,Sussex. He married Kate Pennicard on the 2nd April,1904 in Kirdford,Sussex. She was the daughter of James Pennicard and Jane Stemp,born in 1879. She died on the 5th February,1961 in 8 Butts Mead,Wisborough Green,Sussex.

The records from the Post Office show that William James Belchamber Postman number 181833 was moved from Wisborough Green to Alfold in April,1901.In 1912 he was back in Wisborough Green.

Birth Certificate:
William James Belchamber born 19th April,1881 and registered by George Brookfield Registrar on the 29th May. Father William was a Farm Labourer. The birth took place in Plaistow,Sussex.

Marriage Certificate:
William James Belchamber married Kate Pennicard at Kirdford on the 2nd of April 1904,William aged 22 was a Postman and Kate aged 24 had no occupation listed,their witness`s were Joseph John and Jane Pennicard with Erskine A Burrell the Vicar. Their fathers were William Belchamber a Labourer and James Pennicard a Sawyer.

In the 1911 census William James and Kate were living in Wisborough Green,Sussex. William James was 29 and a Postman,Kate was 31 living with them was their Daughter Lorna Irene Kate 5 and William Whiting aged 26 a Grocers Assistant.

Death Certificates:
William James aged 64 and a postman by profession died of Heart Failure on the 28th of November 1945 at Ivy Cottage,Wisborough Green,Sussex. His son James was informant the death was registered on the 29th.James gave his address as Church Cottage,Stopham,Pulborough.

Private William James Belchamber of the Royal Army Medical Corp. number 80792 was awarded the Victory Medal and The British War Medal during WW1(Citation/roll ramc/101b105,page 8108)

Kate died in number 8 Butts Meadow,Wisborough Green,Sussex. She was 81 years old and listed as widow of William James Belchamber a Postman. Her daughter Lorna Cheeseman of 26 Butts Meadow was informant and present at death. Kate died of heart failure and Myacardial Degeneration certified by W A Kelsey MD. The death was registered by A F Weiry the Registrar on the 7th February in Midhurst and Petworth District.

A story told to me by Cherry Smith

Kate Belchamber nee Pennicard her grandmother would not buy tiolet tissue,she used the tissue paper that fruiterers used to wrap oranges in. This she got from the fruiterers in Horshan Market who saved it up for her.

William James Belchamber and Kate Pennicard had the following children:

i   Lorna Irene Kate Belchamber was born on the 11th October,1905 in Pound Common,Kirdford,Sussex. She died in 1983. She married Reginald Cheeseman on the 18th June,1921.

ii   James Archibald Rudolf Belchamber was born on the 28th June,1916 in Wisborough Green .He died on the 24th May,1985 in 10 Church Cottage,Stopham,Sussex. He married Daisy Grace White on the 29th March,1937 in Stopham,Sussex. She was born on the 2nd December,1908 in Storrington,Sussex. She died on the 20th February,1991 in St.Leonards Hospital,St.Leonards.

Edgar Reginald Belchamber
(Alice11,John10,Edward9,William8,Edward7,Edward6,John5,Thomas4,Robert3,Robert2,John1) was born on the 26th November,1896 in 8 Meadow Brook Road,Dorking,Surrey. He died on the 9th August,1963 in 44 Hale Road,Farnham,Surrey. He married Mary Jane Wakeford on the 6th September,1922 in Kirdford,Sussex. She was born on the 2nd September,1901 in Petworth,Sussex and died on the 16th April,1980 in The Spinney,Reading Road South,Church Crookham.

Birth Certificate:
Alice Belchamber gave birth to a son Edgar Reginald Belchamber in 1896
Edgar Reginald Belchamber was born at 8 Meadow Brook Road,Dorking,Surrey on the 26th of November 1896. No father was recorded,Alice his mother was a Domestic Servant (Housemaid). George Alloway the registrar for Dorking recorded the birth on the 22nd of December.

Marriage Certificate:
Edgar Reginald Belchamber married Mary Jane Wakeford in the parish church,Kirdford on the 6th of September,1922. Edgar was a bachelor aged 25 and a Bakers Assistant,while Mary Jane was a spinster aged 21 with no occupation listed. Witness's were John Wakeford and John Milton. Erskine A Burrells performed the marriage. Mary Jane's father was David Wakeford a Farmer from Butcherlands Farm,Ebernoe,Sussex.

Death Certificates:
Edgar Reginald Belchamber aged 66 died at 44 Hale Road,Farnham,Surrey on the 9th of August,1963. Cause of death was 1a Carcinoma of Stomach certified by E H Roussouny MRCS. Owen Caligan son-in-law was informant of 17 The Glade,Stoneleigh,the death was registered on the 10th of August by B Dewey deputy registrar for Surrey South Western. Edgar's address at the time of death was 3 Woodland Grove,Farnborough, he was listed as a master Grocer.

On the 16th of April,1980 Mary Jane Belchamber passed away at The Spinney,Reading Road South,Church Crookham. Cause of death was Bronchopneumonia and Senile Dementia certified by D Lennox Scott MRCS. Listed as the widow of Edgar Reginald Belchamber a Grocer of 3 Caster Court,Church Crookham,Hants. Her daughter June Hazel Parson of 34 Grove Road,Church Crookham was informant. Deputy Registrar M R Lawrence registered the death for N E Hampshire on the 16th of April.

Private Edgar Belchamber service number 128493 of The Machine Gun Corp. was awarded the Victory Medal and the British War Medal during WW1.(Citation/Roll mgc101b79,page 6280)

Edgar Reginald Belchamber and Mary Jane Wakeford had the following children:

i   Vera Alice Mary Belchamber was born on the 29th June,1922 in 42 Lumley Road,Horley,Surrey. She married Frank Curley on the 20th July,1945 in The Parish Church,Aldershot,Hampshire.

Birth Certificate:
Edgar and Mary Jane's daughter Vera Alice Mary Belchamber was born at 42 Lumley Road,Horley,Surrey on the 29th of June 1922. Her father was Edgar Reginald Belchamber a Baker's Assistant of The Village,Kirdford,Sussex. Mary Jane Wakeford the mother was a shop assistant(Grocers) from Butcherland Farm,Kirdford,Sussex as per declaration dated 27th of July. The birth was registered by W J March the Registrar for Reigate,Surrey.

Marriage Certificate:
Vera Alice Mary Belchamber a spinster aged 23 and Frank Curley a soldier aged 28 and a bachelor were married on the 20th of July,1945 at the Parish Church,Aldershot. Frank was from 11 Harrington Street,Worksop and Vera was living at the Imperial Standard,Aldershot where her father Edgar was a Licence Victualler. Witness's were Mr L Knupp and M Walsh. The vicar J B Rowsell performed the ceremony. Franks father was William Fabery Curley a Miner.

ii   June Hazel Belchamber was born on the 1st June,1934 in 1 Creamery Cottages,Kirdford,Sussex. She married Brian Thomas Parsons on the 19th September,1956 in Christ Church,Church Crookham.Hampshire.

Birth Certificate:
Edgar and Mary Janes second daughter June Hazel Belchamber was born at 1 Creamery Cottages,Kirdford on the 1st of June,1934. Father Edgar Reginald Belchamber was a Milk Lorry Driver and mother Mary Jane Belchamber were living at the same address. The birth was registered on the 28th of June.

Marriage Certificate:
Brian Thomas Parsons a bachelor aged 24 and a Farm Worker married June Hazel Belchamber a 22 year old spinster and Secretary in the Christ Church in Crookham,Southampton County. Brian's father Fred Parsons was a Farmer and Edgar,June;s father a Shopkeeper. Witness's were P Valleley and E N Lee.Brain was

living at 225 Aldershot Road,Church Crookham and June at 3 Woodland Ave.Farnborough.

Bernard John Hugh Belchamber
(JohnWilliam11,John10,Edward9,William8,Edward7,Edward6,John5,Thomas4,Robert3,Robert2,John1) was born on the 13th June,1912 in 11 Brook Road,Chiswick. He died on the 4th January,1996 in Richmond upon Thames. He married Ethel Marjory Guy on the 3rd July,1937 in The Parish Church,Twickenham,Middlesex. She was born on the 20th November,1913 in Twickenham and died on the 11th January,1997.

Birth Certificate:
Bernard John Hugh Belchamber was born at 11 Brook Road,Chiswick the family home on the 13th of June 1912. John William Belchamber his father was a Chauffeur and Jane Elizabeth his mother was listed as late Pearson formerly Nunn. The birth was registered by J B I Baker registrar for Brentford.

Marriage Certificate:
24 year old bachelor and Linotype Operator Bernard John Hugh Belchamber of Garage Cottage,Old Palace Lane,Richmond married Ethel Marjorie Guy a 23 year old spinster and Hairdresser of 69 Kenly Road,East Twickenham on the 3rd of July,1937 in the parish church,East Twickenham. Witness's were Jack Edward Guy and John William Belchamber. Russell B White the vicar performed the marriage. Their fathers were John William Belchamber a Chauffeur and Edward Seacham Guy a Civil Servant.

Death Certificates:
Bernard John Hugh Belchamber born 13th June 1912 died on the 4th of January 1996 at the Memorial Hospital,Hampton Road,Teddington. Bernard J H was a retired Linotype Operator of 36 Craneford Way,Twickenham. His Daughter was in formant and present at death. Cause of death was 1) Carcinoma Prostate and Metaplastic Anaemia which was certified by Diana J M Lister MB. Death was registered on the 5th of January by Brenda A Killingbeck at Richmond Upon Thames.

On the 11 of January 1997 Ethel Marjory Belchamber passed away at the West Middlesex Hospital,Isleworth. Cause of death was Congestive Cardiac Failure,Atrial Fibrillation and Chest Infection certified by M Jackson MB. Listed as the widow of Bernard John Hugh Belchamber Linotype Operator(Retired) of 56 Craneford Way,Twickenham,Middlesex. Her daughter was the informant. Eleanor M Griffith the registrar for Hounslow recorded the death on the 13th of January.

Generation 13

John Richard Belchamber
(John12,John11,Edward10,Edward9,Edward8,Edward7,Edward6,John5,Thomas4,Robert3,Robert2,John1) was born on the 24th July,1885 in 83 New Church Street,Bermondsey,London. He died on the 21st May,1963 in Wokingham Hospital,Wokingham,Berkshire.
He married Amy Nellie Allen Wilkie on the 25th December,1910 in The Parish Church,Aldersgate. She died on the 12th March,1927 in Charing Cross Hospital,London.

He later married Phyliss Louise Holloway on the 4th July,1931 in St.Johns Church,Walthamstow. She was born on the 15th January,1893 in Stoke Newington.London. She died in Weald House Nursing Home,St.Neots,Huntingdon.

Birth Certificate:
John Richard Belchamber came into this world on the 24th of July,1885 in 83 New Church St.Bermondsey. John Belchamber his father was a Grocer's Porter and Elizabeth Ann his mother was formerly Mansfield. W G Hurst Registrar for Southwark recorded the birth on the 13th Of August,George Edward Belchamber and John Richard Belchamber were twins.

Marriage Certificate:Amy Nellie Allen Wilkie
John Richard Belchamber a 25 year old bachelor and Shop Assistant married Amy Nellie Allen Wilkie a 21 year old spinster on the 25th of December,1910 at the parish church,Aldersgate. Witness's were Samuel Carver and Margaret Cox and Maud Belchamber. C O Becker performed the service.Both were living in 85 Aldergate Street. Their fathers were John Belchamber a Tea Merchant and Thomas William Allen deceased.

Death Certificate:Amy Nellie Allen Belchamber
Amy Nellie Belchamber aged 38 died at Charing Cross,Hospital on the 12th of March 1927. Cause of death was cancer of the breast. She was listed as the wife of John Richard Belchamber of 13 Suffolk Street,Pall Mall a Housekeeper. The death was recorded at St.Martins,The Strand on the 13th of March by W Parkhouse the registrar.

Census:
In the 1911 census John and Amy were in living at 36 Gladsmuir Road,Upper Holloway,Highgate. John was aged 25 and a Commissionaire Theatre Attendant and Amy was aged 21.

John Richard Belchamber and Amy Nellie Allen Wilkie had the following children:

i   John Alan Belchamber was born on the 12th May,1912 in 369 Alexandra Park Road,Wood Green.He died in 1998. He married Victoria Garais on the 13th December,1938 in The Registry Office,Willesden,Middlesex. She died on the 22nd October,1944 in 160 Cromwell Road,Kensington.
        He later married Hilda May Brunsdon on the 14th July,1945 in Swindon,Witshire. She was born in 1902 and died in Stoke on the 28th July,1985.
        John Alan Belchamber and Ingeborg Frieda Dorothee Siegert were married probably early 1900's in Gibraltar. She died in Stafford in 1997.

To date I cannot find information on the marriage of John Alan and Ingeborg,I have been told it probably took place in Gibraltrar late 1980's early 1990's.
John Alan died in Estapona,Spain on the 18th February,1998.

ii   Maisie Belchamber was born on the 19th April,1920 in Middlesex Hospital. She married Clarence Jus Von Hoffman on the 3rd January,1942 in The Parish Church,Canvey Island,Essex.

Birth Certificate:
Maisie Belchamber was born at the Middlesex Hospital on the 19th of April 1920.G
H Basset recorded the birth on the 22nd of April for St.Marylebone. Her father was
John Richard Belchamber a Commissionaire(ex army of Westminister). Maisie's
mother was Amy Nellie formerly Allen of 13 Suffolk Street,Westminister.

Marriage Certificate:
Maisie Belchamber and Clarence Jus Von Hoffman married in the parish church
Canvey Island,Essex on the 3rd of January 1942. Clarence was a 35 year old bachelor
in the RAF,and Maisie was 21 a spinster with no occupation given. Witness's
were John Richard Belchamber,Mary Benning and Von Hoffman. The fathers were
John Richard Belchamber a Glass Writer and Clarence Von Hoffman a Jeweller. A W
Swallow the vicar performed the service. Clarence's address at the time of the
marriage was 7 Middleton Drive,Joel Street,Pinner,Middlesex,Maisie was living at
Sunnycliff,May Avenue,Canvey Island,Essex.

Marriage Certificate:Phyliss Louise Holloway
John Richard Belchamber and Phyliss Louise Holloway married at the parish church
St.Johns Walthamstow on the 4th of July 1931 by banns.John Richard was aged 46 a
widower and Telephone Operator. Phyliss Louise was a spinster aged 38 with no
occupation. Both gave their abode as 12 Walthamstow
Avenue,Walthamstow. Witness's were Alfred H Holloway and Sidney John
Kingsley. The fathers were John Richard Belchamber,retired and Harry
Holloway(Deceased) a Glass Driller. The curate Fred.E Lownds performed the
marriage.

Death Certificates:
John Richard Belchamber age 77 died on the 21st May 1963 at Wokingham Hospital,
Wokingham. Cause of death was (1) Recurrent Cerebro Vascular Accidents (2)
Cerebral Arteries Valerious which was certified by Ian W Kerr MB. John Richard was
a retired Glass Writer of 55 Barkham Ride,Wokingham. P L Belchamber his widow
was informant. K Pointon the registrar recorded the death for Wokingham on the 22nd
May.

Phyliss Louisa Belchamber died on the 20th of February,1988 at Weald House
Nursing Home,St.Neots,Huntingdon of Coronary Thrombosis,Arterio Soleroris and
Rheumatiod Arthritis which was certified by T Lyle LRCPvS. The informant was her
daughter-in-law Laurie Eleanor Constance Belchamber of The White House,Hatfield
Heath,Bishops Stortford,Herts. Listed as the widow of John Richard Belchamber a
Signwriter her death was registered on the 22nd of February at Huntingdon,Cambs.

John Richard Belchamber and Phyliss Louise Holloway had the following child:

i   Peter Richard Belchamber was born on the 27th March,1932 in 91 Falmouth
         Avenue,West Ham. He died on the 3rd November,2011. He married Laurie
         Eleanor Constance Acres on the 11th September,1954 in Epping,Essex.

Birth Certificate:
Peter Richard Belchamber was born at 91 Falmouth Avenue,Walthamstow on the
27th of March,1932. His father was John Richard Belchamber a Telephone Operator

of 12 Walthamstow Avenue,Phyllis Louise Belchamber formerly Holloway was the mother of the same address. The birth was registered on the 28th of April.

Marriage Certificate:
22 Year Old Bachelor Peter Richard Belchamber a Solictor's Clerk married 28 year old spinster Laurie Eleanor Constance Acres by banns on the 11th of September,1954 at the parish church,Chingford,Essex. Peter Richard was living at 75 Dale View Avenue,Chingford and Laurie Eleanor at 245 Old Church Road again in Chingford. Witness's were John Richard Belchamber and Daisy Grace Acres. The fathers were John Richard Belchamber a Glass Writer and Bob Acres,retired. J.T.D Davis the assistant priest took the service.

Death Details
Peter Richard Belchamber died on the 3rd of November,2011. He was cremated at The Hastings Crematorium on the 18th November.

William Robert Belchamber
(Edward12,John11,Edward10,Edward9,Edward8,Edward7,Edward6,John5,Thomas4, Robert3,Robert2,John1) was born on the 31st March,1889 in 21 Collett Road,Bermondsey,London. He died on the 13th October,1976 in 32 Ullswater Road,Sompting,Sussex. He married Jessie Morris on the 3rd August,1913 in St.Alban,Holborn. She was born on the 27th November,1892,she died on the 29th March,1979 in Torbay Hospital,Torquay,Devon.

Birth Certificate:
Born on the 31st of March 1889 at 21 Collett Road,Bermondsey,William Robert Belchamber was the son of Edward and Alice Belchamber nee Saunders. Edward Belchamber the father was a Cellarman of 21 Collett Road. The birth was recorded on the 29th of April at St.Olave,Southwark by W J Hurst the registrar.

Marriage Certificate:
William Robert Belchamber and Jessie Morris married by banns on the 3rd of August 1913 at the parish church of St.Alban,Holborn,London.they were both 24 years of age. William Robert was a bachelor and Compositer by trade of 69 Cavendish Buildings. Jessie Morris had no occuption she lived at 49 Grays Inn Buildings. Witness's were Robert and Elizabeth Morris. Their parents were Edward Belchamber a Wine Merchant and Robert Morris a Tailor. The service was performed by the curate E F Russell.

Death Certificates:
Jessie Belchamber aged 86 died of congestive heart failure and myocardial infarction and right femur neck which was certified by Ya Tsai Hsing MB on the 29th of March,1979 at Torbay Hospital,Torquay,Devon. Jessie was listed as the widow of William Robert Belchamber a retired Compositor of 32 Ullswater Road,Lancing,Sussex. The informant was her daughter Phyliss Jessica Daniel of Greynote,Daddyhole Road,Torquay,Devon. W M Wotton the deputy registrar for Torbay,Devon recorded the death on the 30th of March.

William Robert Belchamber a retired Compositer aged 87 died at 32 Ullswater Road,Sompting,Sussex on the 13th of October 1976. Cause of death was Coronary Occlusion,Athero Sclerosis and Osteo Arthritis which was certified by J O Peskett MB. His son Ronald Edward Charles Belchamber was informant of 39 Rowan Way,Rottingdean,Sussex. The registrar E D M Tidmarsh recorded the death on the 13th of October in Worthing,Sussex

William Robert Belchamber and Jessie Morris had the following children:

i   William Robert Belchamber was born on the 11th December,1914 in Camberwell. He died on the 22nd September,1986 in The Royal Surrey County Hospital,Guildford,Surrey. He married Dorothy Emma Greenwood on the 24th December,1938 in The Parish Church,Beckinham,Kent.

ii   Ronald Edward Charles Belchamber was born on the 7th December,1920 in Greenwich. He died on the 11th March,2005 in The Royal Sussex Hospital,Brighton, East Sussex. He married Constance Gertrude Stratton on the 22nd May,1948 in The Parish Church,Beckinham,Kent.
He later married Dorothy Phoebe Dack on the 19th May,1973 in Brighton. She was born on the 15th May,1920 in Norwich,Norfolk. She died in Copper Cliff,Redhill Drive,Brighton.

Birth Certificate:
William Robert and Jessie Belchamber's son Ronald Edward Charles Belchamber was born on the 7th of December 1920 at 9 Casella Road. His father was listed as a Compositer. The birth was recorded by C S Seaman the registrar for Greenwich on the 10th December.

Marriage Certificate:Constance Gertrude Stratton.
Ronald Edward Charles Belchamber a 27 year old bachelor and Clerk married 27 year old Constance Gertrude Stratton a widow on the 22nd of May,1948 by banns,the service took place in the parish church of St.George,Beckenham,Kent. Ronald Edward Charles gave his address as 26 Church Avenue,Beckenham,Kent and Constance Gertrude as 10 Westwood Road,Bexhill,Kent. Their witness's were the fathers William Robert Belchamber a Compositor and George Edward Butler Retired. B Montague Dale the rector performed the ceremony.

Marriage Certificate:Dorothy Phoebe Dack.
Ronald Edward Charles Belchamber and Dorothy Phoebe Belchamber formerly Dack were married in the Register Office Brighton on the 19th of May 1973. Both were aged 52 and both their previous marriages had been dissolved,Ronald was a Bank Official,both were living at 39 Rowan Way,Rottingdean. Witness's were T D Wooley and R H Manser. Their fathers were William Robert Belchamber a retired Compositor and Robert George Dack a deceased Bricklayer. F J Crook the registrar performed the ceremony.

Death Certificates:
Ronald Edward Charles Belchamber died on the 11th of March,2005 at the Royal Sussex Hospital,Brighton. Cause of death was Acute Cardiac Failure,Acute

Myocardial Infarction,Ischaemic Heart Disease and Generalised Atherosclerosis with a Fractured left Femur.Early Brochopneumonia. Which was certified by V Hamilton-Deeley for Brighton and Hove after a post mortem without inquest. Ronald was a retired Bank Clerk of 39 Rowan Way,Rottingdean,Brighton. The informant was his step-daughter Lesley Stace of 6 Whitehawk Way,Brighton.

Ronald Edward Charles Belchamber service number 6346081 of The Infantry and Army Physical Training Corps. was a POW in Stalag XX-B Malbork,Poland his POW number was 1502.

Dorothy Phoebe Belchamber died on the 14th of April,1988 at Copper Cliff,Redhill Drive,Brighton,East Sussex.The cause of death was Cerebral Metalases,Carcinoma Right Breast(Excised 1971) which were certified by J M Kay MB. Date and place of birth were given as 15th May,1920 at Norwich,Norfolk.She was listed as the wife of Ronald Edward Charles Belchamber a retired Bank Clerk of 39 Rowan Way,Brighton who was also the informant.

iii   Phyliss Jessie Belchamber was born on the 1st July,1924 in Greenwich. She
          married John D J Roberts on the 12th April,1947 in Bromley,Kent.

Birth Certificate:
Phyliss Jessie Belchamber was born at 56 Upper Brockley Road,Deptford on the 1st of July 1924. Her father William Robert Belchamber was a Printers Compositor and her mother was Jessie Belchamber formerly Morris. The birth was registered on the 15th of July by the registrar M A White for Greenwich district.

Marriage Certificate;
John David Jendon Roberts and Phyliss Jessie Belchamber were married on the 12th of April,1947 at the parish church of St.George in Beckenham,Kent by banns. John was a bachelor aged 21 and a Manufacturer,while Phyliss was 22,a spinster and Secretary. Witness's were the fathers Edwin Fermot Roberts a manufacturer and William Robert Belchamber a Compositor. John gave his residence as 12 Singlewell Road,Gravesend and Phyliss was living at 26 Church Avenue,Beckenham. The ceremony was performed by R Mayer.

Charles John Belchamber
(CharlesJohn12,John11,Edward10,Edward9,Edward8,Edward7,Edward6,John5,Thomas4,Robert3,Robert2,John1) was born on the 21st May,1883 in 62 Newton Street,Old Hoxton Town,Shoreditch,London. He died on the 9th February,1946 on 20 Hope Street,Halifax,Yorkshire. He married Annie Elizabeth Walker on the 2nd October,1915 in The Registry Office,Halifax,Yorkshire. She was born on the 6th February,1887 in Kimberley,Nottinghamshire. She died on the 7th March,1961 in The Royal Infirmary,Halifax.

Birth Certificate:
At 62 Newton Street,Old Hoxton Town,Shoreditch Elizabeth Phillis Belchamber gave birth to Charles John Belchamber on the 21st of May,1883,Charles John's father also Charles John Belchamber was a Wine Porter. George Pearce the registrar for Shoreditch recorded the birth on the 25th of June.

Marriage Certificate:
On the 2nd of October,1915 at the Registry Office in Halifax,Yorkshire Charles Belchamber and Annie Elizabeth Walker were married.Charles(He had dropped the John) was a 32 year old bachelor and Clerk Warehouseman,Annie Elizabeth was a spinster aged 28 and a Worsted Spinner both were living at 4 Nelson Street,Halifax. Their witness's were George J Verity and Catherine O'Shea. The father's were Charles John Belchamber a Plate Glass Warehouseman and Harry Walker a General Labourer(Deceased). Registrar Fred Jagger performed the wedding.

Note for Annie Elizabeth Walker:
Annie Elizabeth was born Ada Elizabeth Walker on the 6th of February,1887 in Kimberley,Nottinghamshire. Her father was Henry Walker and her mother was Eliza formerly Richards. The birth was registered on the 15th March in the district of Basford,Nottinghamshire.

Death Certificates:
Charles Belchamber jnr aged 62 died at 20 Hope Street,Halifax,Yorkshire on the 9th of February,1946.J McCowan certified cause of death as Syncope,Congestive Heart Failure and Acute Bronchitis. Annie E Belchamber his wife was present at death and informant. The death was registered in Halifax by P P Mitchell Interim Registrar on the 9th February. Charle's occupation was a Wool Warehouseman. Again Charles has dropped the John as he did when he married

On the 7th of March,1961 at the Royal Halifax Infirmary,Halifax Annie Elizabeth Belchamber passed away,cause of death was Carcinoma Colon and Broncho Pueumonia,which was certified by Sued Iftikhar Ali M.B. Annie Elizabeth was 75 years of age and the widow of Charles Belchamber a Woollen Percher,home address was 10 Vickerman Street,Halifax. The informant was a daughter E M Hartley of 20 Hammond Street,Halifax. The death was registered in Halifax by Frank Mallinson the registrar on the 7th of March.

Charles John Belchamber and Annie Elizabeth Walker adopted the following child;

i   May Elizabeth Belchamber was born on the 5th August,1919.

William Henry Belchamber
(CharlesJohn12,John11,Edward10,Edward9,Edward8,Edward7,Edward6,John5,Thomas4,Robert3,Robert2,John1) was born on the 20th August,1886 in 309 Kingland Road,West Hackney,London. He died on the 27th January,1945 in Mackayville,Quebec,Canada. He married Marie Therrien on the 23rd June,1906 in St.Damien,Bedford,Comte Missisquoi,Quebec. She was the daughter of Louis Henri Therrien and Edwidge Chausse.

He later married Marie Alice Marguerite Guillet on the 2nd April,1918 in Ste.Elisabeth Du Portuga,she was the daughter of Philias Guillette and Alphonsine Rheaume.

Birth Certificate:
William Henry Belchamber was born on the 20th of August,1886 in 309 Kingsland,West Hackney. His father Charles John Belchamber was a Wine Porter and

his mother Elizabeth Phillis formerly Potter. The birth was registered on the 11th October by the registrar G R Thepioay.

William Henry Belchamber and Marie Therrien had the following children:

i   Louis Henri Belchamber was born on the 12th April,1906 in Bedford, Comte Missisquoi,Quebec. He died on the 30th December,1968 in Ste.Martine,Comte Chateauquay,Quebec. He married Gemaine Latour on the 24th April,1928 in St.Pauls,Montreal,the daughter of Alexis Latour and Charloote Lapierre.

ii   Victoria Elizabeth Anna Belchamber was born on the 4th February,1911 in St.Jean Sur Richelieu,Quebec. She died there on the 5th September,1911.

iii   Joseph Pierre Armand Belchamber was born on the 6th April,1912 in St.Jean Sur Richelieu,Quebec. He died there on the 3rd January,1917.
Joseph Pierre Fedore Armand Belchamber was baptisted at Cathedrale St.Jean L'Evangeliste on the 8th April,1912 and was buried on the 4th January,1917 at Cimetiere St.Jean L'Evangeliste.

iv   Cecile Blance Clara Belchamber was born on the 26th July,1913 in St.Jean Sur Richelieu,Quebec

v   Anonyme Belchamber was born on the 1st August,1915 in St.Jean Sur Richelieu,Quebec. He died later that day and was buried on the 3rd August,1915 in Cimetiere St.Jean L'Evangeliste.

Charles Frederick Belchamber
(Frederick12,James10,James10,James9,William8,Edward7,Edward6,John5,Thomas4, Robert3,Robert2,John1) was born on the 19th May,1896 in Chuter Cottages,Lion Lane,Shottermill,Surrey. He died on the 4th December,1954 in 48 Selwood Road,Woking,Surrey. He married Elizabeth Bridget Power on the 21st January,1920 in The Church of Aughrim,Dublin,Eire. She was born on the 25th October,1896 in Ireland the daughter of Patrick Power and Bridget Lynch. She died on the 6th July,1992 in St.Peters Hospital,Chertsey,Surrey.

Birth Certificate:
Frederick and Jane Belchamber's only son Charles Frederick Belchamber was born in Shottermill,Frensham,Surrey on the 19th of May 1896. His father Frederick Belchamber was a General Labourer. The birth was registered on the 29th of May in Farnham,Surrey. Jane Belchamber formerly Baker was the mother of Shottermill,Frensham.

Marriage Certificate:
Charles Frederick Belchamber a bachelor married Elizabeth Power a spinster in Dublin, Ireland on the 21st January.1920 in the Catholic Church of Aughrim Street No 3 North City district. Witness`s were John Power and Annie Power. There was no occupation for Elizabeth and Charles was a Sergeant in the 3rd Btn.Worcestershire Regiment. Charles and Elizabeth were both of full age. Father's occupations were Frederick Belchamber a Gardener and Patrick Power was a Cattle Drover.

Death Certificates:
Charles Frederick Belchamber died at 48 Selwood Road,Woking aged 58 of Milignant Hypertension which was certified by J.B.Cargin MB and registered at Woking by S W Cooke on the 6th of December. The informant was his Daughter.His occupation was Omnibus Driver.

Elizabeth Belchamber aged 95 died in St.Peters Hospital,Chertsey,Surrey on the 6th of July 1992. Cause of death was Acute Bronchitis,Cerebral Infraction and Carcinoma of the Rectum certified by M J Clement Burgess Coroner for Surrey after post mortem without inquest. Listed as a Domestic(Retired) and widow of Charles Frederick Belchamber a Bus Driver of 7 Nightingale Court,Inkerman Road,St.Johns,Woking,Surrey.The informant was her son. Registrar M J Cardel Recorded the death on the 8th July for Surrey NW.

Charles Frederick Belchamber and Elizabeth Bridget Power had 6 children of which 5 are still alive to date.

Ivy Alice Belchamber
(George12,James11,James10,James9,William8,Edward7,Edward6,John5,Thomas4,Robert3,Robert2,John1) was born on the 29th August,1895 in The High Street,Petworth,Sussex. She died on the 1973 in Young,Saskatchwen,Canada. She married Roy Steeves on the 9th January,1918 in Chiddingfold,Surrey. He was born on the 19th September,1889. He died on the in Young,Saskatchwen.

Birth Certificate:
Ivy Alice Belchamber was born in the High Street,Petworth,Sussex on the 29th of August,1895. George Belchamber her father was a Blacksmith(Journeyman). Her mother Kate was formerly Horn. The birth was recorded in Petworth on the 26th of September.

Marriage Certificate:
Roy Steeves and Ivy Gladys Belchamber as she called herself then, were married on the 9th of January, 1918 in St.Marys Church; Chiddingfold. Roy was a Canadian soldier who was barracked in Witley Camp while serving in the First World War in the 5th Canadian Division.Roy was aged 28 and Ivy 22 with no occupation listed. Witness's were Kate Belchamber and Ferguson Gladstone Smith. Their fathers were Henry John Steeves a Farmer and George Belchamber an Engineer. C G C Lefroy performed the ceremony.

Roy Steeves and Ivy Alice Belchamber had the following children:

i   Douglas Roy Steeves born 1918 in England

ii   Hazel Ann Steeves born 1923 in Young,Saskatchwen,Canada

iii   George Henry Keith Steeves born 1926 in Young,Saskatchwen,Canada

Family legend says that Roy used to stop and talk to Ivy's father George, where he met her, he liked Ivy but didn't know how to get to ask her out so next day he faked a puncture, so he could take it to Ivy's blacksmith father George to fix, George took Roy home to mend it and, that was his way of meeting Ivy again, and getting up the nerve to ask her out. The Belchamber family was living in Chiddingfold, Surrey at that time.

Roy and Ivy left England in 1919 aboard a troop ship bound for Canada. After letting the troops on board first, it was time for the families, when it was Ivy's turn she was asked if she was Ivy or Gladys Steeves,her heart most probably sank had Roy two wives, but luckily no, there were two Steeves families on board. They landed in Halifax, Nova Scotia, and boarded a train to Nokomis, Saskatchewan where Roy's parents and siblings lived. The Steeves family originally came from New Brunswick, they moved to Nokomis before the First World War and farmed there until Roy's father died in 1935 his mother stayed on until she died in 1943. Roy had seven brothers and five sisters who all fanned out to British Columbia and further south to Carnduff, Saskatchewan and the USA. Before WW1 Roy worked around Watrous,Calgary and south west Alberta where he was logging, he also started a homestead in Oyen,Alberta before he sign up for the army in Calgary. Roy`s parents Henry James(1850-1935) and Alice Lillian(nee Curry)(1859-1943) are both buried in the cemetery in Nokomis

In 1920 Roy and Ivy moved onto their farm 11 miles south of Young, Saskatchewan. For the first year they lived in a granary. They started the farm with the soldier's grant of land it was virgin prairie where only Indians and Buffalo had lived before. Roy and Ivy had three children Douglas Roy born August 30th ,1918 in London,England,Hazel Ann born January 19th,1923 and George Keith born July 2nd,1926 both the latter born on the homestead in Young. By the end of 1923 Ivy's brother Ronald had immigrated to Canada, stayed with them and helped out around the farm, helping to construct the farm buildings, along with Roy, friends and hired help. Ron also helps build the local school at Mornimont, where Doug, Hazel and Keith attended. Families in the district boarded the teachers to cut down on the cost of wages, several stayed with Roy and Ivy over the years.

When Roy and Ivy moved onto the farm they took a team of horses. They grew Wheat, Oats, Barley and Flax.

During the harvest they used a threshing machine; it took a crew to run a threshing rig so farmers in the district helped each other out. Later there were threshing crews who went from farm to farm. Threshing crews were a big chore to the farmer's wives, as they had to feed them three big meals a day, no sandwiches for lunch but three big meals. Crews were up to ten or more men plus a team of at least twelve horses all for the farmer to feed and look after. It was all horsepower until Roy got his first tractor an Oliver 90 in the late 1930`s. It was still horsepower even then, except there used the tractor to power the threshing machine, horses were still used to cut and haul. Roy and Ivy purchased their first combine harvester and Massey Harris in 1945, which cut down the manpower needed to r harvest. In 1920 Roy and Ivy had one quarter which increased to nine quarters altogether.

They used coal oil for lamps and wood and coal for heat and cooking. Later they used gas lamps much like the ones we use for camping now in that you pump up pressure for the lamp to burn. Wood and coal was used in the old house until Doug and Keith sold the farm. They used batteries for light after the 2nd war that was charged by a wind mill. It was a 6 volt system. In the 50s Doug got a motor generator to charge the batteries and then in the late 50s they got power put in. Telephones were around before the war but were local farm systems that ran on the barb wire fence between farms. It wasn't until the late 50s that they had a real telephone system.

Mornimont School was the center of the community it was used like a pubic hall. Christmas Concerts and New Year dances were held there, as were dances at Valentines and Easter. Church services were also held at Mornimont School which ended with a ball game between other schools. The last day of June every year there was a school picnic. The 1st July was always spent in one of the bigger towns Watrous, Young or Davidson where there were celebrations, ball games, and horse racing games, foot races and tug of wars.

In October 1928 Ivy, Hazel and Keith left from Young by train (Canadian Pacific) for Montreal to board a ship(SS Minnedosa) bound for England. Ivy`s brother Ron joined them a few miles down the track in Renown. It took 4/5 days to reach Montreal and a farther 7/8 days to reach Liverpool. They took a cab from Liverpool to Chiddingfold; Surrey. When the cab arrived at the house (Burcot) the driver called out the name Belchamber, to that Kate Belchamber Ivy's Mother retorted "we don't want any hawkers around here" Ivy replied "well don't you want to see us mum?" Hazel who was five then, has great memories of meeting all her English grand parents, aunts, uncles and cousins, especially her uncle Jim and Dennis who she remembers gave her sweets, she really enjoyed the French cream candied mice and rides on their bicycles. Grandfather George also gave her a taste of his home made Parsnip wine. That first night in England she remembers Ivy, Keith and herself all slept in the same bed which was so cold and damp they thought they would freeze. One time Jim Belchamber was taking Hazel and Keith to the sweet shop, when some local children took after them, Ivy had dressed them both in overalls, which was common dress in Canada at that time, Hazel remembers Uncle Jim holding them close and telling the local children to"bugger off". Jim would also play the mouth organ and Hazel would stand on his shoes and dance around the room. It was a great time and sadly it had to end, Ivy, Hazel and Keith returned to Canada in the April of 1929 aboard SS Montcalm.

Although horsepower was for the farm, Roy and Ivy purchased their first car in the early 1920`s, nobody can remember the make, it was a tourer with curtains instead of windows, but on its first trip out, as Roy approached a gate Roy forgot he wasn't driving horses, he pulled back on the steering wheel and yelled whoa, whoa and drove right through it. They later got a new Chevrolet in 1928.Cars could only be driven during the spring and summer as the roads were not kept open during winter. Hazel can remember when in 1947 it snowed so bad, she had to stay on the farm she could not get into Watrous until April the following year.

Ivy made a trip back to England in 1964,both her parents had died by then but there were all her brothers and sisters to visit which she did, she stay with most of us for while, us included in Chiddingfold. Ivy died in 1973,Roy had died ten years earlier in 1963.

Doug. And Keith never married they farmed at Young until they retired in 1973. Hazel married and has a son, who now lives in British Columbia. Keith passed away in 2001; Doug still lives in and around the Young, Saskatchewan area. Hazel Passed away in September 2006.

Frederick George Basil Belchamber
(George12,James11,James10,James9,William8,Edward7,Edward6,John5,Thomas4,Robert3,Robert2,John1) was born on the 21st May,1897 in The High Street,Petworth,Sussex. He died in The Royal Surrey County Hospital,Guildford on

the 18th July,1981. He married Dorothy May Radley at The Registry Office,Guildford on the 15th February,1922,she was the daughter of Albert Henry Radley and Lilian Sarah Elizabeth Denyer. She was born on the 5th October,1900 and died on the 2nd February,1988 in St.Lukes Hospital,Guildford.

Basil's War Record:

Basil Belchamber Service number 2209 Royal Flying Corp.
Basil enlisted and attested on the 16th November, 1914, he was declared fit the same day and approved for military service on the 23rd November at S Farnborough. Basil was 18 years and 178 days old, 5ft 4 inches tall and weighed 125 lbs. He had a fresh complexion, grey eyes and brown hair his chest girth was 35 inches with an expansion of 2 inches. He had a 5 year apprenticeship with Dixon and Burus of Guildford,he had served 3 years when he left to join the army. Herbert Nash witnessed Basil Attestation.

After initial training he was appointed to NO2 RAS RFC on the 1st April,1915,finally being transferred in the Royal Air Force on the 1st April,1918.Promotion: he was made Corporal on the 1st September,1916 and Sergeant on the 1st March,1918. Basil saw active service when he was part of The British Expeditionary Force in France from 7th August,1916 until 24th June,1918,he was then in the UK until the 25th February,1920. He had two medals, the British War Medal and The Victory Medal.

Basil left the RAF on the 25th February, 1920 at RAF Hailscott.

Birth Certificate:
Frederick George Basil Belchamber was born May 21st 1897 the High Street, Petworth the birth was registered July 3rd in the Petworth Southern district of Sussex. George Belchamber his father was a Blacksmith Journeyman and mother Kate was formerly Horn.

Marriage
He married Dorothy May Radley aged 21 a spinster on February 15th 1922 at the Registry Office Guildford. Basil aged 24 ,was listed as a motor mechanic living at Oakleigh, Woodside Road, Chiddingfold, Kate Belchamber his mother and William Huntingfold were witness. Arthur James Langrish registrar performed the ceremony.

Death Certificates:
Basil Frederick Belchamber died in the Royal Surrey County Hospital, Guildford on the 18th of July 1981 of Bronchopneumonia and renal failure. His daughter Barbara was informant.

Dorothy May Belchamber aged 87 died on the 2nd of February,1988 at St.Lukes Hospital,Guildford,Surrey. Cause of death was Bronchopneumonia,Cararnoma of Cervix & Diabetes Mellitus certified by M A Gadkari MB. She was listed as the widow of Frederick George Basil Belchamber an Engineer retired of 2 Hillfield Close,Bushy Hill,Merrow,Surrey. The informant was her daughter. The death was registered on the 3rd of February for Surrey South Western.

Census:

In the 1901 census Dorothy M Radley aged 6 months was living with her mother Lilian Radley aged 24 at Corner Farm, Pickhurst,Chiddingfold with the family of James and Mary Lintott nee Bentley.

Frederick George Basil Belchamber and Dorothy May Radley had 6 children.Of which some family have survived to date.

Robert Leonard Powell Belchamber

(George12,James11,James10,James9,William8,Edward7,Edward6,John5,Thomas4,Robert3,Robert2,John1) was born on the 24th March,1900 in Burningfold,Dunsfold, Surrey. He died on the 3rd February,1963 in Frant,Sussex. He married Ivy Elizabeth Rabson on the 28th February,1928. She was born on the 26th October,1904 in Wadhurst,Sussex She died on the 23 August,1974 in Hastings,Kent.

Birth Certificate:
Robert Leonard Powell Belchamber born 1900 on the 24th of March a whit sunday at Burningfold,Dunsfold,Surrey the birth was registered on the 4th of May by James M G Walder the registrar for Hambledon,Surrey. George Belchamber his father was a Blacksmith Journey and his mother was Kate formerly Horn.

Marriage Certificate:
Robert Leonard Powell Belchamber married Ivy Rabson at the Registry Office in Ticehurst,East Sussex and Kent. The ceremony was performed by Harry J Sancto on the 28th of February,1928. Robert and Ivy`s witness` were Mildred Rabson and Jesse Thomas Edwards,their abode was 15 Osmers Hill,Wadhurst,Sussex. Robert a bachelor was a 27 year old timber carter and Ivy a laundry maid aged 23 and a spinster,there was no father or fathers occupation listed for her.

Death Certificates:
Robert Leonard Powell died in Pembury Hospital on the 3rd February 1964 of a cardiac arrest,his informant was his son Frederick Charles. Robert was 64 years of age and a timber yardman his address at time of death was 33 Warren Ridge,Frant,Sussex. The death was recorded for Tonbridge on the 4th of February by the Registrar.

Ivy Elizabeth Belchamber widow of Robert Baden Powell Belchamber,Timber Haulier of Meadow View,ReedsWood Road,Broad Oak,Rye,East Sussex died on the 23rd of August,1974. Cause of death was Bronchopnemonia,Septicemia and Liver Failure which was certifed by R A Botha MB.Informant was her daughter Beryl Margaret Crouch. A M Bishop registered the death on the 27th of August for Hastings.

Robert Leonard Powell Belchamber and Ivy Elizabeth Rabson had 4 children of which some of the family have survived.

Arthur Dennis Belchamber

(George12,James11,James10,James9,William8,Edward7,Edward6,John5,Thomas4,Robert3,Robert2,John1) was born on the 24th September,1901 in Burningfold,Dunsfold, Surrey. He died on the 11th October,1933 in The Royal Surrey County Hospital.

He married Esther Ellen Jenner on the 27th February,1926 in Guildford,Surrey.

Birth Certificate:
The birth of Arthur Dennis Belchamber took place in Burningfold,Dunsfold on the 24th of September,1901. His father George was a Blacksmith(Journeyman). The birth was recorded on the 8th of November by James M G Walder for Hambledon,Surrey.

Marriage Certificate:
Arthur Dennis Belchamber married Esther Ellen Jenner at the Guildford Registry Office he was a 25 year old bachelor and a general labourer and Esther a 16 year old housemaid and spinster. Arthur was living at Oakleigh,Woodside Road,Chiddingfold and Esther at Hollist Cottage,Chiddingfold. Their witness`s were Clara Jenner and Annie Louise Humphrey. George Belchamber,Arthur`s father was listed as a Engineer and Esther`s father Reuben Charles Jenner as listed as a Carter.

Death Certificate:
32 year old Arthur Dennis Belchamber died in the Royal Surrey County Hospital,Guildford,Surrey. Kate Belchamber his mother was the informant and present at his death of Burcot,Ash Vale,Chiddingfold. Cause of death was Asphyesia,Cancer of the stomach,Multiple secondries in abdominal cavitiy which was certified by Francis G Maitland MB. George Ralph Smith registrar for Guildford recorded the death on the 12th October. The burial took place on the 14th at St.Marys Chiddingfold. His occupation was listed as a domestic gardener.

After Arthur Dennis died,Esther Ellen remarried in 1936 to Harold Elliott.

Marriage Cerificate:
28 year old bachelor Harold Elliott married 27 year old widow Esther Ellen Belchamber at St.Marys Church,Chiddingfold on the 20th of June,1936 by banns. Harold was a Solictors Clerk from Petersfield and Esther had no occupation listed was from Chiddingfold. Witness's were Frank Eric Marshall,Richard Elliott and Kate Belchamber. The fathers were Richard Elliott a Chief Officer in HM Prison Service and Rueben Charles Jenner a Carter.

Arthur Dennis Belchamber and Esther Ellen Jenner had two children,of which some family survive to date.

It was at this wedding that Ronald Smith got talking to Harold's father about the Prison Service and decided to apply to join.

Hugh Gordon Belchamber
(George12,James11,James10,James9,William8,Edward7,Edward6,John5,Thomas4,Robert3,Robert2,John1) was born on the 25th October,1903 in Burningfold,Dunsfold, Surrey. He died on the 6th March,1979 in Chiddingfold,Surrey. He married Lydia Alice Davis on the 17th December,1930 in The Registry Office,Guildford,Surrey. She was born on the 23rd December,1911 in Portsmouth,Hampshire. She died on the 25th March,1998.

Birth Certificate:

Hugh Gordon Belchamber was born at Burningfold,Dunsfold on the 25th of October,1903. George his father was a Blacksmith(Journeyman) his mother Kate Belchamber was formerly Horn and the birth was recorded in Hambeldon by the registrar James M G Walder on the 4th of December.

Marriage Certificate:
Hugh Belchamber as he called himself now age 26 and a bachelor was married to Lydia Alice Davis a spinster age 18 on the 17th February 1930 at the registry office Guildford in the district of Hambledon. Gordon was a gardener living in Burcot,Woodside Road,Chiddingfold and Lydia no occupation listed was living in No.1 St.Peters Road,Old Woking.Gordon and Lydia`s witness` were Ernest Alfred and Ada Lucy Deadman.

Death Certificates:
Hugh Gordon Belchamber died at 20 Queens Mead,Chiddingfold,Surrey on the 6th of March,1979. Cause of death was Myocardiac Infarction and Hypertension certified by D F H Williams MB. His wife Lydia Alice Belchamber was informant of 20 Queens Mead the family home. J Ford registrar for Surrey South Western recorded the death on the 7th of March.

Lydia Alice Belchamber aged 86 died on the 25th of March,1998 at the Tilford Park Nursing Home,Grange Road,Tilford,Surrey. She was the widow of Gordon Hugh Belchamber a retired Water Pump Engineer. The cause of death was Broncopneumonia,Immobility,Parkinson's Disease and Senile Dementia certified by J L Steed MB. The informant was her son.The registrar for West Surrey Patricia I Kent recorded the death on the 26th of March.

Hugh Gordon Belchamber and Lydia Alice Davis had 6 children,of which all survive to date.

James O'brien Belchamber Grandparents
(George12,James11,James10,James9,William8,Edward7,Edward6,John5,Thomas4,Robert3,Robert2,John1) was born on the 14th March,1906 in Maple Tree Cottage, Dunsfold,Surrey. He died on the 28th March,1980 in 3 Coombe View,Chiddingfold, Surrey. He married Dorothy Annie Lawrence on the 11th October,1930 in Northchapel,Sussex. She was the daughter of William George Lawrence and Rose Annie Streeter,born in Colhook,Northchapel on the 18th September,1909. She died on the 12th May,2008 in Eynsham,Oxfordshire.

Birth Certificates:
James O'Brien Belchamber was born in Mapletree Cottage,Dunsfold,Surrey in the year 1906 on the 14th of March.James M G Walder the registrar for Hambledon recorded the birth on the 12th of April. His father George Belchamber was a Blacksmith(Journeyman)

Dorothy Annie Lawrence was born in Colhook,Northchapel,Sussex on the 18th of September,1909. Her father George William was a Farm Labourer and her mother was Rose Annie formerly Streeter. Charles Randall the registrar for Petworth registered the birth on the 5th of November.

Marriage Certificate:
James Belchamber married Dorothy Annie Lawrence at Northchapel parish church on
the 11th October 1930,James was age 24 and Dorothy was 21, the witness` were
Arthur Dennis Belchamber and William George Lawrence the father of Dorothy.
Fathers William George Lawrence was a Roadman and George Belchamber a
Engineer. James was listed as a labourer from Chiddingfold and Dorothy from
Northchapel no occupation listed. R J Burdon the Prebendary of Chichester performed
the marriage.

Death Certificates:
Retired Bricklayer James O'Brien Belchamber died at the Royal Surrey County
Hospital,Guildford,Surrey on the 28th of November,1980. Informant was his wife
Dorothy Annie Belchamber of 3 Coombe View,Chiddingfold the family home. Cause
of death was Bronchopneumonia,Pulmonnale,Chronic Bronchitis and Emphysema
certified by the Coroner for Surrey George Evans. B L Halls the registrar for Surrey
South Western on the 28th of November.

Dorothy Annie Belchamber died at approx.11.45pm on the 12th of May,2008. Cause
of death was Bronchopneumonia certified by S Vigar MBBS. The death was
registered on the 15th of May,the informant was her great granddaughter.

James was cremated at the Guildford Crematorium. Dorothy Annie was cremated at
St John's Chapel,Oxford Crematorium

James O'brien Belchamber and Dorothy Annie Lawrence had three children of which
two siblings and family survive.Their eldest daughter Ivy Muriel Kate Belchamber,
my mother was born on the 3rd November,1930 in Cylinders Lane,Northchapel,
Sussex. She died on the 12th December,1992 in Chichester.

Birth Certificate:
Ivy Muriel Kate Belchamber was born in 1930 on the 3rd of November.The birth took
place at Cylinders,Fisher Street in Northchapel,Sussex the family home. James her
father was a Bricklayers Labourer and her mother was Dorothy Annie formerly
Lawrence. H F Granville the registrar for Petworth recorded the birth on the 3rd of
December.

Marriage Certificate:
Ivy Muriel Kate Belchamber a 37 year old School Cleaner married bachelor Patrick
Vaughan a General Labourer aged 35 at the Registry Office,Guildford on November
the 2nd,1968. B George and Father James O`brien were witness`s. Patricks father
Daniel Vaughan was an Upholsterer and James O`brien a Bricklayer.

Death Certificate:
Ivy Muriel Kate Vaughan died at Hollymead House,DownviewRoad,Felpham,Sussex
on the 12th of December,1992. Cause of death was Left Ventricular Failure,Ischaemic
Heart Disease,DiabetesMellitis Cerebrovascular Accident which was certified by W J
Rogers MRCS. The informant was Norman Robert Brookhouse of 2 Fortunes

Way,Havant,Hampshire of HollymeadHouse. The death was registered by S Pegran the registrar for Chichester on the 14th of December.

Ronald Silas Belchamber

(George12,James11,James10,James9,William8,Edward7,Edward6,John5,Thomas4,Robert3,Robert2,John1) was born on the 22nd March,1908 in Maple Tree Cottage, Dunsfold,Surrey. He died on the 16th August,1976 in Pontrilas,Codette,Saskatchwen, Canada.

Birth Certificate:

Ronald Silas Belchamber was born in Mapletree Cottage,Dunsfold,Surrey the family home on the 22nd of March,1908,his father George was an Estate Blacksmith at Burningfold Manor,Dunsfold.his mother was Kate formerly Horn. The birth was recorded by James M G Walder the registrar for Hambledon,Surrey.

Ron went to Canada at the age of 16 in 1923, for a while he stayed with Roy and Ivy Steeves on their farm in Young, Saskatchewan, helping out around the farm constructing farm buildings etc, he also help build the local school in Mornimont. Ron also worked for different farmers in the district before farming on his own just south of sister Ivy.

Ron and his cousin Hazel were close like brother and sister, Hazel remembers one time Ron was having trouble backing the horse and wagon up to the granary, Hazel learned a new word that day, she thought it such a different word that she was going the tell it at school. When Hazel told her mum Ivy, the word she got a spanking and Ron got hell for using such a word.

Ron and Sister Ivy went back to England in Oct. 1928 and stayed until April 1929.

 Ron met his first wife Ellen when he was in Young; her parents farmed about two miles northeast of Roy and Ivy. Her name was Goodin the Goodins were a very musical family they played Violin and Banjo, Ellen played the piano and Ron played Guitar and sang as well. The Goodin band played at local dances etc.in the area. After they married Ellen refused to live on Rons farm, so they lived with the Goodin family in Snowden. They left young in 1939 with a wagon and two horses called Topsy and Fanny, Elmer Lindgren went with them, they camped along the way. Elmer later took the train back home to Young. Ron worked for a while for the Conservation and Drainage clearing the Carrot River. Ron and Ellen married in 1936 and had a son born Sept 11,1940,they stayed at the farm until WW2,sadly they broke up after the war and Ron moved to Pontrilas,Sask.They divorced in 1949,as a side note Ron's lawyer was John Diefenbaker later to become Prime Minster of Canada in 1957. Ron and Elizabeth (Living) were married on the 28th of Oct 1950; they have three Children of whom all survive to date.

Until he died in 1976 Ron worked the farm in Pontrilas, growing cereal etc.

Kitty Faith Belchamber

(George12,James11,James10,James9,William8,Edward7,Edward6,John5,Thomas4,Robert3,Robert2,John1) was born on the 7th July,1911 in Maple Tree Cottage,Dunsfold, Surrey. She died on the 8th October,1993 in Maidstone,Kent. She married Ronald Herbert Smith on the 23rd October,1937 in Chiddingfold,Surrey. He was born on the 11th November,1911 and died in Maidstone on the 24th November,1993.

Birth Certificate:
The birth of Kitty Faith Belchamber took place in Mapletree Cottage,Dunsfold,Surrey on the 7th of July,1911. Her father George was a Blacksmith(Journeyman) and her mother Kaye was formerly Horn. The birth was registered on the 12th of September by James M G Walder for Hambledon,Surrey.

Marriage Certificate:
Kitty Faith Belchamber married Ronald Herbert Smith a 25 year old prison officer of 8 Ellington St.,Bansbury on the 23rd of October 1937 at St.Marys Church,Chiddingfold,Surrey. Kit had no occupation listed but her address was Burcot,Chiddingfold the family home. Their witness`s were E.J.Munday and C.W.Brooks. The rector Charles Baldwin performed the ceremony. They started their married life living in Wandsworth,finally settling in Maidstone,Kent.

Death Information:
Kitty Faith Smith died on the 8th Oct,1993 aged 82 and Ronald on the 24th October the same year aged 81.

Note for Kitty Faith:
One story related to me by George Belchamber(born 1933),was when Kitty Faith bought a new pair of shoes,and her mother Kate gave them away to someone who she thought was in more need of them,understandably Kitty Faith was not amused and made her mother retrieve them from the person to whom they had been given.

Annie Elizabeth Belchamber
(William12,James11,James10,James9,William8,Edward7,Edward6,John5,Thomas4,Robert3,Robert2,John1) was born on the 3rd February,1910 in Plaistow,Sussex. She married Alec Mitchell on the 6th November,1933 in Swindon,Wiltshire.

Birth Certificate:
Annie Elizabeth Belchamber was born on the 3rd of February 1910 in Plaistow,Sussex. William Belchamber the father was a General Labourer and Louisa Jane her mother was formerly Remnant. Charles Randall registrar for Petworth recorded the birth on the 4th of March

Marriage Certificate:
Alec Mitchell a bachelor aged 23 and a private in the Royal Tank Corp. Annie Elizabeth Belchamber was aged 23 also and a domestic cook working at Belchambers Farm,Kirdford they married at the Registry Office,Swindon,Wiltshire on the 10th of November 1933. Witness were W M Houslow and M L Tyler. The ceremony was conducted by Harry Y Kirby and William Davey Registrars.

Alec Mitchell and Annie Elizabeth Belchamber had one surviving child.

Bertha Florence Belchamber
(William12,James11,James10,James9,William8,Edward7,Edward6,John5,Thomas4,Robert3,Robert2,John1) was born on the 4th September,1916 in Golden Cross Cottage, Plaistow,Sussex. She married Andrew Hamilton Forrest on the 19th February,1940 in

Plaistow,Sussex.

Birth Certrificate:
Bertha Florence Belchamber was born in Golden Cross Cottage,Plaistow,Sussex on the 4th of September 1916. William her father was a Farm Labourer and her mother was Louisa Jane formerly Remnant. J W Pugley the registrar for Petwoth recorded the birth on the 6th of October.

Marriage Certificate:
James Dalglish Forrest's son Andrew Hamilton Forrest a 25 year old bachelor married Bertha Florence Belchamber a spinster aged 23 at the parish church Plaistow, Sussex on the 19th of February,1940. Andrew J Young performed the ceremony and Thomas Remnant and Charles Henderson were witness`s. Andrews occupation was a Forester, his residence at the time was Shorncliffe Camp, while Bertha was living in Golden Cross Cottage. The fathers were James Dalgleish Forrest who was retired and William Belchamber a Farm Labourer

Andrew Hamilton Forrest and Bertha Florence Belchamber had two children of which some survive.

Reginald Clonard Leslie Belchamber
(Alfred12,William11,James10,James9,William8,Edward7,Edward6,John5,Thomas4,Robert3,Robert2,John1) was born on the 3rd March,1898 in The Common,Dunsfold, Surrey. He died on the 10th November,1967 in Ashford Hospital,Stanwell,Middlesex. He married Elsie Caister Beauchamp on the 5th November,1921 in St.Marys Church,Staines,Middlesex. She was born on the 17th July,1897 in Staines,Middlesex. She died on the 12th October,1970 in 26 Victoria Street,Englefield Green,Surrey.

Birth Certificate:
Reginald Clonard Leslie Belchamber the second son of Alfred and Sarah Jane was born on the 3rd of March 1898 at The Common,Dunsfold,Surrey the birth was registred by James M G Walder the Registrar on the 9th of April at Hambledon. Father Alfred was a Domestic Gardener.

Marriage Certificate:
He married widow Elsie Caister Beachamp(nee Prangley) in St.Marys Church,Staines by banns on November 5th,1921.Reginald was a 23 year old bachelor and Motor Mechanic,living at 20 Church Street,Staines. Elsie was 24 with no occupation listed and she was living in 148 Wendover Road,Staines. Witness's were H.W Taylor and A Prangley. Fathers Alfred Belchamber was a Head Gardener and Arthur Prangley was deceased. John R James performed the ceremony.

Death Certificates:
Reginald C L was aged 69 when he died of Chronic Bronchitis & Emphysema. He was living at 26 Victoria Street,Englefield Green. Deputy Coroner D M Paul certified the death after post mortem without inquest,which was registered on the 13th of November by L H Webb the Registrar. His son was informant..Reginald C L was a garage proprietor.

Elsie Caister Belchamber died of Recurrent Coronary Thrombosis aged 73 on the 12th of October 1970,which was certified by George M McEwan Coroner, after a post mortem without Inquest. She died at home which was 26 Victoria Street,Englefield Green,Surrey.Her son was the informnant at the same address. Elsie was listed as the widow of Reginald Clonald Leslie Belchamber a Company Director. The registrar for Chertsey D R Grover registered the death on the 16th of October

Reginald Clonard Leslie Belchamber and Elsie Caister Beauchamp had two children,and some are still alive.

Private Reginald C.L Belchamber service number M2/147206 of The ASC was awarded the Victory Medal and The British War Medal in the First World War(Citation/Roll rasc/107b100,page 10734)

Stanley Aubrey Alec Belchamber
(Alfred12,William11,James10,James9,William8,Edward7,Edward6,John5,Thomas4,Robert3,Robert2,John1) was born on the 18th September,1904 in Northcroft Cottage,Englefield Green,Surrey. He died on the 2nd June,1999 in Westmorland General Hospital,Kendal,Cumbria. He married Marjorie Violet Crane on the 30th January,1932 in The Church Of St.Michaels,Highgate,Middlesex. She was born on the 13th April,1906 and died on the 27th January,1978 in 1Torrington,Berkhampstead.

Birth Certificate:
Alfred and Sarah's son Stanley Aubrey Alec Belchamber was born in Northcroft Cottage,Englefield Green on the 18th of September 1904,the birth was registered at Windsor on the 26th of October by M.Gardener the Registrar. Father Alfred was a Gardener/Domestic Servant.

Marriage Certificate:
On the 30th of January 1932 the marriage by banns took place at St Michaels church,Highgate,Middlesex of Stanley Aubrey Alec Belchamber and Marjorie Violet Crane.He was aged 27 and a bachelor and she was a spinster aged 25. Stanley was a Gardener by trade,like his father Alfred. There was no occupation for Marjorie only her father Henry Crane who was a Gardener. Both lived at Casewood Towers Stanley at The Bothy and Majorie at The Gardens. Witness`s were Henry Crane and Alfred Belchamber both fathers. The rector J.T.T.Robinson performed the ceremony.

Death Certificates:
Stanley Aubrey Alec Belchamber was a Landscape Gardener(Retired) when he died,his son was the informant. His address at time of death was 50 Kentsford Road,Grange-over-sands,Cumbria. The death was registered on the same day by Barbara E Airey Registra and the death was certified by A Suman MB. Stanley Aubrey Alec was a Landscape Gardener(Retired) when he died.

Marjorie Violet Belchamber of 17 Torrington Road,Berkhampstead died there on the 27th of January,1978. She died of Myocardial Infarction,Ischaemic Heart Disease,Hypertension and Left Ventricular Failure Bronchitis which was certified by

Lyn Jenkins B M.Majorie was the widow of Stanley Aubrey Alec Belchamber a retired Horticulturalist. The informant was her son. B H Hible deputy registrar for Dacorum recorded the death on the 27th of January.

Stanley Aubrey Alec Belchamber had one child,who is still living.

Cedric Cecil Guy Belchamber
(Alfred12,William11,James10,James9,William8,Edward7,Edward6,John5,Thomas4,Robert3,Robert2,John1) was born on the 10th September,1907 in Northcroft Cottage, Englefield Green,Surrey. He died on the 18th May,1997 in Surbiton Hospital,Surbiton,Surrey. He married Marion Harris on the 1st August,1938 in The Baptist Church,Church Road,Teddington,Middlesex. She was born on the 7th September,1905 in Teddington and she died on the 13th May,1992 in Crawley,Sussex.

Birth Certificate;
Cedric Cecil Guy Belchamber was born in Northcroft Cottage,Englefield Green the family home on the 10th of September 1907,Alfred his father was a Domestic Gardener. M Gardener registrar of Egham recorded the birth on the 16th October.

Marriage Certificate:
In Teddington,Middlesex in the Baptist Church, Church Road. Cedric Cecil Guy Belchamber married Marion Harris on the 1st of August,1938. Cedric was a bachelor aged 30 and a Master Greengrocer,he was living at 20 Long Lane,Stanwell while Dressmaker Marion was 32 years of age and a spinster she lived at 33 Cambridge Crescent,Teddington. Fathers Alfred Belchamber was a retired Gardener and David Harris a Master House Decorator. Ada May Harris and Sarah Jane Belchamber were witness`s and the vicar Henry John Morley performed the marriage.

Death Certificates:
Marion Belchamber aged 86 died on the 13th of May 1992 at the Crawley Hospital,Crawley,West Sussex. Cause of death was Acute Mycardial Infraction which was certified by S Chandrara MB. Marion was the widow of Cedric Cecil Guy Belchamber a retired Interior Decorator of Wardecot,Church Lane,Itchingfield,Horsham,West Sussex who was the informant. Wendy Hall the deputy registrar for Crawley recorded the death on the 1st June.

Cedric Cecil Guy died in Surbiton Hospital on the 18th of May 1997 he was 98 years of age. Cause of death was Bronchopneumonia and multiple Myeloma which was certified by Nassis Mansour MB. His son was informant of the same address as his father. Registrar S A Lecky the deputy registrar registered the death on the 19th May.

Cedric Cecil Guy Belchamber and Marion Harris had one child who is still living.

Victor Charles Belchamber
(Walter Charles12,William11,James10,James9,William8,Edward7,Edward6, John5,Thomas4,Robert3,Robert2,John1) was born on the 2nd January,1906 in Mill Cottage,Dunsfold,Surrey. He died on the 7th Febuary,1995 in Cranleigh Village Hospital,Cranleigh,Surrey. He married Gwendolin Marjorie Killick on the 29th April,1933 in Ewhurst,Surrey. She was born on the 27th June,1908. She died on the 13th January,1994 in 21 Parsonage Road,Cranleigh,Surrey.

Birth Certificate:
Victor Charles Belchamber was born in Mill Cottage,Dunsfold,Surrey on January the 2nd 1906. The birth was registered at Hambledon,Surrey by James M.G Walder the Registrar on the 12th of February. Father Charles Belchamber was a Domestic Gardener.

Marriage Certificate:
Charles Belchamber and Gwendolin Marjorie Killick married at St Peter and Paul Church Ewhurst on the 29th Of April,1933 Victor C aged 27 a bachelor and Postman of Cranleigh and Gwendolin aged 24 a spinster and Telephonist of Ewhurst. Witness`s were S V Killick and Alice Winifred Belchamber. Fathers occupations were Walter Charles was a Taxi Driver and Fred William Killick a Painter. The marriage was performed by the Rector Joseph B Doller.

Death Certificates:
Gwendoline Marjorie Belchamber died at 21 Parsonage Road,Cranleigh,Surrey on the 13th of January,1994. Informant and present at death was her hushand Victor Charles Belchamber a retired Postal Inspector. Cause of death was Ruptured thoracic aortic aneurysm,Ischaemic heart disease and hypertension certified by R Fawner-Corbett MB. Judith Breach the registrar for Surrey SW recorded the death on the 31st of January.

Victor Charles Belchamber died at Cranleigh Village Hospital,Cranleigh,Surrey on the 7th of Febraury,1995 listed as a Postal Inspector(Retired) of 21 Parsonage Road,Cranleigh,Surrey. Cause of death was cerebrovascular accident and hypertension. The informant was his daughter. The death was recorded on the 8th of Febraury by Judith Breach registrar for Surrey SW.

The records from the Post Office show that Victor Charles Belchamber became a Postman Messenger at Guildford in August 1922 employment number 124385/22,by April,1926 he made Postman and in November, 1928 he was in Ewhurst,Surrey. He was still a Postman in July,1935 back at Guildford.

Victor Charles Belchamber and Gwendolin Marjorie Killick had three children of whom some are alive.

Jack Belchamber
(Walter Charles12,William11,James10,James9,William8,Edward7,Edward6, John5,Thomas4,Robert3,Robert2,John1) was born on the 26th July,1908 in Mill Cottage,Dunsfold,Surrey. He died on the 12th June,1943 in North Afica. He married Nellie Elizabeth Howick on the 17th November,1929 in The Registry Office,Guildford,Surrey. She was the daughter of William John Howick born on the 17th April,1909 in Ellens Green,Rudgwick,Sussex. She died on the 20th April,2000 in Honeywood House,Rowhook,Horsham,Sussex.

Birth Certificate:

Jack Belchamber was born in Mill Cottage,Dunsfold on July 26,1908 the birth was registered by Registrar James M G Walder on the 18th of September at Hambledon,Surrey. Father Charles was a Domestic Gardener.

Marriage Certificate:
On the 20th of November 1929 Jack Belchamber and Nellie Elizabeth Howick married at the Registry Office,Guildford. The witness`s were Alice Winifred Belchamber and Edith Sturt. Arthur James Langrish the registrar performed the ceremony. Jack a bachelor aged 21 and Grocers Assistant of Elston,St James Place,Cranleigh. His father Walter Charles was a Taxi Driver. Nellie Elizabeth a spinster aged 20 with no occupation listed of Bury St Austens,Ewhurst her father William John Howick was a Farm Labourer.

Death Certificates:
Nellie Elizabeth Belchamber widow of Jack Belchamber died at Honeywood House,Rowhook,Horsham on the 20th of April,2000. Cause of death was just listed as Old Age. Her son was informant.Nellie was listed as a retired Domestic Worker.

Death Certificate:
Jack Belchamber aged 34 died in North Africa of "injuries sustained in Accident" on the 12th of June,1943.
1736100 L/Bdr Jack Belchamber died from injuries sustained in accident aged 34.Jack of the Royal Artillery 50 Bty.17 Lt.A.A Regt. is buried in Enfidaville War Cemetery.Tunisia(I.D 13).

Lorna Irene Kate Belchamber
(William James12,William11,James10,James9,William8,Edward7,Edward6,John5, Thomas4,Robert3,Robert2,John1) was born on the 11th October,1905 in Pound Common,Kirdford,Sussex. She died in 1983 in Wisborough Green,Sussex. She married Reginald Cheesman on the 18th June,1921 in The Registry Office,Petworth,Sussex.

Birth Certificate;
William and Kate had two children Lorna Irene Kate born 11th of October 1905 and James Archibald Rudolf born June 28th 1916. At the time of James`s birth William was a private serving in the 1st Company,Royal Medical Corp.

Birth Certificate:
Lorna Irene Kate Belchamber was born on the 11th of October,1905 at Pound Common,Kirdford,Sussex. Her Father William James was a postman of Elms Cottage,Wisborough Green,Sussex. The birth was registered on the 18th of November by the registrar for Petworth Charles Randall.

Marriage Certificate:
Lorna Irene Kate Belchamber aged only 16 years married Reginald Cheeseman aged 23 and a bachelor at the registry Office in Petworth on the 18th of June 1921. Reginald was a Carpenter,the son of John Cheeseman(Deceased) and living at Institute Cottages,Wisborough Green. Lorna had no occupation listed and was livng at

2 Ivy Cottages,Wisborough Green. Witness`s were William James Belchamber and Nellie Elizabeth Cheeseman.Lorna`s father was a postman.

Reginald Cheesman and Lorna Irene Kate Belchamber had three children.

James Archibald Rudolf Belchamber
(William James12,William11,James10,James9,William8,Edward7,Edward6,John5, Thomas4,Robert3,Robert2,John1) was born on the 28th June,1916 in Petworth,Sussex. He died on the 24th May,1985 in 10 Church Cottages,Stopham,Sussex. He married Daisy Grace White on the 29th March,1937 in Stopham,she was born in Storrington,Sussex on the 2nd December,1908 and died on the 20th Febuary,1991 in St.Leonards Hospital,St.Leonards,Sussex.

Birth Certificate:
James Archibald Rudolf Belchamber was born in Ivy Cottage,Wisborough Green,Sussex on the 28th of June 1916. William James Belchamber his father was a private in the Royal Army Medical Corp.(J company). J W Pugeley the registrar for Petworth recorded the birth on the 15th of July.

Marriage Certificate:
James Archibald Rudolf Belchamber a bachelor aged 20 and Daisy Grace White aged 27 and a spinster were married by banns on the 29th of March 1937 at the parish church Stopham,Sussex. Their witnesss were Dorothy Belchamber,Dorothy Jenner and William E Hazelman. Daisy`s father William was a forester from Stopham.

Death Certificates:
Retired Aircraft Fitter James Archibald Rudolf Belchamber died on the 24th of May 1985 at 10 Church Cottages,Stopham,West Sussex. Cause of death was Ischaemic heart disease and Atheroseterous which was certified by M.G Calvert-Lee coroner for West Sussex after postmortem without inquest and registered by registra B Rickard. The informant was his widow Daisy Grace Belchamber.

Daisy Grace Belchamber died at St.Leonards Hospital on the 20th of February,1991 cause of death was bronchopuemonia and carcinoma bronchus certifed by P P Ramachandran MB. Listed as the widow of James Archibald Rudolf Belchamber a retired Mechanical Engineer of 4 Simmonds Close,Oakdale,Poole,Dorset. Her informant and present at her death was her daughter. O L Ryan deputy registrar for Poole recorded the death on the 22nd February.

James Archibald Rudolf Belchamber and Daisy Grace White had two children. One daughter living and a son who died at birth.

Generation 14

John Alan Belchamber
(John Richard13,John12,John11,Edward10,Edward9,Edward8,Edward7,Edward6, John5,Thomas4,Robert3,Robert2,John10) was born on the 12th May,1914 in 369 Alexandra Park Road,Wood Gren,Essex. He died in Estapona,Spain on the 18th

Febuary,1998. He married Victoria Garais on the 13th Decemebr,1938 in The Registry Office,Willesden,Middlesex. She was born in 1902 and died on the 22nd October,1944 in 160 Cromwell Road,Kensington. After Victoria's death he remarried to Hilda May Brunsdon on the 14th July,1945 in Swindon,Wiltshire. Hilda May was born on the 9th November,1912 in Swindon. She died on the 28th July,1985 in Stoke. He later married Ingeborg Frieda Dorothee Siegert date not known,but it was sometime between 1985 and 1998 because Ingeborg died on the 20th December,1997 in Stafford,she was born in Germany on the 24th July,1921.

Birth Certificate:
John Alan Belchamber was born at 369 Alexandra Park Road,Wood Green on the 12th of May,1914. His father John Richard Belchamber was a Fruit Market Commissionaire and his mother was Amy Nellie formerly Wilkie of the above address the family home. The birth was recorded by A J Stacey the registrar for Edmonton on the 16th of June.

Marriage Certificate:
John Alan Belchamber and Victoria Garais were married on the 13th December 1938 by licence at the Registry Office,Willesden,Middlesex. John Alan Belchamber was a 24 year old Bachelor and Clerk(International Commitee) of 58 Brondesbury Villas,Kilburn NW6. Victoria Garais was a spinster aged 36 with no occupation she was living at 4 Edith Road,West Kensington. Witness's were E J Partridge and S C Levan. Their fathers were John Richard Belchamber no occupation and Julos Garais he was of Independant Means. Lena H Rhodes the registrar and Hubert W Jobbing Interim Sup.Registra perform the ceremony.

Victoria Garais was born in either France or Argentina(they were listed as French on the Passenger list),she came to England in 1915 from Argentina aboard the Araquary from Buenos Aires to Liverpool with her parents,landing on the 11th July 1915.Her parents were Julio Garais 44,Maria Garais 32 and her brother Alexandrio Garais 11, Victoria was aged 13.Julio Garais was an engineer.Underneath the list is an address which looks like 44 Chailot,St Johns,London.The Araquary belonged to the Royal Mail Steam Packet Company Ltd. no 120716

Death Certificate:
Victoria Belchamber aged 42 Died at 160 Cromwell Road,Kensington on the 22nd of October 1944. Cause of death was Asphyxia due to coal gas poisoning. She killed herself while the balance of her mind was disturbed. The certificate was issued by J W Hulme deputy Coroner for the county of London on the 26th of October after an inquest was held. She was listed as the wife of John Alan Belchamber,Captain Royal Artillery of 34 Ridgeton Road,Woolton,Liverpool. The registrar C H Stark recorded the death on the 28th October.

Victoria Belchamber's Administration
In His Majesty's High Court Of Justice
The District Probate Registry of Harwich
BE IT KNOWM that Victoria Belchamber of
34 RidgetonRoad,Woolton,Liverpool in the county of Lancaster.

Died   on the 22nd day of October 1944

At the Hotel Majestic Kensington London W8

Intestate

AND BE IT FURTHER KNOWN that at the date hereunder written letters of Administration of all Estate which by law devolves to and vests in the personal representative of the said intestate were granted by his Majestry's High Court of Justice at the District Probate Registry thereof at Harwick

To John Alam Belchamber of 34 Ridgeton Road aforesaid captain HM Army the lawful husband.

Of the said intestate

AND IT IS HEREBY CERTIFIED that an Affidavit for Inland Revenue has been delivered wherein it is shewn that the gross value of the said Estate in Great Britain.

(exlusive of what the said deceased may have been possessed of or entitled to as a Trustee and not beneficially)
Amount to £229.4.8
And that the said Affidavit bears a stamp of £1.10.6

Dated the 12th day of December 1944

District Registrar   Max J Pemberton

Marriage Certificate:
John Alan Belchamber a Captain in the Royal Artillary and a bachelor aged 31 married 32 year old Hilda May Brunsdon a spinter with no occupation listed on the 14 of July 1945 at the parish church,Swindon,Wiltshire by license. John Alan gave his address as 75 Dale View,Chingford,Essex and Hilda May was at 16 Burford Avenue,Swindon,Wiltshire. The witness's were Herbert Brunsdon the bride's father who was a Stationary Engine Man,and Ewart Albert John Knighton. John Richard Belchamber the groom's father was a Glass Sign Writer. C A G Saunders performed the service.

Death Certificates:
Retired Teacher,Hilda May Belchamber died at The North Stafford Royal Infirmary,Harts Hill,Stoke on Trent on the 28th of July 1985. The cause of death was Carcinomatosis and Carcinoma Breast which was certified by S Ramakrishnan MB. Hilda was listed as the Wife of John Alan Belchamber a Local Goverment Office(Retired) of 34 Beechwood Close,Clayton,Newcastle under Lyme. Her husband John Alan was also informant and in attendance. The deputy registrar B Cartlidge recorded the death on the 29th of July for Stoke on Trent.

Ingeborg Frieda Dorothee Belchamber died at the Staffordshire General Hospital,Stafford on the 20th of December,1997. Cause of death was Congestive cardiac failure,Atrial fibrillation and Hypertension which was certified by P.Krishnamoorthy MB. Ingeborg was listed as a retired Catering Supervisor and the widow of John Alan Belchamber,Accountant and Club Secretary(Retired) of Maple Lodge,Rotherwood Drive,Rowley Park,Stafford. The informant was Eleanor Ethel Bruce her daughter of 83 First Avenue,Stafford. Registrar K M Green recorded the death on the 20th December for Stafford.

To date I cannot find information on the marriage of John Alan and Ingeborg,I have been told it probably took place in Gibraltrar late 1980's early 1990's.

John Alan died in Estapona,Spain on the 18th February,1998.

John Alan Belchamber and Hilda May Brunsdon had two sons,one son is living,the other son died in 1947.

Peter Richard Belchamber
(John Richard13,John12,John11,Edward10,Edward9,Edward8,Edward7,Edward6, John5,Thomas4,Robert3,Robert2,John10) was born on the 27th March 1932 in 91 Falmouth Avenue,West Ham. He died on the 3th November,2011 in East Sussex. He married Laurie Eleanor Constance Acres on the 11th September,1954 in Epping,Essex. She was born on the 22nd September,1922 in Epsom,Surrey. She died in 2003 in Hastings.

Birth Certificate:
Peter Richard Belchamber was born at 91 Falmouth Avenue,Walthamstow on the 27th of March,1932. His father was John Richard Belchamber a Telephone Operator of 12 Walthamstow Avenue,Phyllis Louise Belchamber formerly Holloway was the mother of the same address. The birth was registered on the 28th of April.

Marriage Certificate:
22 Year Old Bachelor Peter Richard Belchamber a Solictor's Clerk married 28 year old spinster Laurie Eleanor Constance Acres by banns on the 11th of September,1954 at the parish church,Chingford,Essex. Peter Richard was living at 75 Dale View Avenue,Chingford and Laurie Eleanor at 245 Old Church Road,Chingford. Witness's were John Richard Belchamber and Daisy Grace Acres. The fathers were John Richard Belchamber a Glass Writer and Bob Acres,retired. J.T.D Davis the assistant priest took the service.

Death details for Peter Richard Belchamber who died peacefully on the 3rd November,2011 at home. The funeral was on the 18th November at 11am in Hastings Crematorium

Death Certificate:
Laurie Eleanor Constance Belchamber died in 2003 on the 14th of June at St.Michaels Hospice,25 Upper Maze Hill,St.Leonards on sea,East Sussex. Cause of death was Non-Hodgkins Lymphoma certified by R Board MB. Listed as the wife of Peter

Richard Belchamber,Solicitor Retired of High Chimneys,Whatlington Road,Battle,East Sussex,who was also informant.

William Robert Belchamber
(WilliamRobert13,Edward12,John11,Edward10,Edward9,Edward8,Edward7, Edward6,John5,Thomas4,Robert3,Robert2,John1) was born on the 11th December,1914 in Camberwell. He died on the 22nd September,1986 in The Royal Surrey County Hospital,Guildford,Surrey. He married Dorothy Emma Greenwood on the 24th December,1938 in The Parish Church,Beckinham,Kent.

Birth Certificate:
William Robert Belchamber the son of William Robert and Jessie Belchamber nee Morris was born on the 11th of December 1914 at 17 Ansdell Road,Camberwell. His father was a Printer Compositer by trade. The birth was registered by A G Quaif Registrar on the 1st January 1915.

Marriage Certificate:
William Robert Belchamber a bachelor aged 24 and a Printer married Dorothy Emma Greenwood a spinster aged 25 by banns on the 24th December 1938. The marriage took place at the parish church Beckenham,Kent by the assistant Curate E P Field. Their witness's were both the fathers William Robert Belchamber a Printer and Frederick Lyon Greenwood a Steward. William Robert was living at 26 Church Avenue and Dorothy Emma at 56 Ravenscroft Road both in Beckenham.

Death Certificate:
William Robert Belchamber a retired Printer Compositer of 5 Sheldon Court,Lower Edgeborough Road,Guildford died on the 22nd of September,1986 at The Royal Surrey Hospital,Guildford. Myocardial Infarction was the cause of death,which was certified by M.Coleby MB. His son was informant. The death was recorded on the 22nd of September for Guildford.

William Robert Belchamber and Dorothy Emma Greenwood had two children,both of whom are alive.

May Elizabeth Belchamber
(Charles John13,Charles John12,John11,Edward10,Edward9,Edward8,Edward7, Edward6,John5,Thomas4,Robert3,Robert2,John1) was born on the 5th August,1919 in 164 Herndean Road,Caversham,Reading,Berkshire. She died on the 19th December,1993 in The General Hospital,Halifax,Yorkshire. She married Donald Hartley on the 4th November,1939 in The Registry Office,Halifax. He died on the 31st March,1986.

Birth Certificate:
May Elizabeth Belchamber was adopted by Charles and Annie Belchamber. She was born 5th August 1919, in Reading, Berkshire.
I have a copy of her birth certificate, her given name at birth was Jean Marcia Woollcott, the place of birth is stated as being 164, Hemdean Road, Caversham, Reading. The name of her birth mother was Marian Francis Woollcott there is no name of the father on the certificate.

Marriage Certificate;
19 year old bachelor and Dyers Operative Donald Hartley married May Elizabeth Belchamber a 20 year old spinster and Worsted Winder at the Registry Office,Halifax,Yorkshire on the 4th of November,1939. Donalds residence was 4 Stansfield Street,Halifax and May was living at 20 Hope Street,Halifax the family home. Their witness's were May's parents Charles and Annie Belchamber. The fathers were Charles Belchamber a Textile Warehouseman and Albert Hartley was a Labourer in a Brassworks. Registrar Harold Walkin performed the Service.

Death Certificate:
May Elizabeth Hartley died at the General Hospital,Halifax on the 19th of December,1993. The cause of death was Respiratory failure,chest infection,chronic obstructive airways disease and left ventricular failure which was certified by A M Wilsom MB. The informant and present at the death was her daughter Jean Jones of 33 Lindrick Way,Bradshaw,Halifax. May Elizabeth was listed as a Machinist of 3 West Parade Flats,Kings Cross,Halifax the widow of Donald Hartley Textile worker retired. Jennifer M Featherstone the registrar for Halifax recorded the death on the 21st of December.

Louis Henri Belchamber
(William Henry13,Charles John12,John11,Edward10,Edward9,Edward8,Edward7 Edward6,John5,Thomas4,Robert3,Robert2,John1) was born on the 12th April,1906 in Bedford,Comte Missisquoi,Quebec,Canada. He died on the 30th December,1968 in Ste.Martine,Comte Chateauquay,Quebec. He married Germaine Latour on the 24th April,1928 in St.Pauls,Montreal,she was the daughter of Alexis Latour and Charlotte Lapierre.

Louis Henri was baptisted on the 13th April,1906 in St.Damien,Bedford,Comte Missisquoi,Quebec.He was buried on the 2nd January,1969 in St.Damien,Bedford, Comte Chateauquay.

Louis Henri Belchamber and Germaine Latour had three children.

i   Bruce Belchamber

ii   Louise Belchamber

iii   Ronald Vilbert Belchamber
All born in Quebec,Canada.

Cecile Blance Clara Belchamber
(William Henry13,Charles John12,John11,Edward10,Edward9,Edward8,Edward7 Edward6,John5,Thomas4,Robert3,Robert2,John1) was born on the 26th July,1913 in St.Jean,Sur Richelieu,Quebec,Canada.

Cecile Blanche Clara Belchamber was baptisted on the 27th July,1915 in Cathedrale St.Jean L'Evangeliste,St.Jean Sur Richelieu,Quebec.

Cecile Blanche Clara Belchamber had the following child:

i   Joseph Gaetan Belchamber was born on the 14th April,1935 in Montreal Aide a la Femme.

The Belchambers of Quebec are another side of the family that needs more research.

I hope you have enjoyed your trip through the family tree,please do come again. If there is something you would like to add,or disagree with,please do get in touch with me. My email address is jbelchamber@live.co.uk I would love to hear from you.

Source References

Petworth General Register
PAR/149/1/1/1 1559-1794

Archive-West Sussex Record Office

Wills

Robert Payne Northchapell Vol.7 Page.168 Year.1551

John Belchamber Northchaple Vol.7 Page.123 Year 15507 Year.1582(orig.K.8)

Robert Belchamber Petworth Vol.M.Dean Page.19 Year.1612

Constance Belchamber Petwoth Vol.M.Dean Page.24 Year.1621

Robert Belchamber Petworth Vol.23 Page.315b Year.1666

Adminstrations

Robert Belchamber Northchappell Vol.B Page.3 Year.1575

Richard Belchamber Petworth Vol.H Page.54 Year 1637

John Belchamber Northchappell Vol.H Page.233 Year.1661

Probate Account

Robert Belchamber Petworth AC.ep.1/33/1617

Inventories

Contance Belchamber,widow 142/010 8.021622 £0.00 M.Dean 24

Richard Belchamber   142/021   15.12.1637 £83.15.0 STCII H F.54

Robert Bellchamber Yeoman 142/041 29.050166 £357.10.0 STCI/23 F.315

Bishops Transcipts Northchapel EP.1/24/85A

Kirdford Parish Registers

116/1/1/1   General Register   1558-1693

116/1/1/2   General Register   1693-1746

116/1/1/3	General Register	1747-1791
116/1/1/4	Marriages and Banns	1745-1788
116/1/1/5	Banns and Marriages	1788-1812
116/1/1/6	Baptisms and Burials	1792-1812
116/1/2/1	Baptisms	1812-1840
116/1/2/2	Baptisms	1841-1869
116/1/2/3	Baptisms	1869-1876
116/1/3/1	Marriages	1813-1837
116/1/3/2	Marriages	1837-1875
116/1/3/3	Marriages	1875
116/1/5/1	Burials	1813-1872
116/1/5/2	Burials	1872-1900

www.ancestry.co.uk

www.familysearch.com

Bishops Transcripts Kirdford EP.1/24/66A

Kirdford Some Parish History   Hugh Kenyon 1971

Kirdford The Old Parish Discovered Janet Austin
ISBN 0 9516547 0 5 Published by Ifold and District Local History Society.

Northchapel A Parish History   Pamela Bruce 2000
ISBN O 9538291 0 3 Published by Northchapel Parish Council

(c) John Belchamber 2012

<u>Notes</u>

<u>Notes</u>